CliffsNotes®

*SAT
CRAM PLAN™

CliffsNotes®

*SAT CRAM PLAN™

William Ma and Jane R. Burstein

Houghton Mifflin Harcourt

Boston   New York

CliffsNotes® *SAT Cram Plan™

Copyright © 2009 Houghton Mifflin Harcourt Publishing Company

www.hmhco.com

Library of Congress Cataloging-in-Publication Data
Ma, William.
   Cliffsnotes SAT cram plan / by William Ma and Jane R. Burstein.
     p. cm.
  Includes bibliographical references.
        ISBN 978-0-470-47058-9
1. SAT (Educational test)--Study guides. I. Burstein, Jane R. II. Title.
 LB2353.57.M22 2009
 378.1'662--dc22
                    2009014911
Printed in the United States of America
DOC 10 9 8 7 6
4500464491

About the Authors

William Ma was chairman of the Math Department at the Herricks School District on Long Island for many years before retiring. He also taught as an adjunct math instructor at Baruch College, Columbia University, and Fordham University. He is the author of two calculus review books and an online review course for the New York State's Math A Regents Exam. He is currently a math consultant.

Jane Burstein taught English at Herricks High School in New Hyde Park, New York, for 36 years. She has been an SAT tutor for 25 years, an instructor at Hofstra University, and a reader for AP exams.

Acknowledgments

William Ma would like to thank his wife, Mary, and daughters, Janet and Karen, who gave him much help in putting the book together; Roberta Melendy, a retired math teacher from Herricks, who edited many parts of the book; and Elizabeth Kuball and Abraham Mantell for their patience and editorial assistance.

Jane Burstein would like to thank her husband, David, and children, Jessica, Jonathan, Beth, and Seth for their encouragement and helpful suggestions. Many thanks also to English teacher Barbara Hoffman and her students at Herricks High School.

Editorial

Acquisition Editor: Greg Tubach

Project Editor: Elizabeth Kuball

Copy Editor: Elizabeth Kuball

Technical Editor: Abraham Mantell

Composition

Proofreader: ConText Editorial Services, Inc.

Wiley Publishing, Inc., Composition Services

Table of Contents

Appendix: Using the TI-89 Graphing Calculator. 285

Introduction

That time in every high school student's life has arrived: The SAT hovers on the horizon. Your SAT score, along with your high school transcript, your résumé of extracurricular activities, your letters of recommendation, and your application essays, is an important factor in the college admission process, so you know how important it is to prepare. You're determined to do whatever it takes to get your best possible score on the test. All you need to begin to work is a helpful study plan, one that's simple, organized, and doable—in other words, one you'll be able to stick to as you embark on the path to SAT success. No problem. Whether you have two months, one month, or one week, you can achieve your goals if you're organized and diligent.

About the Test

Section	Subject	Type of Questions	Time Allotted
1	Writing	1 essay	25 minutes
2	Mathematics	20 multiple-choice questions	25 minutes
3	English	Sentence-completion questions Passage-based reading questions	25 minutes
4	Writing	11 improving-sentences questions 18 identifying-sentence-errors questions 6 improving-paragraphs questions	25 minutes
5	Experimental	Critical reading, mathematics, or writing	25 minutes
6	Mathematics	8 multiple-choice questions 10 grid-in questions	25 minutes
7	English	Sentence-completion questions Passage-based reading questions	25 minutes
8	Mathematics	16 multiple-choice questions	20 minutes
9	English	Sentence-completion questions Passage-based reading questions	20 minutes
10	Writing	14 improving-sentences questions	10 minutes

The SAT is comprised of ten sections: one essay section, three mathematics sections, three critical reading sections, and two multiple-choice writing sections. These sections may occur in any order, but Section 1 is always the essay, and Section 10 is always a ten-minute multiple-choice writing section. In addition, somewhere between Section 2 and Section 7, you'll have an experimental section which will not be identified as such and will not count toward your SAT score. The SAT Test Development Committee uses this section to field test new questions that they'll use on future tests. The whole test takes 3 hours and 45 minutes.

The three critical reading sections consist of sentence-completion questions and passage-based reading questions. In one section, you'll find a set of short paired reading passages; in another section, you'll find a set of long paired reading passages.

All questions in the mathematics portion of the SAT can be solved without a calculator; however, using a calculator, particularly a graphing calculator, can help solve a problem more quickly and prevent careless errors. The TI-89 graphing calculator is one of the most versatile and easy-to-use calculators permitted for use in the math sections of the SAT. In this book, every question that can be solved with the help of a graphing calculator is indicated by a Calculator icon. The appendix at the end of this book explains how to use the TI-89 graphing calculator to solve SAT math questions. (*Note:* On the actual SAT, you won't see this icon. We're using it here so you're familiar with the types of questions for which you should use a calculator.)

Go to www.collegeboard.com and search on "SAT calculator policy" for the latest information on which calculators are permitted on the SAT.

About This Book

The first step in getting ready for the SAT is determining exactly how much time you have and following the appropriate plan: the two-month plan, the one-month plan, or the one-week plan. Each plan has a schedule for you to follow along with approximate time you'll need to allot to each task. In addition, each subject-review chapter will give you strategies for that part of the test. Included in each subject-review chapter are practice exercises to assist you in the areas in which you're weakest and to help you continue to maximize your strengths.

Begin by taking the diagnostic test to pinpoint your strengths and weaknesses. The explanation of answers will guide you to the specific chapters that cover the topics in which you need the most help. After the diagnostic test, you'll find a scoring guide that will give you an indication of your current score on each section of the SAT. Then you can begin to focus on the subject-review chapters. At the end of the book, you'll find a practice test, a simulated SAT with a scoring guide to give you an authentic test-taking experience.

Online Extras at CliffsNotes.com

As an added bonus to this *CliffsNotes SAT Cram Plan,* you can get some additional practice by visiting www.cliffsnotes.com/go/SATCram. There you'll find:

- Vocabulary practice exercises
- Grid-in math practice
- Common writing errors to watch for
- A list of common prefixes, suffixes, and roots
- And more!

I. Diagnostic Test

This Diagnostic Test, excluding the essay, is half the length of a full-length SAT Test. The Diagnostic Test has four sections: The Essay, Critical Reading, Mathematics, and Writing. The tests are designed to measure your ability in these four areas and to predict your success in college. Each question on the test is numbered. Choose the best answer for each question and fill in the corresponding circle on the answer sheet provided.

When you take this exam, try to simulate the test conditions by following the time allotments carefully. On the actual SAT, if you finish a section before the allotted time runs out, you may not work on any other section. You may not go back to a previous section or move ahead to work on the next section.

You will need 1 hour and 53 minutes to complete the Diagnostic Test:

Essay: 25 minutes
Critical Reading: 35 minutes
Mathematics: 35 minutes
Writing: 18 minutes

Answer Sheet

Section 1

CUT HERE

CUT HERE

CUT HERE

Section 2

1	Ⓐ Ⓑ Ⓒ Ⓓ Ⓔ	21	Ⓐ Ⓑ Ⓒ Ⓓ Ⓔ
2	Ⓐ Ⓑ Ⓒ Ⓓ Ⓔ	22	Ⓐ Ⓑ Ⓒ Ⓓ Ⓔ
3	Ⓐ Ⓑ Ⓒ Ⓓ Ⓔ	23	Ⓐ Ⓑ Ⓒ Ⓓ Ⓔ
4	Ⓐ Ⓑ Ⓒ Ⓓ Ⓔ	24	Ⓐ Ⓑ Ⓒ Ⓓ Ⓔ
5	Ⓐ Ⓑ Ⓒ Ⓓ Ⓔ	25	Ⓐ Ⓑ Ⓒ Ⓓ Ⓔ
6	Ⓐ Ⓑ Ⓒ Ⓓ Ⓔ	26	Ⓐ Ⓑ Ⓒ Ⓓ Ⓔ
7	Ⓐ Ⓑ Ⓒ Ⓓ Ⓔ	27	Ⓐ Ⓑ Ⓒ Ⓓ Ⓔ
8	Ⓐ Ⓑ Ⓒ Ⓓ Ⓔ	28	Ⓐ Ⓑ Ⓒ Ⓓ Ⓔ
9	Ⓐ Ⓑ Ⓒ Ⓓ Ⓔ	29	Ⓐ Ⓑ Ⓒ Ⓓ Ⓔ
10	Ⓐ Ⓑ Ⓒ Ⓓ Ⓔ	30	Ⓐ Ⓑ Ⓒ Ⓓ Ⓔ
11	Ⓐ Ⓑ Ⓒ Ⓓ Ⓔ	31	Ⓐ Ⓑ Ⓒ Ⓓ Ⓔ
12	Ⓐ Ⓑ Ⓒ Ⓓ Ⓔ	32	Ⓐ Ⓑ Ⓒ Ⓓ Ⓔ
13	Ⓐ Ⓑ Ⓒ Ⓓ Ⓔ	33	Ⓐ Ⓑ Ⓒ Ⓓ Ⓔ
14	Ⓐ Ⓑ Ⓒ Ⓓ Ⓔ		
15	Ⓐ Ⓑ Ⓒ Ⓓ Ⓔ		
16	Ⓐ Ⓑ Ⓒ Ⓓ Ⓔ		
17	Ⓐ Ⓑ Ⓒ Ⓓ Ⓔ		
18	Ⓐ Ⓑ Ⓒ Ⓓ Ⓔ		
19	Ⓐ Ⓑ Ⓒ Ⓓ Ⓔ		
20	Ⓐ Ⓑ Ⓒ Ⓓ Ⓔ		

Section 3

1	Ⓐ Ⓑ Ⓒ Ⓓ Ⓔ	21	Ⓐ Ⓑ Ⓒ Ⓓ Ⓔ
2	Ⓐ Ⓑ Ⓒ Ⓓ Ⓔ	22	Ⓐ Ⓑ Ⓒ Ⓓ Ⓔ
3	Ⓐ Ⓑ Ⓒ Ⓓ Ⓔ	23	Ⓐ Ⓑ Ⓒ Ⓓ Ⓔ
4	Ⓐ Ⓑ Ⓒ Ⓓ Ⓔ	24	Ⓐ Ⓑ Ⓒ Ⓓ Ⓔ
5	Ⓐ Ⓑ Ⓒ Ⓓ Ⓔ	25	Ⓐ Ⓑ Ⓒ Ⓓ Ⓔ
6	Ⓐ Ⓑ Ⓒ Ⓓ Ⓔ	26	Ⓐ Ⓑ Ⓒ Ⓓ Ⓔ
7	Ⓐ Ⓑ Ⓒ Ⓓ Ⓔ	27	Ⓐ Ⓑ Ⓒ Ⓓ Ⓔ
8	Ⓐ Ⓑ Ⓒ Ⓓ Ⓔ		
9	Ⓐ Ⓑ Ⓒ Ⓓ Ⓔ		
10	Ⓐ Ⓑ Ⓒ Ⓓ Ⓔ		
11	Ⓐ Ⓑ Ⓒ Ⓓ Ⓔ		
12	Ⓐ Ⓑ Ⓒ Ⓓ Ⓔ		
13	Ⓐ Ⓑ Ⓒ Ⓓ Ⓔ		
14	Ⓐ Ⓑ Ⓒ Ⓓ Ⓔ		
15	Ⓐ Ⓑ Ⓒ Ⓓ Ⓔ		
16	Ⓐ Ⓑ Ⓒ Ⓓ Ⓔ		
17	Ⓐ Ⓑ Ⓒ Ⓓ Ⓔ		
18	Ⓐ Ⓑ Ⓒ Ⓓ Ⓔ		
19	Ⓐ Ⓑ Ⓒ Ⓓ Ⓔ		
20	Ⓐ Ⓑ Ⓒ Ⓓ Ⓔ		

Section 4

1	Ⓐ Ⓑ Ⓒ Ⓓ Ⓔ	21	Ⓐ Ⓑ Ⓒ Ⓓ Ⓔ
2	Ⓐ Ⓑ Ⓒ Ⓓ Ⓔ	22	Ⓐ Ⓑ Ⓒ Ⓓ Ⓔ
3	Ⓐ Ⓑ Ⓒ Ⓓ Ⓔ	23	Ⓐ Ⓑ Ⓒ Ⓓ Ⓔ
4	Ⓐ Ⓑ Ⓒ Ⓓ Ⓔ	24	Ⓐ Ⓑ Ⓒ Ⓓ Ⓔ
5	Ⓐ Ⓑ Ⓒ Ⓓ Ⓔ	25	Ⓐ Ⓑ Ⓒ Ⓓ Ⓔ
6	Ⓐ Ⓑ Ⓒ Ⓓ Ⓔ		
7	Ⓐ Ⓑ Ⓒ Ⓓ Ⓔ		
8	Ⓐ Ⓑ Ⓒ Ⓓ Ⓔ		
9	Ⓐ Ⓑ Ⓒ Ⓓ Ⓔ		
10	Ⓐ Ⓑ Ⓒ Ⓓ Ⓔ		
11	Ⓐ Ⓑ Ⓒ Ⓓ Ⓔ		
12	Ⓐ Ⓑ Ⓒ Ⓓ Ⓔ		
13	Ⓐ Ⓑ Ⓒ Ⓓ Ⓔ		
14	Ⓐ Ⓑ Ⓒ Ⓓ Ⓔ		
15	Ⓐ Ⓑ Ⓒ Ⓓ Ⓔ		
16	Ⓐ Ⓑ Ⓒ Ⓓ Ⓔ		
17	Ⓐ Ⓑ Ⓒ Ⓓ Ⓔ		
18	Ⓐ Ⓑ Ⓒ Ⓓ Ⓔ		
19	Ⓐ Ⓑ Ⓒ Ⓓ Ⓔ		
20	Ⓐ Ⓑ Ⓒ Ⓓ Ⓔ		

CUT HERE

Section 1: Writing—Essay

Time: 25 minutes

Directions: This essay gives you a chance to develop your own ideas and express them in essay form. Read the question carefully, think about your point of view, present your ideas clearly in logical fashion, and be sure to use standard written English.

You must write your essay in the space provided; you must use only the lines within the margin. You should write on every line (do not skip lines), avoid wide margins, and keep your handwriting to a reasonable size. You may write or print, but try to write as legibly as you can.

You will have 25 minutes for this section. Be sure to write on the topic. An off-topic essay, no matter how well written, will receive a score of zero.

Think about the issue presented below:

> Some students of human nature say people are driven by selfish desires. They say every action is motivated by a self-serving impulse. Others disagree and point to all the selfless and humanitarian deeds done by people throughout the ages. Human actions, they say, are primarily motivated by the desire to help others.

Assignment: Are human beings by nature primarily selfish or unselfish? Plan and write an essay in which you develop your point of view on this question. Be sure to support your position with reasons and examples taken from personal experience, observation, reading, or studies.

Be sure to write only in the space provided on your answer sheet.

IF YOU FINISH BEFORE TIME IS CALLED, CHECK YOUR WORK ON THIS SECTION ONLY. DO NOT WORK ON ANY OTHER SECTION IN THE TEST.

Section 2: Critical Reading

Time: 25 minutes

Directions: Each sentence below has either one or two blanks. Each blank indicates that a word has been left out. Beneath the sentence are five words or sets of words labeled A through E. Choose the word or set of words that, when inserted in the sentence, *best* fits the meaning of the sentence as a whole.

EXAMPLE:

The regeneration of the Pine Barrens after the devastating wildfire did not take place overnight; on the contrary, the regrowth was _____.

- **A.** expected
- **B.** encouraged
- **C.** gradual
- **D.** infinite
- **E.** rapid

The correct answer is C.

1. Charlie preferred to remain unnoticed in the crowd, for his natural _____ led him to shun attention.

   - **A.** dogmatism
   - **B.** affability
   - **C.** jocularity
   - **D.** slyness
   - **E.** diffidence

2. Rather than _____ the signs warning picnickers to remain on the paths, Ella and Alex decided to spread their blanket on the rocky cliff.

   - **A.** disregard
   - **B.** apply
   - **C.** appease
   - **D.** heed
   - **E.** evade

3. Although they are twins, Jessica and Jonathan are nothing alike; Jessica is reserved and _____ while her brother is _____ and extroverted.

   - **A.** distant . . . guileful
   - **B.** insightful . . . unskillful
   - **C.** introspective . . . ebullient
   - **D.** congenial . . . reticent
   - **E.** jolly . . . amiable

4. Not an _____ by nature, Sophie declined to _____ her ideals for a quicker, more expedient solution to the problems plaguing her community.

   - **A.** organizer . . . denounce
   - **B.** enabler . . . supplant
   - **C.** opportunist . . . compromise
   - **D.** authoritarian . . . discern
   - **E.** instigator . . . incite

5. In his most recent book, *A Concise Pocket Guide to Birds,* Dr. Gonzalez includes all the species of North America; hence, while his work is _____, it lacks _____.

   A. compendious . . . independence
   B. unique . . . energy
   C. comprehensive . . . depth
   D. serious . . . frivolity
   E. useful . . . pragmatism

6. Edgar Allan Poe's much-vaunted detective C. Auguste Dupin often astonishes his cohort with his acumen: this _____ sleuth often reveals the solution with an uncanny display of _____.

   A. acclaimed . . . perspicacity
   B. gullible . . . equanimity
   C. notorious . . . mettle
   D. nondescript . . . ostentation
   E. officious . . . astuteness

7. In his later, more secular verse, the Cavalier poet leavens the _____ piety of his youthful religious sonnets with irreverent and suggestive _____.

   A. sober . . . wit
   B. devout . . . indictment
   C. flippant . . . accuracy
   D. urbane . . . provincialism
   E. callow . . . cacophony

8. The sophists, Greek philosophers who used the art of rhetoric to deceive, were often accused of _____ reasoning.

   A. munificent
   B. propitiatory
   C. hapless
   D. specious
   E. salutary

9. Because computer-generated digital painting is still neither totally accepted nor completely rejected as an art form by curators, its placement in museums remains _____.

   A. aggrandized
   B. arbitrary
   C. ubiquitous
   D. evanescent
   E. perfidious

Directions: Carefully read the following passages and answer the questions that follow each passage. The questions after the pair of related passages may ask you about the relationship between the passages. Answer the questions based on the content of the passages: both what is stated and what is implied in the passages as well as any introductory material before each passage.

Questions 10-11 are based on the following passage.

This passage is taken from the introduction to a British novel published in 1766.

There are an hundred faults in this thing and an hundred things might be said to prove them beauties. But it is needless. A book may be amusing with numerous errors, or it may be
(5) very dull without a single absurdity. The hero of this piece unites in himself the three greatest characters upon earth: he is a priest, an husbandman, and the father of a family. He is drawn as ready to teach, and ready to obey; as
(10) simple in affluence, and majestic in adversity. In this age of opulence and refinement whom can such a character please? Such as are fond of high life will turn from the simplicity of his country friends. Such as mistake ribaldry for
(15) humour will find no wit in his harmless conversation; and such as have been taught to deride religion will laugh at one whose chief stores of comfort are drawn from futurity.

10. The author refers to the "faults in this thing" (line 1) in order to

A. suggest that the novel needs to be revised.
B. recommend ways to make the novel beautiful.
C. acknowledge that the novel is not a perfect work.
D. apologize for the displeasing nature of the characters.
E. mock those critics who found fault with this novel.

11. The reference in line 11 to "this age of opulence and refinement" is used to

A. indicate that the main characters will be drawn from the aristocracy of the time.
B. set up a contrast to the modest life of the main character.
C. refer to the wealth accumulated by the church.
D. amuse the reader with an irrelevant detail.
E. satirize the hero of the novel.

Questions 12–13 are based on the following passage.

In 1966, Eddie Arnold earned induction into the Country Music Hall of Fame. With his long string of hits, Arnold ranked among the most popular country singers in U.S. his-
(5) tory. Arnold used his smooth voice to escape from poverty. When his father died, the family farm was lost to creditors and the Arnolds were forced to become sharecroppers. Even when Arnold achieved his lifelong dream of
(10) becoming a top-selling artist, this country boy never lost touch with his roots. Although he gained a rather sophisticated fan base with his succession of hits, he always referred to himself as the "Tennessee Plowboy." In his mind,
(15) his background as a hard-working farm hand prepared him for the demanding role of successful singer. From the beginning, he cut a different figure from most of his contemporaries in the world of country singers. Unlike
(20) most of the country singers who appeared either in jeans and plaid shirts or glittering sequins and spangles, Arnold always dressed in debonair attire. When he died in May 2008, the music world lost an immensely popular
(25) crooner of romantic ballads.

12. By stating that "Arnold never lost touch with his roots" (line 11), the author implies that

   A. Arnold remained connected to the family farm and continued to pursue agriculture.
   B. Arnold eschewed his humble beginnings and indulged in a more sophisticated lifestyle.
   C. Arnold liked to be known as a farm hand and favored jeans and cowboy boots when he performed.
   D. Arnold continued to identify himself with the attitudes and values of hardworking rural Americans.
   E. Arnold's smooth singing voice was a direct contrast to the roughness of his upbringing.

13. The primary purpose of the passage is to

   A. contrast the world of country singers with that of the more urbane pop singers.
   B. explain the method by which poor farm children can become successful singers.
   C. argue that only by rejecting their poverty can entertainers reach the height of popularity.
   D. depict the specific conditions that caused a young boy to escape the life of a sharecropper.
   E. present an overview of an artist who accomplished his goals while remaining unspoiled by his success.

Questions 14–23 are based on the following passage.

The following is an excerpt from a novel written in 1921 by an American author.

There is another sound in the room now—a sound no one could have noticed before, it is so small and monotonous—the sound of even breathing. It comes from the great oak bed by (5) the wall and the chair rocked close to the grate. Hearing it makes the room seem stiller and warmer. The fire shifts suddenly, throwing a gay flare on the face of the drowser before it, and the procession of dull-blue pea- (10) cocks that parade the ivory chintz of the deep chairs and tall curtains. From the bed comes an indistinguishable sleepy sound that, finding itself nonsense, stops, and a little later begins again, this time enough waked up to be (15) in words.

"Nurse!" it says. "Oh, Nurse!"

The rumple of starched linen in the rocker moves infinitesimally and relapses without answering.

(20) "Nurse!" repeats the voice from the bed, this time with a tickle of laughter in it. "Miss Hollis! Sorry to wake you!"

And now the linen hears and crackles. The figure in the chair rises, a tall strapping girl (25) with a tumble of blond hair coming out from under her nurse's cap. She looks as vigorous and healthy as a young tree, but the pulled-down droop of the corners of her mouth shows that she recently has been thoroughly tired. (30) She stands now with her arms over her head, yawning magnificently, and then suddenly realizing what she is doing, straightens and starts to look very professional. But the next minute her hands are at her eyes again, trying (35) desperately to rub away the sleep.

The voice from the bed is contrite.

"I'm awfully sorry. I know I shouldn't have waked you. I've been counting peacocks and peacocks getting the cruelty to. Because if you (40) were as sleepy as I was—"

"You should have waked me long ago, Mrs. Sellaby." The full dignity of an expert has been recovered. "I had no business to sleep like that. I don't know how I—"A yawn splits (45) this in the middle, but she goes on determinedly, "I don't know what I—" Again the annihilating yawn. This time she gives up. "Oh, dear," she says frankly, "I *was* so tired. . . ."

She busies herself with bottle and trays and (50) pillows, hiding what yawns will come behind four fingers. The girl in the bed lies flat back, looking at the ceiling. Her hair, which is the color of pine smoke, is in thick, soft waves about her face.

(55)   It is a face with that delicate tense strength you may see in the hands of a great surgeon— the soul beneath it has been tempered steely, is as exquisitely balanced and direct at the long springing blade of an old rapier. And at pres-

(60) ent, in spite of the weight and heaviness of exhaustion upon it, so deep as to be almost visible and clinging like a netted veil, it is over- whelmed with peace, absorbed with peace.

14. The passage can primarily be described as

A. a confrontation between two hostile characters.

B. a reconciliation between previously estranged women.

C. a narration that establishes a sympathetic relationship.

D. an account of an employer reprimanding a lazy employee.

E. a satire of a situation from a bystander's point of view.

15. The first paragraph (lines 1–15) sets the mood of

A. grandeur.

B. quietude.

C. disappointment.

D. nostalgia.

E. melodrama.

16. The phrase *finding itself nonsense* (lines 12–13) suggests that

A. the listener does not understand the speaker.

B. the speaker does not understand herself.

C. the speaker is unable to hear the listener.

D. the noise of the fire drowns out the speaker's words.

E. the peacocks are making an indistinguishable sound.

17. The phrase *the rumple of starched linen* (line 17) suggests that

A. the sick woman is sleeping on linen sheets.

B. the rocking chair is covered in linen fabric.

C. the peacocks parade across the deep chairs of linen.

D. the nurse wears a uniform of stiff linen.

E. the linen curtains move in the breeze.

18. The second call to the nurse (line 20) suggests that the speaker is

A. impatient with the lack of response.

B. amused that the nurse is sleeping.

C. dissatisfied with the nursing care she receives.

D. experiencing severe pain and needs attention.

E. feeling vigorous and wishes to get out of bed.

19. The initial description of the nurse ("The figure . . . tired"; lines 23–29) suggests

A. an exhausted but healthy young woman.

B. a sleepy waif who tries to shirk her duties.

C. an arrogant girl who believes that caring for others is beneath her.

D. a strong and energetic professional who takes pride in her work.

E. an expert who is brusque and aloof from those in her care.

20. The word *annihilating* (lines 46–47) most nearly means

A. killing.

B. colliding.

C. defeating.

D. definitive.

E. abolishing.

21. The phrase *tempered steely* (line 57) refers to

    A. the volatile anger of the girl in the bed.

    B. the weapons displayed on the wall of the room.

    C. the heaviness of the illness that weighs upon the patient.

    D. the patient who, although ill, has inner strength.

    E. the exquisite skill of the surgeon who has operated on the patient.

22. The language of the last paragraph (lines 55–63) is best described as

    A. objective.

    B. metaphorical.

    C. histrionic.

    D. sardonic.

    E. vitriolic.

23. This passage reveals all of the following emotions EXCEPT

    A. enervation.

    B. contrition.

    C. serenity.

    D. somnolence.

    E. indignation.

Questions 24–33 are based on the following passages.

Passage 1

The magnificent polar bear, the world's largest terrestrial carnivore, lives most of its life on the ice floes in the Arctic cap and feeds mostly on seals. Recently, the United States

(5) government has listed the polar bear as a "threatened species." Under the Endangered Species Act, the designation "threatened" indicates that, without some form of protection, this species likely faces extinction. The

(10) threat to these bears does not come from predators, but from global climate changes. Increased burning of fossil fuels has caused an unprecedented warming, which in turn has caused a loss of sea ice. As their habitat

(15) shrinks, the polar bears follow the retreating ice; some bears then find themselves stranded on land. Many animal lovers are disturbed by reports that this awesome, and for thousands of years self-sufficient, creature has been

(20) forced to rummage around garbage pails and camp sites for scraps of food. According to the U.S. Fish and Wildlife Service, "In the declining polar bear population of Canada's Western Hudson Bay, extensive scientific

(25) studies have indicated that the increased observation of bears on land is a result of changing distribution patterns and a result of changes in the accessibility of sea ice habitat." Clearly, to ensure the survival of these beloved

(30) symbols of the Arctic, we must take action to prevent the diminution of their habitat.

Passage 2

Some climatologists investigating the claim that global warming threatens to cause polar bear extinction find little basis for fear. The study finds that for the most part, polar bear

(5) populations are intact. The polar bear population in the southern Beaufort Sea off Alaska's North Slope, for example, has been relatively stable for 20 years, according to a federal analysis. Some government agencies fear that

(10) environmentalists are using the polar bear as an excuse to influence policy. One government official states, "While the legal standards under the ESA compel me to list the polar bear as threatened, I want to make clear that

(15) this listing will not stop global climate change or prevent any sea ice from melting. Any real solution requires action by all major economies for it to be effective. That is why I am taking administrative and regulatory action to

(20) make certain the ESA isn't abused to make global warming policies." Moreover, since the Earth has undergone climatic fluctuations for thousands of years and the polar bears have survived, there is insufficient evidence that

(25) polar bears are in danger of becoming extinct within the foreseeable future.

24. According to the author of passage 1, the greatest threat faced by polar bears is

   A. the increased population of large predators that prey on polar bears.
   B. the encroachment of human settlements into the territories previously inhabited solely by the polar bears.
   C. the declining herds of seals that provide the major food source to the polar bears.
   D. the diminishment of the ice shelves.
   E. the researchers who invade the ice floes and displace the polar bears.

25. The "animal lovers" in passage 1 (line 17) are most likely "disturbed" because

   A. they are afraid that the hungry polar bears might attack people.
   B. they see the food-scavenging behavior as demeaning to the polar bears.
   C. they believe the change in diet may cause physiological damage to the polar bears.
   D. they believe the natural world and the modern world have reached an accommodation.
   E. they fear an imbalance in Arctic sea life as a result of the loss of a natural predator.

26. The tone of the last sentence of passage 1 (lines 29–31) is best described as

   A. respectful and exigent.
   B. admiring and cautious.
   C. curious and impatient.
   D. indignant and whimsical.
   E. frustrated and irascible.

27. Which of the following statements, if true, would most undermine the primary argument of passage 1?

   A. There are approximately 20,000 polar bears currently living in the Arctic cap.
   B. Large carnivores are often sensitive indicators of the health of an ecosystem.
   C. Climate fluctuations have occurred at regular intervals with little or no effect on animal populations.
   D. Environmentalists want the government to be more stringent in its restrictions on greenhouse emissions.
   E. Researchers have found that the thickness of the layers of fat under the polar bears' skin has declined.

28. The word *basis* in passage 2 (line 3) most nearly means

   A. core.
   B. foundation.
   C. beginning.
   D. center.
   E. component.

29. The word *abused* in passage 2 (line 20) most nearly means

   A. treated harshly.
   B. overstepping limits.
   C. strictly prevented.
   D. denounced scathingly.
   E. taken advantage of.

30. The author of passage 1 would most likely respond to the position stated in passage 2 ("Some . . . policy"; lines 9–11) by stating that

    A. the continuation of an endangered species warrants a change in policy.

    B. the climate of the Arctic has natural fluctuations that are not influenced by human actions.

    C. the policies of the government are subjected to the will of the populace.

    D. each state should make its own laws regarding the protection of indigenous species.

    E. evidence indic.ating the possible extinction of the polar bear is insufficient to warrant government action.

31. It can be inferred from the government official's comments (passage 2, lines 12–21) that

    A. he does not regard the state of the polar bear population as justification for a change in government position on global warming.

    B. he feels forced to rely on insufficient data to make necessary policy changes.

    C. he believes we do the polar bears an injustice by our reliance on fossil fuels.

    D. the economy of the nation will suffer if we no longer allow humans to hunt polar bears.

    E. no evidence exists that links climate fluctuations with the extinctions of Arctic mammals.

32. The authors of both passages would support which of the following statements?

    A. It is not the role of the government to regulate conditions that have led to global warming.

    B. Human interference is the direct cause of declining polar bear populations.

    C. The ecosystem of the Arctic is so fragile that the rise in one species at the expense of another is inevitable.

    D. Nature has the power to self-correct an imbalance to ecosystems.

    E. Certain situations necessitate human interference to rectify conditions in nature.

33. Compared with the tone of passage 1, the tone of passage 2 is

    A. less objective.

    B. more detached.

    C. more impassioned.

    D. less satirical.

    E. more defiant.

IF YOU FINISH BEFORE TIME IS CALLED, CHECK YOUR WORK ON THIS SECTION ONLY. DO NOT WORK ON ANY OTHER SECTION IN THE TEST.

Section 3: Math

Time: 35 minutes
27 questions
Calculator allowed

Reference Information

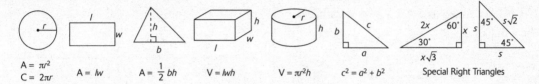

$A = \pi r^2$
$C = 2\pi r$

$A = lw$

$A = \frac{1}{2}bh$

$V = lwh$

$V = \pi r^2 h$

$c^2 = a^2 + b^2$

Special Right Triangles

The complete arc of a circle measures 360°.

The sum of the measures of the angles of a triangle is 180°.

---

1. If George has 3 jackets and 4 ties, how many combinations of 1 jacket and 1 tie can George have?

   A.   3
   B.   4
   C.   7
   D.   12
   E.   14

2. If $5(x - 2) = 10$, what is the value of $x - 2$?

   A.   2
   B.   4
   C.   6
   D.   8
   E.   10

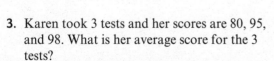

3. Karen took 3 tests and her scores are 80, 95, and 98. What is her average score for the 3 tests?

   A.   84
   B.   89
   C.   91
   D.   95
   E.   96

4. Given a number n, if $\frac{2}{3}$ of $\frac{1}{2}$ of n is 36, what is the value of n?

   A.   12
   B.   24
   C.   48
   D.   108
   E.   216

5. Set A = {10, 20, 30, 40}, and Set B = {30, 40, 50}. If a number is randomly picked from Set A, what is the probability that the number picked is divisible by 4 and is also a member of Set B?

   A. $\frac{1}{6}$

   B. $\frac{1}{5}$

   C. $\frac{1}{4}$

   D. $\frac{1}{3}$

   E. $\frac{1}{2}$

6. In an algebra class, the ratio of boys to girls is 3 to 4. Which of the following could be the total number of students in the class?

 A. 18
 B. 24
 C. 28
 D. 32
 E. 36

7. If $x \# y$ is defined as $x \# y = x^2 + xy$, what is the value of $\dfrac{2 \# 3}{3 \# 2}$?

 A. -1
 B. 1
 C. $\dfrac{2}{3}$
 D. $\dfrac{3}{2}$
 E. $\dfrac{4}{9}$

8. Given the sequence 10, 15, 20, 25, . . . , what is the value when the 11th term is divided by the 5th term?

 A. 2
 B. 4
 C. 6
 D. 10
 E. 12

9. In the accompanying diagram, the graphs of $p(x)$ and $q(x)$ are shown. What is the value of $p(q(2))$?

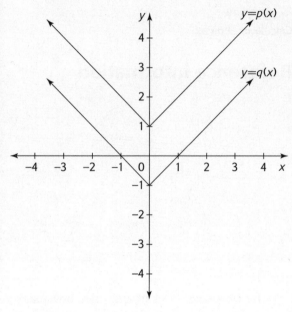

 A. -1
 B. 0
 C. 1
 D. 2
 E. 3

10. If Karen, Janet, Mary, and Bill are given assigned seats labeled A, B, C, and D, how many different seat assignments are possible with Karen given seat C?

 A. 3
 B. 6
 C. 9
 D. 24
 E. 27

11. In the accompanying figure, what is the value of $x + y$?

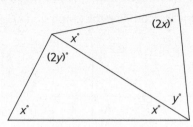

(Not drawn to scale)

A. 60
B. 90
C. 120
D. 150
E. 180

12. If a, b, and c are nonzero numbers, and $a = 2b$, $b = 3c$, and $c = ak$, what is the value of k?

A. $\frac{1}{6}$

B. $\frac{1}{3}$

C. 3
D. 6
E. Cannot be determined

13. If the area of a square is $36x^2$, what is the perimeter of the square in terms of x?

A. $12x$
B. $18x$
C. $24x$
D. $24x^2$
E. $36x$

14. In a coordinate plane, an equation of line l is $y = 2x + 4$. If line m is the reflection of line l about the y-axis, which of the following is an equation of line m?

A. $y = 2x - 4$
B. $y = -2x + 4$
C. $y = -2x - 4$
D. $y = 4x + 2$
E. $y = -4x - 2$

15. In the accompanying figure, $ABCD$ and $DEFG$ are both squares. If $AD + DE = 10$, and $GC = 2$, what is the perimeter of the shaded figure?

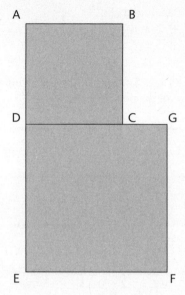

A. 30
B. 32
C. 36
D. 38
E. 40

16. At 6 p.m., Karen and Janet are standing side by side in a park. Karen, who is 5 feet 6 inches tall, casts a shadow 11 feet long. Janet is 5 feet tall. How long is her shadow in feet?

A. 9
B. 10
C. 11
D. 12
E. 12.1

17

17. If $f(x) = x(x - 1)(x + 2)$, what are all the possible roots of $f(x)$?

  A. 0
  B. 1 and –2
  C. 0, –1, and 2
  D. 0, 1, and 2
  E. 0, 1, –2

18. If $2 \leq |x| \leq 5$, which of the following graphs show all the possible values of x?

  A.
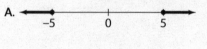

  B.
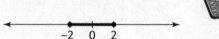

  C.
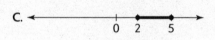

  D.
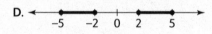

  E.
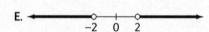

19. In the accompanying figure, if $\overline{AB} \perp \overline{AC}$ and $\overline{DE}$ intersects $\overline{AB}$ and $\overline{AC}$ at M and N respectively, what is the value of $x + y$?

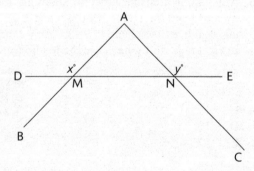

  A. 90
  B. 120
  C. 180
  D. 210
  E. 270

20. If $f(x) = x^2 + bx + c$, where b and c are positive integers and $c = \left(\dfrac{b}{2}\right)^2$, which of the following could be the graph of $f(x)$?

  A.
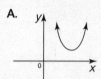

  B.

  C.
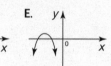

  D.

  E.
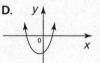

21. The table summarizes the number of students having 0 to 4 calculators in a class of 20 students. What is the sum of the mode and the median number of calculators?

Number of Calculators per Student in Class	
Number of Calculators	**Number of Students**
0	0
1	12
2	4
3	3
4	1

  A. 1
  B. 2
  C. 3
  D. 4
  E. 5

22. A container in the shape of a cube with the length of one of its edges being 6 inches is completely filled with water. If all the water in this cube is completely poured into a rectangular container whose length is 8 inches, width is 3 inches, and height is 10 inches, how high will the water level reach?

- **A.** 6
- **B.** 8
- **C.** 9
- **D.** 10
- **E.** 12

23. If $p(x) = x^2 + 2x$, and $p(2h) = 8h$, and $h > 0$, what is the value of h?

- **A.** −4
- **B.** −1
- **C.** 0
- **D.** 1
- **E.** 4

24. Bill paid $100 to rent a lawn mower for the weekend to mow lawns in his neighborhood for pay. He charges the same price for all his neighbors. If he mows 6 lawns, his net profit is $140. What is his net profit if he mows 12 lawns?

- **A.** 200
- **B.** 280
- **C.** 300
- **D.** 380
- **E.** 480

25. A square is inscribed in a circle whose circumference is $2\sqrt{2}\pi$. What is the perimeter of the square?

- **A.** 4
- **B.** $4\sqrt{2}$
- **C.** 8
- **D.** $8\sqrt{2}$
- **E.** 16

26. If the median of the three terms $\sqrt{x}$, $4x$, and x^2 is $\sqrt{x}$, which of the following could be the value of x?

- **A.** $\dfrac{1}{9}$
- **B.** 2
- **C.** $\dfrac{9}{4}$
- **D.** 4
- **E.** 9

27. Using 2 identical machines, a manufacturer can produce 60 toy trucks in 6 hours. If the manufacturer uses 3 such machines, how many hours would it take him to produce 75 toy trucks?

- **A.** 1
- **B.** 3
- **C.** 5
- **D.** 7
- **E.** 9

IF YOU FINISH BEFORE TIME IS CALLED, CHECK YOUR WORK ON THIS SECTION ONLY. DO NOT WORK ON ANY OTHER SECTION IN THE TEST.

STOP

Section 4: Writing

Time: 18 minutes
25 questions

Directions: Read each of the following questions carefully. Then select the best answer from the choices provided. Fill in the corresponding circle on your answer sheet.

The following sentences test your ability to recognize correctness and effectiveness of expression. In each sentence, part of the sentence or the entire sentence is underlined. Underneath each sentence, you'll find five ways of phrasing the underlined material. Choice A is the same as the original sentence in the question; the other four choices are different. If you think the original sentence is correct as written, select Choice A; if not, carefully consider choices B, C, D, and E and select the one you think is the best.

In making your selection, follow the requirements of standard written English. Carefully consider the grammar, diction (word choice) sentence construction, and punctuation of each sentence. When you make your choice, select the most effective sentence, the one that is clear and precise, without any awkwardness or ambiguity.

EXAMPLE:

The high fuel efficiency and low emissions of a newly released hybrid car <u>account for its attractiveness to</u> those who are environmentally aware.

    A. account for its attractiveness
    B. accounts for its attractiveness
    C. account for their attractiveness
    D. are the reason why it has attractiveness
    E. accounts for their attractiveness

The correct answer is A.

---

1. Last week, Principal Gertrude Studious honored many seniors, <u>especially while achieving high grades on their final exams.</u>

    A. especially while achieving high grades on their final exams.
    B. especially those who achieved high grades on their final exams.
    C. and especially those achieving high grades on their final exams.
    D. especially those whom achieved high grades on their final exams.
    E. especially the achieving of high grades on their final exams.

2. Although it was recently refurbished, <u>the new theater in Weston can accommodate fewer people than Hartford.</u>

    A. the new theater in Weston can accommodate fewer people than Hartford.
    B. the new theater in Weston can accommodate less people than Hartford.
    C. the new theater in Weston can accommodate less people than that of Hartford's.
    D. the new theater in Weston can accommodate fewer people than that in Hartford.
    E. the new theater in Weston is good for accommodating fewer people that in Hartford.

3. The world's best-known photographer of Native Americans, a powerful and evocative collection of Edward S. Curtis is available for sale in New York.

A. The world's best-known photographer of Native Americans, a powerful and evocative collection of Edward S. Curtis is available for sale in New York.

B. The world's best-known photographer of Native Americans, Edward S. Curtis's powerful and evocative collection is available for sale in New York.

C. Edward S. Curtis's powerful and evocative collection are available for sale in New York, and he is the world's best-known photographer of Native Americans.

D. The world's best known photographer of Native Americans, Edward S. Curtis's collection, powerful and evocative, is available for sale in New York.

E. A powerful and evocative collection of photographs by Edward S. Curtis, the world's best-known photographer of Native Americans, is available for sale in New York.

4. In the French Sculpture Galleries in the city museum, there is two bronzes by Edgar Degas, each of which depicts a young ballet dancer.

A. there is two bronzes by Edgar Degas, each of which depicts a young ballet dancer.

B. there are two bronzes by Edgar Degas, each of which depict a young ballet dancer.

C. there are two bronzes by Edgar Degas, each of which depicts a young ballet dancer.

D. there are two bronzes by Edgar Degas, each of who depict a young ballet dancer.

E. two bronzes by Edgar Degas, each of which depict a young ballet dancer.

5. While the Tokyo String Quartet has been performing together for almost 40 years, their latest incarnation is renowned for a warm richness of tone, an elegant phrasing, and their playing avant-garde pieces.

A. a warm richness of tone, an elegant phrasing, and their playing avant-garde pieces.

B. a warm richness of tone, an elegant phrasing, and their being willing to play an avant-garde repertoire.

C. using a warm richness of tone, having an elegant phrasing, and their willingness to play avant-garde pieces.

D. a warm richness of tone, their phrasing elegantly, and their playing avant-garde pieces.

E. a warm richness of tone, an elegant phrasing, and an avant-garde repertoire.

6. The European shag, a seabird whose susceptibility to parasite infections has been studied by scientists who discovered that more male chicks are infected than females.

A. a seabird whose susceptibility to parasite infections has been studied by scientists who discovered that more male chicks are infected than females.

B. a seabird who is susceptible to parasite infections, has been studied by scientists who discovered that more male than female chicks are infected.

C. a seabird, being susceptible to parasite infections, has been studied by scientists who discovered that more male chicks are infected than females.

D. a seabird who scientists have studied as to their susceptibility to parasite infections, discovered that more male chicks are infected than females.

E. a seabird whose susceptibility to parasite infections are being studied by scientists who had discovered that more male chicks are infected than females.

7. Botanists have learned that the peculiar qualities <u>that help the chili pepper survive are identical to those that attract potentially harmful
or even fatal bacteria.</u>

   A. that help the chili pepper survive are
   identical to those that attract potentially
   harmful or even fatal bacteria.
   B. that helps the chili pepper survive are
   potentially identical to that which
   attracts harmful or even fatal bacteria.
   C. that help the chili pepper survive are
   identical to those that have been
   attracting potentially harmful or even
   fatal bacteria.
   D. is identical to the one that attract
   potentially harmful or even fatal
   bacteria.
   E. is identical to those that attracts
   potentially harmful or even fatal
   bacteria.

8. Some people are reluctant to purchase a new
computer because the technology <u>of them is
changing so quickly.</u>

   A. of them is changing so quickly.
   B. is in a quick change.
   C. is changing so quickly.
   D. is quick in its changes.
   E. is on a quick change.

9. <u>Each of the scientists involved in studying the
brain have found that memory is stored in
neurons and may be retrieved</u> by stimulating
the same neurons that fired when the recalled
event first occurred.

   A. Each of the scientists involved in
   studying the brain have found that
   memory is stored in neurons and may
   be retrieved
   B. Each of the scientists who studies the
   brain have found that memory is stored
   in neurons and may be retrieved
   C. Each of the scientists involved in
   studying the brain has found that
   memory is stored in neurons and may
   be retrieved
   D. Each scientist involved in studying the
   brain have found that memory will be
   stored in neurons and may be retrieved
   E. Scientists involved in studying the brain
   has found that memory is stored in
   neurons and may be retrieved

10. Dashing madly for the taxi, <u>Seth's folder full
of papers fell from his briefcase.</u>

   A. Seth's folder full of papers fell from his
   briefcase.
   B. Seth's folder full of papers falling from
   his briefcase.
   C. papers fell from the folder in Seth's
   briefcase.
   D. Seth dropping a folder full of papers
   from his briefcase.
   E. Seth dropped a folder full of papers
   from his briefcase.

11. Acclaimed cellist Yo-Yo Ma, a brilliant musi-cian who is famed for his virtuoso perfor-mances that stimulate the imagination as he seeks to explore music as a means of communication.

    A. Acclaimed cellist Yo-Yo Ma, a brilliant musician who is famed for his virtuoso performances
    B. Acclaimed cellist Yo-Yo Ma, who is a brilliant musician who is famed for his virtuoso performances
    C. Acclaimed cellist Yo-Yo Ma is a brilliant musician famed for his virtuoso performances
    D. Acclaimed cellist Yo-Yo Ma, being a brilliant musician who is famed for his virtuoso performances
    E. A brilliant musician, Yo-Yo Ma, who is famed for his virtuoso performances

12. The lovely Indian dancer Madhavi Mudgal, a member of a family deeply committed to the classical arts, is the epitome of elegance and grace, her style blends ancient Hindustani traditions with a modern sensibility.

    A. is the epitome of elegance and grace, her style blends ancient Hindustani traditions with a modern sensibility.
    B. is the epitome of elegance and grace: her style blends ancient Hindustani traditions with a modern sensibility.
    C. the epitome of elegance and grace, her style blends ancient Hindustani traditions with a modern sensibility.
    D. is the epitome of elegance and grace and her style blends ancient Hindustani traditions with a modern sensibility.
    E. who is the epitome of elegance and grace, her style blends ancient Hindustani traditions with a modern sensibility.

13. Monticello, a fine example of Roman neo-classic architecture, was home to Thomas Jefferson; he began to build it when he was 26 years old.

    A. Thomas Jefferson; he began to build it when
    B. Thomas Jefferson, he began to build it when
    C. Thomas Jefferson who was building it when
    D. Thomas Jefferson; building it when
    E. Thomas Jefferson, in addition, he began building it when

Directions: In the following questions, you will be tested on your ability to recognize errors in grammar and usage. Every sentence below contains either one error or no errors. None of the sentences contains more than one error. If the sentence contains an error, it will be in one of the underlined parts of the sentence. You should find the part of the sentence that needs to be changed to make the sentence correct. If you think the sentence is correct as written, select Choice E. Keep the requirements of standard written English in mind as you read the sentences carefully.

EXAMPLE:

As the doors to Carnegie Hall <u>slowly opened</u> and the audience <u>began to</u> flow in, each of the musi-
                                     A   B

cians <u>in the orchestra</u> tuned <u>their</u> instrument before striking the opening chords of the symphony.
           C   D

<u>No error.</u>
  E

The correct answer is D.

---

14. Pie safes, <u>used during</u> the 19th century to
            A
store cooling baked goods, <u>are</u> prized by
                      B
collectors for <u>its value</u> as reminders of
            C
American life before the <u>advent of</u> the
                    D
refrigerator. <u>No error.</u>
         E

15. Agronomists experimenting with hybrid
vegetables <u>have been unable</u> to grow many
           A
<u>of these</u> plants in the desert <u>because</u> there is
  B   C
not <u>sufficient enough</u> rainfall in the area.
       D
<u>No error.</u>
  E

16. American aviation pioneer Amelia Earhart,
the first woman to receive the Distinguished
Flying Cross, <u>flew</u> solo across the Atlantic
        A
Ocean <u>to prove</u> to <u>skeptics that</u> a woman
      B   C
was just as <u>capable to fly</u> airplanes as men.
           D
<u>No error.</u>
  E

17. <u>Because of</u> the judge's <u>glacial</u> attitude and
  A   B
arrogant commentary, many petitioners
found her so <u>irreproachable</u> that <u>they were</u>
        C   D
too intimidated to present their requests to
her. <u>No error.</u>
    E

18. <u>Just as</u> some parents feel the cellphone
       A

    <u>has enhanced</u> communication within <u>their</u>
         B   C

    families, so others find <u>them</u> a nuisance and
                            D

    an unnecessary expense. <u>No error.</u>
                             E

19. <u>On a warm day</u> last June, I <u>discovered</u>
         A   B

    hand-knitted baby blankets <u>browsing</u> the
                              C

    country flea market <u>with</u> my Aunt Pearl.
                      D

    <u>No error.</u>
     E

20. Many students <u>found</u> that if they
                A

    <u>would have taken</u> out loans for their college
          B

    studies, they would <u>have been</u> in a better
                    C

    financial situation <u>when</u> they finished their
                   D

    education. <u>No error.</u>
              E

21. <u>Because</u> hurricane season was <u>rapidly</u>
       A   B

    approaching, the owners of the small hotel

    on the beach <u>decided to</u> take precautions
                 C

    <u>as outlined</u> in their hurricane handbook and
       D

    pack up all the outdoor furniture. <u>No error.</u>
                                      E

22. Professor North, along <u>with many</u> of his
                           A

    colleagues, <u>have</u> recently attended the
               B

    <u>conference on</u> coelacanths <u>sponsored</u> by
       C   D

    the marine biology department of the

    University of South Florida. <u>No error.</u>
                           E

Questions 23–25 are based on the following passage.

Directions: The following passage is an early draft of an essay that needs some editing and revision. First, read the passage; then consider the questions that follow. Some will ask you to revise a particular sentence or will ask you to find the best version of the sentence. Other questions will ask you about the structure or organization of the essay. Always consider your revisions in the context of the whole essay. In choosing your answers, follow the requirements of standard written English.

---

(1) This has been a historic year for sports fans in New York who must bid a fond farewell to a shrine of America's favorite sport. (2) Shea Stadium, home of the Mets since 1964, is slated for demolishment. (3) Since the ballpark is not a particularly impressive architectural construction, fans have been seen to become teary as the date of destruction nears.

(4) Shea Stadium has been the home of the Amazin' Mets since 1964. (5) The steel and concrete structure in Flushing was originally going to be named "Flushing Meadows Stadium." (6) However, the decision was made to name it in honor of William A. Shea, an attorney who led the campaign to bring a National League team back to the Big Apple. (7) One of the most distinctive features of the stadium is the big scoreboard, which provides scores from out-of-town games, shows color slides, and leading the crowd in sing-a-longs. (8) No one who has been to a game and witnessed the Mets score a home run can forget the sight of the big apple rising out of a top hat behind the scoreboard or the unfailingly optimistic antics of Mr. Met, the fuzzy baseball mascot.

(9) The Shea good-bye ceremony brought back great players from past teams who were honored as they crossed home plate for the last time.

23. Which of the following is the best version of the underlined portion of sentence 3 (reproduced below)?

Since the ballpark is not a particularly impressive architectural construction, fans have been seen to become teary as the date of destruction nears.

A. As it is now

B. However, the ballpark is not a particularly impressive architectural construction,

C. Although the ballpark is not a particularly impressive architectural construction,

D. The ballpark is not a particularly impressive architectural construction; consequently,

E. Because the ballpark is not a particularly impressive architectural construction,

24. Which is the best version of sentence 7 (reproduced below)?

One of the most distinctive features of the stadium is the big scoreboard, which provides scores from out-of-town games, shows color slides, and leading the crowd in sing-a-longs.

A. As it is now

B. One of the most distinctive features of the stadium is the big scoreboard, which is providing scores from out-of-town games, showing color slides, and leading the crowd in sing-a-longs.

C. One of the most distinctive features of the stadium is the big scoreboard provides scores from out-of-town games, shows color slides, and leads the crowd in sing-a-longs.

D. One of the most distinctive features of the stadium is the big scoreboard, which is one that provides scores from out-of-town games, shows color slides, and leads the crowd in sing-a-longs.

E. One of the most distinctive features of the stadium, the big scoreboard, provides scores from out-of-town games, shows color slides, and leads the crowd in sing-a-longs.

25. Which of the following is the best sentence to follow sentence 9 (reproduced below)?

The Shea good-bye ceremony brought back great players from past teams who were honored as they crossed home plate for the last time.

A. If you were there, you would have been moved to tears by the remarkable ceremony.

B. Fans may say farewell to the old stadium but not to the many memories of triumphant victories and troubling defeats.

C. Even though the Mets lost, I wish could have been there for the last game.

D. Shea Stadium is a great ballpark and should not be demolished.

E. The new stadium will be built nearby and will have many more modern amenities.

IF YOU FINISH BEFORE TIME IS CALLED, CHECK YOUR WORK ON THIS SECTION ONLY. DO NOT WORK ON ANY OTHER SECTION IN THE TEST.

Scoring the Diagnostic Test

Answer Key

Section 2: Critical Reading

1. E	10. C	19. A	28. B
2. D	11. B	20. C	29. E
3. C	12. D	21. D	30. A
4. C	13. E	22. B	31. A
5. C	14. C	23. E	32. E
6. A	15. B	24. D	33. B
7. A	16. B	25. B	
8. D	17. D	26. A	
9. B	18. B	27. C	

Section 3: Mathematics

1. D	8. A	15. B	22. C
2. A	9. D	16. B	23. D
3. C	10. B	17. E	24. D
4. D	11. B	18. D	25. C
5. C	12. A	19. E	26. A
6. C	13. C	20. C	27. C
7. C	14. B	21. B	

Section 4: Writing

1. B	8. C	15. D	22. B
2. D	9. C	16. D	23. C
3. E	10. E	17. C	24. E
4. C	11. C	18. D	25. B
5. E	12. B	19. C	
6. B	13. A	20. B	
7. A	14. C	21. E	

Answer Explanations

Section 1: The Essay

First, reread your essay. Then look at the rubric below and see which description best fits your essay. Try to be objective as you evaluate how well you did in each area listed under the score in the rubric.

Look at the sample essays and compare your essay to the samples provided. If you think your essay is better than the 2, but not as good as the 4, give yourself a 3. If you think your essay is better than the 4, but not as good as the 6, give yourself a 5. (*Tip:* Because grading your own essay can be difficult, ask an English teacher at your school to grade it for you, based on the rubric below.)

The SAT essay is scored on a scale of 1 to 6 points. Two scorers read each essay, and their scores are added together, so the highest score an essay can receive is a 12. This essay score counts as one-third of your total writing score. The multiple-choice grammar sections (there are two on the SAT) count as the other two-thirds.

Essays are scored holistically by experienced high school and college English teachers; graders read the essays rather quickly and get an impression of the entire essay. You don't lose points for grammatical errors; in fact, grammar is only one of the factors the graders consider. Because the graders know that you're writing this essay in a stressful situation under time constraints, your essay is graded as if it were the first draft of an essay.

After you have scored your essay and the multiple-choice writing section, use the worksheets later in this chapter to help you determine your writing score.

Rubric for the SAT Essay

6	5	4
Addresses the task in a perceptive and exemplary manner, which demonstrates exceptional critical thinking Supports the position with well-chosen and well-developed examples Uses transitional words effectively to organize and achieve coherence Uses lively and appropriate vocabulary Effectively varies sentence structure Is free of serious grammatical errors	Addresses the task proficiently and demonstrates clear critical thinking Supports and develops the position with good examples Shows evidence of a coherent organizational plan Uses appropriate vocabulary Has evidence of sentence variety Has a few grammatical and usage errors	Addresses the task satisfactorily Takes a position and has sufficient examples to support the position competently Demonstrates a functional organizational plan Uses appropriate but routine or "flat" vocabulary Is inconsistent in its use of sentence variety Contains grammatical and usage errors, but not so many as to prevent understanding

3	2	1
Does not address the task proficiently, but shows some developing capability of critical thinking	Is very vague or incomplete in its position; critical thinking is weak or absent	Does not take a position or display any evidence of critical thinking skills
Is inconsistent in the development of the position; examples are not particularly apt or well-developed	Lacks adequate development of examples to support the position	Shows no evidence of support; no appropriate examples are presented
Shows little evidence of an organizational structure	Is unfocused and lacks coherence	Lacks focus and has no organizational plan
Uses "flat" or unsuitable vocabulary	Shows little evidence of skill with language; vocabulary is weak and inappropriate	Shows no evidence of skill with language; vocabulary is badly chosen
Does not demonstrate skill in sentence variety	Demonstrates frequent difficulty with sentence construction	Demonstrates serious errors in sentence construction
Has numerous and obvious errors in grammar and usage	Is rife with such serious errors in grammar and usage that meaning is unclear	Is rife with such serious and glaring grammatical and usage errors that meaning is lost

If your essay does not approach the topic and answer the question, it will receive a grade of 0 (no matter how well-written it may be).

Sample Essays

Sample A (Score: 2)

All human beings have selfish desires without even noticing it themselves. It is perfectly natural to always relate certain things to yourself. People work, go to school, study, and do things that they specifically do not like for themselves. Being selfish is defined as only thinking for yourself and no others. Some examples are not sharing, not thinking of others in certain situations like that.

At most times, people are more selfish when they are younger. For example, kids not sharing their toys with other kids because they want it for themselves. I think selfishness has a lot to do with fear and they are scared to have things taken away so therefore they are selfish. Even at this age, 16 years old, sharing is enormously difficult.

Shakespeare's play, Macbeth, the main character shows much selfishness, he does unimaginable things to the king. His selfish desires leads him to kill innocent people, and even kills the people that trusted him. Selfishness is capable of making anyone do anything.

Explanation of score: Although this essay attempts to take a position ("all human beings have selfish desires"), it never develops the thesis. The critical thinking is weak in that it never actually addresses the duality of human nature. It does not offer any concrete examples, but only presents general statements and some vague and underdeveloped examples ("kids not sharing their toys with other kids because they want it for themselves"). When the essay does attempt to offer a specific example, it remains poorly developed ("Macbeth, the main character shows much selfishness, he does unimaginable things to the king. His selfish desires leads him to kill innocent people, and even kills the people that trusted him.") The writer uses awkward language ("Selfishness is capable of making anyone do anything") and has difficulty with sentence structure (fragments and run-ons). While this essay falls into the upper range of a score of 2, it does not have enough solid evidence to merit a 3.

Sample B (Score: 4)

There will always be people who are driven by selfish desires, but there are good people in the world who put the needs of others before their own needs. Most people, I believe, are unselfish by nature.

People who put others before themselves have a love of helping others. A single parent who works two jobs to support his or her family puts their needs before his or her own. These parents will buy clothes and other things for their children and do without it themselves. Some kids will even give their allowance to charity for no reason other than they want to help another person who does not have what they have.

The TV show *Extreme Makeover* does a good job portraying those who do extraordinary things for others and their community. In one episode, a mother and a father have four children. Two are disabled and use wheelchairs. Their house is small and hard for them to get around. These parents work very hard and run a day-care center to help their children, but they cannot afford to move to a bigger house. This is where *Extreme Makeover* comes in to grant this family a new home that is specially created so the kids can get around easily. Because this family has been helping their community by having a day-care center, the TV people help them with a reward of a new house.

Some people are motivated by selfishness and are determined to provide more for themselves. Others are driven by the desire to help people in need. People who are unselfish inspire other people to follow their example and make the world a better place.

Explanation of score: This essay takes a position and addresses the task competently. The thesis statement ("Most people, I believe, are unselfish by nature") is supported with two examples. The first example, "A single parent who works two jobs to support his or her family," is somewhat of a generalization and is not as specific as it should be. The second example shows more evidence of critical thinking in that it is more detailed and explains the "rewards" of unselfishness. The writing is straightforward, but lacks precision and liveliness. Most sentences are simple, and there is little variety in vocabulary and sentence structure. There are no major grammatical errors, just an occasional awkwardness: "These parents will buy clothes and other things for their children and do without it themselves." Overall, this essay fits the criteria for a score of 4.

Sample C (Score: 6)

Human nature is difficult to define, primarily because it is unpredictable and inconsistent. While one person may be driven by selfish impulses, another may be completely altruistic. Both may involve themselves in alleviating the plight of others, but for contradictory reasons.

Patriotic acts reveal the dichotomy in human nature. Some soldiers, for example, may enlist in the military for personal gain and glory. They thrive on the glamour of uniforms, the adulation of their friends and families, and the respect of their countrymen. Other s join out of love for their fellow man, to save some unfortunate from a harsh dictator or a repressive regime. While both soldiers put their lives on the line and face the possibility of death or injury, only one of the two is truly unselfish.

The same principle holds true for ordinary citizens. Do we give up our holiday to help serve meals in a soup kitchen because of our concern that other human beings are homeless and hungry or because it makes us feel good about ourselves? When teenagers spend time in a nursing home entertaining the elderly or spend summers working for Habitat for Humanity are they selfless, or are they collecting their community service hours?

Perhaps, then, it is impossible to conclude that human nature is definable as selfish or selfless. Yet, I, for one, am not ready to give up on altruism. The history of mankind is filled with innumerable acts of selfless compassion and benevolence. Strangers who risk their lives and jump onto subway tracks to help someone who has fallen, doctors who give up their lucrative practices and spend one month every year in impoverished nations, and teachers who stay after school on their own time to help students—everyone knows someone who is driven by kindness rather than by personal gain.

Clearly, human nature is as diverse as human beings themselves. Nevertheless, it is the cooperative spirit that has helped us evolve. Had our ancestors not sacrificed self-interest and worked together for the common good, they would have starved. Thus, humanity has a long history of compassion, one that we must nurture in a world often driven by self rather than by selflessness.

Explanation of score: This well-written essay shows outstanding critical thinking. The writer chose to investigate human nature rather than to definitively state one position or another. She did this thoughtfully and insightfully, using apt examples such as soldiers and ordinary citizens to illustrate different motivations for charitable actions. The writing is precise and effective, and the vocabulary is lively and appropriate: "They thrive on the glamour of uniforms, the adulation of their friends and families, and the respect of their countrymen." The essay shows impressive control and smooth transitions from one idea to the next. The writer concludes with her optimistic opinion backed up with evidence: "Had our ancestors not sacrificed self-interest and worked together for the common good, they would have starved." This essay clearly deserves a score of 6.

Section 2: Critical Reading

1. **E** Sentence 1 is a one-blank definitional sentence *(see Chapter V, Section B)*. To answer this question, you must find the clue in the sentence ("shun attention") and know that Choice E, *diffidence,* means shyness *(see Chapter VII)*.

2. **D** Sentence 2 is a one-blank logic-based sentence *(see Chapter V, Section D)*. To answer this question correctly, you must note the signal words (see Chapter V, Section A) that set up the logic of the sentence. The signal words *Rather than* set up an opposition. The logic of the sentence indicates that "Ella and Alex" did not pay attention to "the signs warning picnickers to remain on the paths." Choice D, *heed* (to pay attention), will fit the logic of the sentence.

3. **C** Sentence 3 is a two-blank definitional sentence *(see Chapter V, Section C)*. It begins with a signal word, *Although,* which is followed by the clue, "nothing alike." You're given additional clues in the characteristics of each of the twins: "Jessica is reserved" and "her brother is extroverted." You look through the choices knowing the definitions of the two words: the first word will be similar in meaning to *reserved* and the second word will be similar in meaning to *extroverted.* You also know the words will be opposites. Choice C, *introspective . . . ebullient,* fits all the clues.

4. **C** Sentence 4 is a two-blank logic-based sentence *(see Chapter V, Section E)*. This sentence is a bit tricky because you must note that it has two negative words, *not* and *declined.* In addition, you must understand the logic of what it means to "decline ideals for a more expedient solution." *Expedient (see Chapter VII)* means something that is advantageous, often for practical reasons. Thus, Sophie is the kind of person who would *not* give up her ideals to gain an advantage. An opportunist is a person who will take advantage of any situation to gain in some way *(see Chapter VII)*. Clearly, *not an opportunist* accurately describes Sophie. The verb *to compromise* means to put something in jeopardy or to lessen its value *(see Chapter VII)*. If Sophie is not an opportunist, then she would not want to compromise her ideals.

5. C Sentence 5 is a two-blank logic-based sentence *(see Chapter V, Section E)*. In the first half of the sentence, you're given the information that Dr. Gonzalez's book is concise, yet it "includes all species" of North American birds. Logically, a concise guide to *all* species cannot cover the topic in great depth. The signal word *hence* indicates that the second half of the sentence is a result of the statement in the first half of the sentence. So, while the guide is comprehensive *(see Chapter VII)*, it does not go into great detail and lacks depth. Choice C fits the logic of the sentence.

6. A Sentence 6 is a two-blank definitional sentence *(see Chapter V, Section C)*. As on the actual SAT, the questions get more difficult as you progress through the section. This sentence presents a challenge in that the definitions embedded in the sentence are difficult vocabulary words. To answer this question correctly, you should know the meaning of two key words, *much-vaunted* (highly praised) and *acumen* (keenness of insight) *(see Chapter VII)*. However, even if you aren't sure of the exact definitions of these words, you should be able to get the impression that the sentence is a positive portrayal of C. Auguste Dupin. Armed with that impression, you can eliminate any answer with a negative word and be left with Choice A.

7. A Sentence 7 is a combination of the two-blank definitional sentence *(see Chapter V, Section C)* and the two-blank logic-based sentence *(see Chapter V, Section E)*. The definitions of the clues within the sentence—*secular, leavens, piety*, and *irreverent*—provide the logic of the sentence. By stating that the poet's later verse is *secular* (nonreligious), while his youthful verse displays *piety* (religious devotion) *(see Chapter VII)*, the logic leads you to find words that are opposites to fill in the blanks. The first word is one associated with religious devotion, while the second word suggests secular irreverence, since the verb *leavens* means "to enliven or lighten the mood." In Choice A, *sober* suggests seriousness, and *wit* means "clever humor"; both words fit the logic of the sentence.

8. D Sentence 8 is a one-blank definitional sentence *(see Chapter V, Section B)*. The definition of the missing word is embedded in the sentence "used the art of rhetoric to deceive." Choice D, *specious,* means something that has the appearance of truth, but is actually false *(see Chapter VII)*.

9. B Sentence 9 is a one-blank logic-based sentence *(see Chapter V, Section D)*. The sentence begins with a signal word, *Because,* which sets up a cause-and-effect relationship between the two clauses in the sentence. The statement that "digital painting is still neither totally accepted nor completely rejected" tells you that museums might or might not include this art in their collections. Because the inclusion is not a definite yes or no, the implication is that the museum can decide for itself. Based solely on individual choice, the decision becomes an arbitrary one.

10. C Question 10 is a line reference/author's purpose question *(see Chapter VI, Section F)*. It requires you to understand what the author is trying to accomplish when he states that his novel has "faults." If you just read the first sentence, you may be tempted by choices A or D. Be sure to read beyond the sentence that is referenced in the question. In fact, the best clue is in the third sentence, which states that "a book may be amusing with numerous errors." Thus, the author admits a book does not have to be perfect to be interesting. Choice C is then more accurate than Choice A or Choice D.

11. B Question 11 is a line reference/author's purpose question *(see Chapter VI, Section F)*. To answer correctly, you must ascertain the purpose of a specific phrase. Ask yourself why the author chose to use the words *age of opulence and refinement.* Read before and after the phrase to find evidence in the text to help you. The sentence after the reference suggests that the hero is a simple country man, which would contrast with the "age of opulence and refinement," so Choice B is the only answer that indicates contrast.

12. D This is a line reference/inference question *(see Chapter VI, Section E)*. You need to understand the phrase *touch with his roots* and know that it suggests or implies that Arnold remained firmly "rooted" in the values he had as a child. The passage states that Arnold grew up poor and lived a hard life on a farm, so Choice D is the best answer.

13. E Question 13 is a main purpose question *(see Chapter VI, Section B)*. Think about *why* the author wrote this passage. Ask yourself what he was trying to accomplish. Since this passage is about more than one particular aspect of Arnold's life, *present an overview* is the best answer.

14. C This primary purpose question *(see Chapter VI, Section B)* asks you to consider the entire passage and characterize it as a whole. For this type of question, you should not focus on one small segment of the piece, but look at it in its entirety. Since the characters display no hostility toward each other, and there is no satirical point of view, Choice C is the best answer.

15. B This mood question *(see Chapter VI, Section G)* asks you to think about the atmosphere of the first paragraph of the passage and select the word that best describes the mood. ***Remember:*** This question asks you to look at the first paragraph *only,* not the whole passage. The words *stiller* and *sleepy sound* are the key to the quiet mood in the first paragraph.

16. B To answer this question, you need to read closely and understand the context of the phrase *finding itself nonsense.* This is a line reference/purpose question *(see Chapter VI, Section F)*. The source of the phrase is the voice from the bed. Therefore, it must emanate from the bed-ridden woman. That leaves only choices B and C. Since the voice in the bed is the speaker, it must be Choice B because the voice from the bed is the speaker, not the listener.

17. D To answer this question, you must read the context closely. The phrase in question precedes the rising of the figure who is sitting in the chair. Clearly, the sound arises from this figure, the nurse whose uniform is made of stiff linen.

18. B The second call to the nurse is made by a voice "with a tickle of laughter in it." This clue should lead you to Choice B, because laughter suggests that the speaker is amused, not impatient, dissatisfied, in pain, or vigorous.

19. A To answer this question, you must consider your first picture of the nurse. She is described as "a tall strapping girl" and "as vigorous and healthy as a young tree." Then she yawns and rubs her eyes. These context clues lead you to Choice A.

20. C This is a vocabulary-in-context question *(see Chapter VI, Section H)*. Use the context to select the best meaning of the word as it is used in the passage. Immediately after the "annihilating yawn," the nurse "gives up." She tries to suppress the yawn, but she's too tired to hold it in. This suggests that the yawn is defeating.

21. D This question tries to trick you into missing the metaphorical use of the phrase *tempered steely.* The soul of the woman on the bed is compared to the blade of a *rapier*, a thin-bladed sword, which suggests her inner strength. There are no weapons in the room (as far as the passage indicates), and the woman is not angry. The reference to the surgeon is a distracter, a choice meant to lead you off base.

22. B This is a language question that asks you to take note of the series of similes in this paragraph. The language is metaphorical, not literal *(see Chapter VI, Section G)*. For definitions of the words in choices A, C, D, or E, see Chapter VII.

23. **E** In an *except* question *(see Chapter VI, Section A)*, you must remember that four of the answers will be correct. You're now looking for the incorrect answer. It's also a vocabulary question; to answer correctly, you should know the meanings of all the words *(see Chapter VII)*. All the feelings are present in the passage except indignation.

24. **D** If the question says, "According to the author," you should be able to find this detail in the text *(see Chapter VI, Section E)*. The author specifically says: "The threat to these bears does not come from predators, but from global climate changes. Increased burning of fossil fuels has caused an unprecedented warming, which in turn has caused a loss of sea ice." Follow the logic of the two sentences. It should lead you to Choice D, the loss of the ice that is home to the polar bears.

25. **B** This question requires you to do some interpretation. The animal lovers referred to in line 17 are disturbed by reports that "this awesome, and for thousands of years self-sufficient, creature has been forced to rummage around garbage pails and camp sites for scraps of food." This context clue should lead you to understand that the animal lovers are upset at the food-scavenging behavior of the bears. By describing the bears as "awesome and previously self-sufficient," the author suggests that they are no longer so, as evidenced by the fact that they're forced to eat garbage. This behavior has *demeaned* (lowered the status) of the bears.

26. **A** This tone question *(see Chapter VI, Section G)* tests both your ability to detect the author's attitude toward his subject and your vocabulary. It is important to remember that *both* words in the answer must be correct. It's also important to note that the question refers to the last sentence of passage 1, not the whole passage: "Clearly, to ensure the survival of these beloved symbols of the Arctic, we must take action to prevent the diminution of their habitat." The author expresses admiration for the polar bears, but he is not cautious; in fact, he strongly urges action to protect the polar bears. Thus, Choice A, *respectful . . . exigent* (demanding immediate action), is the most accurate description of the tone.

27. **C** To find the correct statement that would *undermine* (weaken) the primary argument of passage 1, you must first know what the primary argument is. The primary argument of passage 1 is that global climate changes have posed a danger to the polar bears that live on ice shelves in the Arctic. Thus, if it were discovered that climate fluctuation did not affect animal populations, the argument of passage 1 would be weakened.

28. **B** This is a vocabulary-in-context question *(see Chapter VI, Section H)*. Try substituting each word in the choices for the word in the passage. *Foundation* makes the most sense in the sentence as it is used in the passage.

29. **E** Another vocabulary-in-context question *(see Chapter VI, Section H)*. Follow the same technique as in the preceding question. Substitute the phrases in the answers for the word *abused* in the passage. Since the remarks in the passage refer to a government agency being used to make policy, the phrase *taken advantage of* best fits the meaning of the sentence in the passage.

30. **A** To answer this synthesis question *(see Chapter VI, Section I)*, you must understand the position of the author of passage 1 and consider how he would respond to the "fear that environmentalists are using the polar bear as an excuse to influence policy." Since you already know that the author of passage 1 advocates a policy that helps the polar bears, you can safely assume he would welcome a change in policy that would secure the continuation of the polar bears.

31. **A** This is an inference question *(see Chapter VI, Section D)*. You need to reread the government official's comments (passage 2, lines 12–21) and think about his position. He makes a point to separate the "endangered" status for the polar bears from any government policy regarding global warming.

He wants to make it clear that his action on the polar bears does not mean he believes global warming is the cause of the problem nor does he want his position on the bears to be taken as a statement of policy.

32. **E** Another synthesis question *(see Chapter VI, Section I)*, this question asks you to find a statement with which *both* authors would agree. Some of the statements in the choices would be acceptable to one of the authors, while other statements are not mentioned by either of the authors. Only on Choice E would both authors agree. The action of putting polar bears on the endangered species list acknowledges a condition that must be rectified and constitutes human interference.

33. **B** This tone question *(see Chapter VI, Section G)* tests both your ability to detect the author's attitude toward his subject and your vocabulary. It also amps up the difficulty by using the words *more* and *less* before the tone words. Passage 1 is more subjective *(magnificent, awesome, beloved)* as it expresses great admiration for the polar bears and urges strong action to protect the species. Thus it is *less detached* (impartial) than passage 2.

Section 3: Mathematics

1. **D** For each jacket, George can pick 4 ties to match—thus, (3)(4) = 12 combinations. *(See Chapter XIII, Section A.)*

2. **A** Since $5(x - 2) = 10$, divide both sides of the equation by 5 and you have $x - 2 = 2$. *(See Chapter XI, Section B.)*

3. **C** The average score can be obtained by $\frac{80 + 95 + 98}{3} = \frac{273}{3} = 91$. *(See Chapter XIII, Section C.)*

4. **D** Use the equation $\left(\frac{2}{3}\right)\left(\frac{1}{2}\right)N = 36$. Simplify and you have $\left(\frac{1}{3}\right)N = 36$ or $n = 108$. *(See Chapter XI, Section B.)*

5. **C** Note that 20 and 40 are both divisible by 4, but only 40 is a member of Set B. Thus, the probability is $\frac{1}{4}$. *(See Chapter XIII, Section B.)*

6. **C** The ratio of boys to girls is 3 to 4. Thus $3x$ and $4x$ could represent the numbers of boys and girls, respectively. Thus, the total number of students is $7x$. So, the number of subjects has to be divisible by 7, which means 28 is the right answer. *(See Chapter X, Section B.)*

7. **C** Begin with 2 # 3, and you have $(2)^2 + 2(3) = 10$. Then 3 # 2 = $(3)^2 + 3(2) = 15$. Thus, $\frac{2 \# 3}{3 \# 2} = \frac{10}{15}$ or $\frac{2}{3}$. *(See Chapter XIV, Section A.)*

8. **A** This is an arithmetic sequence with a common difference of 5. The nth term is $a_0 + (n - 1)d$, where a_0 is the first term. Thus, the 11th term is $10 + (11 - 1)5 = 60$, and the 5th term is $10 + (5 - 1)5 = 30$. The quotient is $\frac{60}{30} = 2$. *(See Chapter X, Section E.)*

9. **D** Begin with $q(2)$, and you have $q(2) = 1$. Thus, $p(q(2)) = p(1) = 2$. *(See Chapter XI, Section H.)*

10. **B** With Karen in seat C, there are 3 choices for one of the seats (say, seat A), 2 choices for another seat (say, seat B), and 1 choice for the remaining seat (seat D). Thus, the total number of assignments is (3)(2)(1) = 6. *(See Chapter XIII, Section A.)*

11. **B** The sum of the measure of the angles of a triangle is 180°. Thus, $x + x + 2y = 180°$ or $2x + 2y = 180°$ or $x + y = 90°$. Also, $2x + x + y = 180°$, or $3x + y = 180°$. From $3x + y = 180°$, subtract $x + y = 90°$, and you have $2x = 90°$ or $x = 45°$. Substitute $x = 45°$ in $x + y = 90°$, and you have $y = 45°$. Thus,

$x + y = 90°$. *(See Chapter XII, Section A. Also see Appendix on Solving a System of Equations.)*

12. **A** Since $a = 2b$ and $b = 3c$, $a = 2(3c)$ or $a = 6c$. You're also given $c = ak$. Substitute $c = ak$ in $a = 6c$, and you have $a = 6(ak)$ or $a = 6ak$ or $\frac{1}{6} = k$. *(See Chapter XI, Section E and see Appendix on Solving A System of Equations.)*

13. **C** If the area is $36x^2$, then a side of the square is $6x$. Thus, the perimeter is $4(6x) = 24x$. *(See Chapter XII, Section D.)*

14. **B** For a reflection about the y-axis, you substitute $-x$ for x. Thus, $f(-x) = 2(-x) + 4 = -2x + 4$. *(See Chapter XII, Section I.)*

15. **B** If $AD + DE = 10$, then $AB + EF = 10$ and $BC + GF = 10$. Thus, the perimeter is the sum of $(AD + DE) + (AB + EF) + (BC + GF) + GC = 10 + 10 + 10 + 2 = 32$. *(See Chapter XII, Section D.)*

16. **B** Note that 5 feet 6 inches is equivalent to 5.5 feet. Set up a proportion, $\frac{5.5}{11} = \frac{5}{x}$, where x is the length of Janet's shadow. Thus, $5.5x = 5(11)$ or $x = \frac{5(11)}{5.5}$ or $x = 10$. *(See Chapter X, Section B.)*

17. **E** To find the roots of $f(x)$, set $f(x) = 0$. Thus, $x(x - 1)(x + 2) = 0$ or $x = 0, 1$, and -2. *(See Chapter XI, Section H.)*

18. **D** Rewriting $2 \leq |x| \leq 5$, you have $|x| \geq 2$ and $|x| \leq 5$. Since $|x| \geq 2$, you have $x \geq 2$ or $x \leq -2$. Also, $|x| \leq 5$, so you have $-5 \leq x \leq 5$. Thus, numbers that satisfy both conditions are $-5 \leq x \leq -2$ and $2 \leq x \leq 5$. *(See Chapter XI, Section D.)*

19. **E** If $\overline{AB} \perp \overline{AC}$, then $m\angle A = 90°$. Thus $m\angle AMN + m\angle ANM = 90°$. Note that $\angle AMD$ and $\angle AMN$ are supplementary. So are $\angle ANE$ and $\angle ANM$. Thus, $x° + m\angle AMN + m\angle ANM + y° = 360°$, or $x + y + 90° = 360°$ or $x + y = 270°$. *(See Chapter XII, Section A.)*

20. **C** Since $f(x) = x^2 + bx + c$, the coefficient of x^2 is 1, which means $f(x)$ is concave up. Also, $c = \left(\frac{b}{2}\right)^2$, then $f(x) = x^2 + bx + \left(\frac{b}{2}\right)^2$ or $f(x) = \left(x + \frac{b}{2}\right)^2$. Set $f(x) = 0$, and you have $x = -\frac{b}{2}$. Since b is positive, $f(x)$ has one negative root. *(See Chapter XII, Section I.)*

21. **B** The *mode* is the number that appears most often. In this case, the mode is 1. The median is the middle number, and in this case, it's also 1. Thus, the sum of the mode and median number of calculators is $1 + 1 = 2$. *(See Chapter XIII, Section C.)*

22. **C** The volume of the cube is $(6)^3 = 216$. The volume of the rectangular container is $v = lwh$. Set $216 = (8)(3)(h)$ and you have $216 = 24h$ or $h = 9$. *(See Chapter XII, Section E.)*

23. **D** Since $p(x) = x^2 + 2x$, $p(2h) = (2h)^2 + 2(2h) = 4h^2 + 4h$. Set $4h^2 + 4h = 8h$, and you have $4h^2 - 4h = 0$ or $4h(h - 1) = 0$. Thus, $h = 0$ or $h = 1$. Since $h > 0$, $h = 1$. *(See Chapter XI, Section H.)*

24. **D** Let x be the price for moving one lawn. Then $6x - 100 = 140$, or $6x = 240$ or $x = 40$. So, Bill charges \$40 per lawn. Thus, 12 lawns $= 12(\$40) = \$480$. His net profit is $\$480 - \$100 = \$380$. *(See Chapter XIV, Section B.)*

25. **C** If the circumference of a circle is $2\sqrt{2}\pi$, then $2\pi r = 2\sqrt{2}\pi$ or $r = \sqrt{2}$, and the diameter is $2\sqrt{2}$. Note that the diameter is also a diagonal of the square. Thus using the Pythagorean theorem (or the 45-45 right-triangle relationship), you have $x^2 + x^2 = \left(2\sqrt{2}\right)^2$ or $2x^2 = 8$. Thus, $x^2 = 4$ or $x = 2$. Therefore, the perimeter of the square is $2(4) = 8$. *(See Chapter XII, Section F.)*

26. **A** Substitute $x = \frac{1}{9}$ in the 3 terms $\sqrt{x}$, $4x$, and x^2 and you have $\sqrt{\frac{1}{9}}$, $4\left(\frac{1}{9}\right)$, and $\left(\frac{1}{9}\right)^2$ or $\frac{1}{3}$, $\frac{4}{9}$, and $\frac{1}{81}$. Note that $\sqrt{x} = \frac{1}{3}$. Arranging them from smallest to largest, you have $\frac{1}{8}$, $\frac{1}{3}$, and $\frac{4}{9}$. Thus, $\sqrt{x}$ is the median. *(See Chapter XIII, Section C.)*

27. **C** If 2 machines can produce 60 trucks in 6 hours, then 1 machine can produce 30 trucks in 6 hours, or 5 trucks in 1 hour. Thus, 3 machines can produce 15 trucks in 1 hour. Therefore, it takes 3 machines 5 hours to produce 75 toy trucks. *(See Chapter XIV, Section B.)*

Section 4: Writing

1. **B** This sentence has a modification problem *(see Chapter IX, Section E)*. The participle *achieving* is dangling in the original sentence and implies that the principal is achieving rather than the students. Adding the phrase *those who* clears up the ambiguity.

2. **D** The error is lack of parallel comparison *(see Chapter IX, Section I)*. You can only compare the theater in Weston to the theater (or that) in Hartford. You must also know usage rules regarding *fewer* and *less*. *Less* is used for whole quantities; *fewer* is used for anything you can count. Since you can count people, *fewer* is correct.

3. **E** The sentence has a misplaced modifier *(see Chapter IX, Section E)*. The opening phrase describes Edward S. Curtis: his name must immediately follow the comma, or the entire sentence must be reconfigured. Only Choice E is grammatically correct.

4. **C** The original sentence contains an error in subject-verb agreement: the plural subject *bronzes* needs the plural verb *are (see Chapter IX, Section J)*. In reading the choices, you must be careful to note that choices B, D, and E contain agreement errors in the second half of the sentence. Since the pronoun *each* is singular, you must select the sentence that has the singular form of the verb *depicts*.

5. **E** The original sentence contains an error in parallel structure *(see Chapter IX, Section F)*. The phrases *richness of tone* and *elegant phrasing* must be parallel to an *avant-garde repertoire*.

6. **B** The original phrasing is a sentence fragment *(see Chapter IX, Section L)*. The correct choice must provide a verb for the subject, "European shag." You must also avoid the awkward phrasing, *being susceptible* and *as to their susceptibility* in choices C and D.

7. **A** The original sentence is grammatically correct. The pronoun *those* must be in the plural form because it replaces the plural noun *qualities (see Chapter IX Section B)*.

8. **C** The sentence contains a pronoun error *(see Chapter IX, Section B)*. The plural pronoun *them* is used to refer to the singular noun *computer*. Actually, the whole phrase *of them* is unnecessary and wordy. Choice C is clear and concise.

9. **C** The sentence contains an agreement error *(see Chapter IX, Section J)*. The pronoun *each* is singular and must take the singular form of the verb *has found*. Choice E has the correct verb form, but the subject has been changed to *scientists,* which is a plural subject, so this choice also has an agreement error.

10. **E** This sentence contains a modification error *(see Chapter IX, Section E)*. *Dashing madly for the taxi* must be followed by the word it modifies, *Seth*. It is neither the folder that is dashing for the taxi, as the sentence suggests, nor *papers* (as in Choice C).

11. **C** This is a sentence fragment *(see Chapter IX, Section L)*. It has no verb for the subject Yo-Yo Ma. Only Choice C contains a verb for the subject.

12. **B** This is a comma splice error that results in a run-on sentence *(see Chapter IX, Section L)*. The comma between *grace* and *her style* cannot be used to join two main clauses. Choice B uses the colon correctly to join two main clauses when the second clause is an explanation of the first clause.

13. **A** This sentence correctly uses the semicolon to join two closely related main clauses *(see Chapter IX, Section L)*.

14. **C** This sentence has a pronoun agreement error *(see Chapter IX, Section B)*. The singular pronoun *its* is incorrectly used to refer to the plural noun *safes*. The correct pronoun to replace *its* is *their*.

15. **D** The phrase *sufficient enough* is a redundancy *(see Chapter IX, Section C)*. Both words have the same meaning.

16. **D** This sentence has an idiom error. The phrase *capable to fly* should be changed to *capable of flying* *(see Chapter IX, Section D)*.

17. **C** This sentence contains a diction error *(see Chapter IX, Section H)*. The word *irreproachable* does not mean "unapproachable." *Irreproachable* means "unable to be reproached or criticized."

18. **D** This sentence has a pronoun agreement error *(see Chapter IX, Section B)*. The plural pronoun *them* is used to refer to the singular noun *phone*. The correct pronoun to refer to the cellphone is *it*.

19. **C** This sentence has a vague modification error *(see Chapter IX, Section E)*. The participle *browsing* is misplaced: in this position, it is incorrectly modifying the baby blankets. The proper replacement is *while I browsed*.

20. **B** The tenses in this sentence are inconsistent *(see Chapter IX, Section K)*. The correct use of the past subjunctive tense is *If they had . . . would have*.

21. **E** This sentence is grammatically correct.

22. **B** This sentence has a subject-verb agreement error *(see Chapter IX, Section J)*. The subject, *Professor North,* is singular and does not agree with the plural verb *have*.

23. **C** The logic of the sentence is not correct: *Since* is not the correct word to begin a sentence that establishes a relationship of contrast between the two clauses. Only Choice B or Choice C sets up a contrast relationship. Choice B does not have proper sentence construction. The only way *however* would be correct would be to place it between the two clauses, preceded by a semicolon and followed by a comma. Therefore, only Choice C is correct.

24. **E** The sentence as it is lacks parallelism *(see Chapter IX, Section F)*. The verb *leading* is not parallel to the series of verbs *provides* and *shows*. Choice B makes the verbs parallel, but it uses the awkward construction *which is providing*. Choice C also creates parallel verbs, but *is the big scoreboard provides* does not have correct syntax (word order). Choice D is too wordy; *which is the one that provides* uses too many words. Choice E is correct; it is parallel and concise.

25. **B** A good concluding sentence should refer to the main topic of the essay and should be similar in tone to the rest of the essay. Choice A inappropriately addresses the reader *(you)*. Choice C incorrectly shifts to the first person pronoun *I* for the first time in the essay. Choice D is rather silly because it expresses the writer's opinion about a foregone conclusion. Choice E is not relevant. Choice B nicely ties together the elements of the essay: the response of the fans and the history of many years of baseball at Shea Stadium.

Scoring Worksheets

Critical Reading

	Number Right	Number Wrong
Section 2		
Total		

Raw score = Number right – (Number wrong ÷ 4) = _____ – _____ = _____

Round the raw score to the nearest integer: _____.

Rounded raw score × 2 = _____

Scaled score range: _____

Note: To find your scaled score range, use the following chart.

Critical Reading Raw Score Conversions							
Raw Score	Scaled Score Range	Raw Score	Scaled Score Range	Raw Score	Scaled Score Range	Raw Score	Scaled Score Range
67	800	48	580–640	29	470–520	10	340–400
66	760–800	47	580–640	28	460–520	9	330–390
65	740–800	46	570–630	27	450–510	8	320–380
64	720–800	45	570–620	26	450–510	7	300–380
63	700–790	44	560–620	25	440–500	6	290–370
62	680–780	43	550–610	24	430–500	5	280–370
61	670–770	42	540–610	23	430–490	4	260–360
60	660–760	41	540–600	22	420–480	3	250–340
59	660–740	40	530–590	21	410–480	2	230–330
58	650–720	39	530–580	20	410–470	1	220–320
57	640–720	38	520–580	19	400–460	0	200–300
56	630–710	37	520–570	18	400–450	–1	200–290
55	630–700	36	510–570	17	390–450	–2	200–270
54	620–700	35	500–560	16	380–440	–3	200–240
53	610–680	34	500–560	15	380–440	–4	200–230
52	600–680	33	490–550	14	370–430	–5	200–210
51	610–670	32	480–540	13	360–420	–6 and below	200
50	600–660	31	480–540	12	350–410		
49	600–650	30	470–530	11	340–410		

Mathematics

	Number Right	Number Wrong
Section 3		
Total		

Raw score = Number right – (Number wrong ÷ 4) = _____ – _____ = _____

Round the raw score to the nearest integer: _____.

Rounded raw score × 2 = _____

Scaled score range: _____

Note: To find your scaled score range, use the following chart.

Mathematics Raw Score Conversions					
Raw Score	**Scaled Score Range**	**Raw Score**	**Scaled Score Range**	**Raw Score**	**Scaled Score Range**
54	800	34	530–610	14	390–450
53	760–800	33	520–600	13	380–440
52	720–780	32	520–580	12	360–430
51	700–780	31	520–580	11	350–430
50	680–770	30	510–570	10	320–420
49	680–750	29	500–560	9	300–420
48	670–730	28	490–550	8	300-410
47	660–720	27	480–540	7	300–400
46	650–700	26	480–530	6	290–380
45	630–700	25	470–530	5	280–380
44	610–680	24	460–520	4	270–370
43	620–670	23	460–520	3	260–340
42	610–670	22	440–510	2	240–340
41	600–650	21	440–490	1	230–320
40	580–650	20	430–490	0	210–310
39	570–650	19	430–480	−1	200–290
38	550–640	18	420–480	−2	200–280
37	550–630	17	410–460	−3	200–250
36	540–630	16	400–460	−4	200–220
35	540–610	15	400–450	−5 and below	200

Writing

	Number Right	Number Wrong
Section 4		
Total		

Raw score = Number right – (Number wrong ÷ 4) = _____ – _____ = _____

Round the raw score to the nearest integer: _____.

Rounded raw score × 2 = _____

Multiple choice subscore range: _____

Writing Multiple Choice Raw Score Conversions					
Raw Score	**Scaled Score Range**	**Raw Score**	**Scaled Score Range**	**Raw Score**	**Scaled Score Range**
49	800	30	540–640	11	360–450
48	770–800	29	530–630	10	350–440
47	740–800	28	520–620	9	340–430
46	720–800	27	510–610	8	330–420
45	700–790	26	500–600	7	310–400
44	680–780	25	490–590	6	300–390
43	670–770	24	480–580	5	300–380
42	660–760	23	470–570	4	290–340
41	660–740	22	460–560	3	280–330
40	650–720	21	450–550	2	270–320
39	640–720	20	450–540	1	250–300
38	630–710	19	440–540	0	200–290
37	630–700	18	430–530	–1	200–270
36	620–700	17	420–520	–2	200–240
35	590–680	16	410–510	–3	200–280
34	580–680	15	400–500	–4	200–260
33	570–670	14	390–490	–5	200–230
32	560–660	13	380–480	–6 and below	200–220
31	550–650	12	370–470		

To find your total writing score, estimate your essay score using the rubric (or have your English teacher score your essay).

Essay score (1–6): _____

To find your total writing scaled score range, use the following chart. Locate your multiple choice raw score in the first column. Then find your essay score across the top. The point of intersection is your total writing scaled score.

Writing Conversions							
Multiple Choice Raw Score	**0**	**1**	**2**	**3**	**4**	**5**	**6**
49	650–700	670–720	690–740	710–770	750–800	770–800	800
48	630–690	640–720	660–740	690–770	720–800	740–800	770–800
47	600–690	620–720	640–740	660–770	700–800	730–800	750–800
46	580–690	600–710	620–730	650–750	680–770	700–790	720–800
45	570–690	580–720	600–740	630–750	660–760	680–770	690–790
44	560–680	570–710	590–730	620–740	660–750	670–760	680–780
43	540–660	560–690	580–710	610–730	640–740	650–750	660–770
42	530–660	550–680	570–700	600–720	630–730	640–740	650–760
41	530–650	540–670	560–690	590–700	620–720	640–730	640– 750
40	520–640	530–670	550–690	580–710	620–710	630–730	640–740
39	510–630	520–660	540–680	570–700	610–700	620–720	630–730
38	500–620	510–650	530–670	560–700	600–690	610–710	620–720
37	490–610	500–640	520–660	550–690	590–680	600–700	610–710
36	480–600	490–630	510–650	540–680	580–670	590–690	600–700
35	480–590	490–620	500–640	520–650	550–660	570–670	580–680
34	470–590	480–600	500–620	510–630	530–640	560–660	570–670
33	450–570	470–600	490–610	500–620	540–630	550–650	560–660
32	440–570	460–590	470–600	490–610	520–620	540–640	550–650
31	440–560	460–570	470–590	480–600	510–610	530–630	540–640
30	430–550	450–560	460–580	470–590	500–600	520–620	530–630
29	430–540	440–550	450–570	460–580	490–600	510–610	520–620
28	420–530	430–540	440–560	450–570	470–590	500–600	510–610
27	410–520	420–540	430–550	440–560	460–580	480–590	500–600
26	400–510	410–530	420–540	430–550	450–570	470–580	490–590
25	390–500	400–520	410–530	420–540	440–560	460–570	480–580

Multiple Choice Raw Score	0	1	2	3	4	5	6
24	380–490	390–510	400–520	410–530	430–550	450–560	470–570
23	370–480	380–510	400–510	400–520	420–540	440–550	460–560
22	370–470	380–500	390–510	390–520	410–510	430–540	450–550
21	370–470	380–500	390–500	390–510	410–510	430–530	450–550
20	360–460	370–490	380–500	390–500	400–510	420–520	440–540
19	350–460	360–490	380–500	390–500	400–510	420–520	430–530
18	340–450	350–480	370–490	380–490	390–500	410–510	420–520
17	330–440	340–470	360–480	370–480	380–500	400–510	410–510
16	320–440	340–460	350–480	360–480	370–490	400–500	410–510
15	310–430	330–450	340–480	350–470	360–490	390–490	400–500
14	300–420	320–440	330–460	340–470	350–480	390–490	400–500
13	300–410	310–430	320–450	330–460	340–470	380–480	390–490
12	290–400	300–420	310–440	320–450	330–460	370–470	380–480
11	280–390	290–410	300–430	310–440	320–450	360–460	370–470
10	270–390	280–400	290–420	300–430	310–440	350–450	360–460
9	260–380	270–380	280–410	290–420	300–430	340–440	350–450
8	260–370	270–370	280–400	280–410	290–420	330–430	340–440
7	250–370	270–360	280–390	280–410	290–410	320–420	340–430
6	240–360	250–350	270–380	270–400	280–400	310–410	330–420
5	220–350	240–340	260–370	260–390	270–390	300–400	320–410
4	210–340	230–330	250–360	250–380	260–380	290–390	310–400
3	210–310	220–320	240–330	240–370	250–370	280–380	290–390
2	210–300	220–310	220–320	230–350	240–360	270–370	280–380
1	200–290	210–300	220–310	230–340	240–350	250–350	260–370
0	200–270	210–280	210–300	210–320	220–320	230–330	240–350

II. Two-Month Cram Plan

Two-Month Cram Plan			
	Mathematics	**Critical Reading**	**Writing**

8 weeks before the test	**Study Time:** 2½ hours
	❑ Take **Diagnostic Test** and review answer explanations.
	   ❑ Compare your essay to the rubric and the samples and target areas to improve.
	   ❑ Based on your errors on the Diagnostic Test, identify difficult topics and their corresponding chapters. These chapters are your targeted chapters.		

7 weeks before the test	**Study Time:** 2 hours
	❑ **Working with Numbers:** Chapter X
	   ❑ Read sections A–F.
	   ❑ Do practice questions 1–2 in each section.
	   ❑ For targeted areas, do practice questions 1–4 in each section.
	❑ **Algebra and Functions:** Chapter XI
	   ❑ Read sections A–H.
	   ❑ Do practice questions 1–2 in each section.
	   ❑ For targeted areas, do practice questions 1–4 in each section.
	❑ **Geometry:** Chapter XII
	   ❑ Read sections A–I.
	   ❑ Do practice questions 1–2 in each section.
	   ❑ For targeted areas, do practice questions 1–4 in each section.
	❑ **TI-89 Calculator:** Appendix
	   ❑ Do practice questions 1–2.
		Study Time: 1½ hours
		❑ **Sentence Completions:** Chapter V
		   ❑ Read sections A–B.
		   ❑ Do 3 practice questions in each section.
		   ❑ For targeted areas, do 5 questions in each section.
		❑ **Vocabulary Study:** Chapter VII
		   ❑ Read aberration–extraneous.
		   ❑ Highlight unfamiliar words; divide them into 5 equal groups, and study 1 group each night.
		   ❑ Review all 5 groups for 2 nights.
			Study Time: 1 hour
			❑ **The Essay:** Chapter VIII
			   ❑ Read chapter.
			   ❑ Practice writing 5 sentences using transitional words.
			❑ **Grammar and Usage:** Chapter IX
			   ❑ Read sections A–B.
			   ❑ Do half the practice questions in each section.
			   ❑ For targeted areas, do all the practice questions.

continued

	Mathematics	Critical Reading	Writing

6 weeks before the test	**Study Time:** 2 hours
	❏ **Probability, Statistics, and Data Analysis:** Chapter XIII
	  ❏ Read sections A–D.
	  ❏ Do practice questions 1–2 in each section.
	  ❏ For targeted areas, do practice questions 1–4 in each section.
	❏ **Logic and Problem Solving:** Chapter XIV
	  ❏ Read sections A–C.
	  ❏ Do practice questions 1–2 in each section.
	  ❏ For targeted areas, do practice questions 1–4 in each section.
	❏ **TI-89 Calculator:** Appendix
	  ❏ Do practice questions 3–4.
		Study Time: 1½ hours
		❏ **Sentence Completions:** Chapter V
		  ❏ Read sections C–D.
		  ❏ Do 3 practice questions in each section.
		  ❏ For targeted areas, do 5 practice questions in each section.
		❏ **Vocabulary Study:** Chapter VII
		  ❏ Read facetious–itinerant.
		  ❏ Highlight unfamiliar words; divide them into 5 equal groups, and study 1 group each night.
		  ❏ Review all 5 groups for 2 nights.
			Study Time: 1 hour
			❏ **The Essay:** Chapter VIII
			  ❏ Choose one of the sample essay topics at the end of Chapter VIII. Brainstorm and plan the essay.
			❏ **Grammar and Usage:** Chapter IX
			  ❏ Read sections A–C.
			  ❏ Do half the practice questions in each section.
			  ❏ For targeted areas, do all the practice questions.

5 weeks before the test	**Study Time:** 2 hours
	❏ **Working with Numbers:** Chapter X
	  ❏ Read sections A–F.
	  ❏ Do practice questions 3–4 in each section.
	  ❏ For targeted areas, do practice questions 1–4 in each section.
	❏ **Algebra and Functions:** Chapter XI
	  ❏ Read sections A–H.
	  ❏ Do practice questions 3–4 in each section.
	  ❏ For targeted areas, do practice questions 1–4 in each section.
	❏ **Geometry:** Chapter XII
	  ❏ Read sections A–I.
	  ❏ Do practice questions 3–4 in each section.
	  ❏ For targeted areas, do practice questions 1–4 in each section.
	❏ **TI-89 Calculator:** Appendix
	  ❏ Do practice questions 5–6.
		Study Time: 1½ hours
		❏ **Critical Reading Passages:** Chapter VI
		  ❏ Read sections A–C.
		  ❏ Do practice questions in each section.
		  ❏ For targeted areas, do additional practice questions at the end of Chapter VI.
		❏ **Vocabulary Study:** Chapter VII
		  ❏ Read jocular–ostracism.
		  ❏ Highlight unfamiliar words; divide them into 5 equal groups, and study 1 group each night.
		  ❏ Review all 5 groups for 2 nights.
			Study Time: 1 hour
			❏ **The Essay:** Chapter VIII
			  ❏ Choose one of the sample essay topics at the end of Chapter VIII. Brainstorm and plan the essay.
			❏ **Grammar and Usage:** Chapter IX
			  ❏ Read sections D–E.
			  ❏ Do half the practice questions in each section.
			  ❏ For targeted areas, do all the practice questions.

	Mathematics	Critical Reading	Writing

4 weeks before the test	**Study Time:** 2 hours
	❏ **Probability, Statistics, and Data Analysis:** Chapter XIII
	  ❏ Read sections A–D.
	  ❏ Do practice questions 3–4 in each section.
	❏ **Logic and Problem Solving:** Chapter XIV
	  ❏ Read sections A–C.
	  ❏ Do practice questions 3–4 in each section.
	❏ **TI-89 Calculator:** Appendix
	  ❏ Do practice questions 7–8.
		Study Time: 1½ hours
		❏ **Critical Reading Passages:** Chapter VI
		  ❏ Read sections D–E.
		  ❏ Do practice questions in each section.
		  ❏ For targeted areas, do additional practice questions at the end of Chapter VI.
		❏ **Vocabulary Study:** Chapter VII
		  ❏ Review all the highlighted words in aberration–ostracism.
			Study Time: 1 hour
			❏ **The Essay:** Chapter VIII
			  ❏ Choose one of the sample essay topics at the end of Chapter VIII. Brainstorm and plan the essay.
			❏ **Grammar and Usage:** Chapter IX
			  ❏ Read sections F–G.
			  ❏ Do half the practice questions in each section.
			  ❏ For targeted areas, do all the practice questions.

3 weeks before the test	**Study Time:** 2 hours
	❏ **Working with Numbers:** Chapter X
	  ❏ Read sections A–F.
	  ❏ Do practice question 5 in each section.
	❏ **Algebra and Functions:** Chapter XI
	  ❏ Read sections A–H.
	  ❏ Do practice question 5 in each section.
	❏ **Geometry:** Chapter XII
	  ❏ Read sections A–I.
	  ❏ Do practice question 5 in each section.
	❏ **Probability, Statistics, and Data Analysis:** Chapter XIII
	  ❏ Read sections A–D.
	  ❏ Do practice question 5 in each section.
	❏ **Logic and Problem Solving:** Chapter XIV
	  ❏ Read sections A–C.
	  ❏ Do practice question 5 in each section.
	❏ **TI-89 Calculator:** Appendix
	  ❏ Do practice questions 9–10.
		Study Time: 1½ hours
		❏ **Critical Reading Passages:** Chapter VI
		  ❏ Read sections F–G.
		  ❏ Do practice questions at the end of the section.
		  ❏ For targeted areas, do additional practice questions at the end of Chapter VI.
		❏ **Vocabulary Study:** Chapter VII
		  ❏ Read palatial–punctilious.
		  ❏ Highlight unfamiliar words; divide them into 5 equal groups, and study 1 group each night.
		  ❏ Review all 5 groups for 2 nights.
			Study Time: 1 hour
			❏ **The Essay:** Chapter VIII
			  ❏ Choose one of the sample essay topics at the end of Chapter VIII. Brainstorm and plan the essay.
			❏ **Grammar and Usage:** Chapter IX
			  ❏ Read sections H–I.
			  ❏ Do half the practice questions in each section.
			  ❏ For targeted areas, do all the practice questions.

continued

	Mathematics	Critical Reading	Writing
2 weeks before the test	**Study Time:** 4½ hours ❏ Take **Practice Test** and review answer explanations. ❏ Based on your errors on the Practice Test, identify difficult topics and their corresponding chapters. These chapters are your targeted areas.		

	Study Time: 2 hours
	❏ Based on Practice Test, review topic summaries for all targeted areas.
	❏ Redo those questions that you answered incorrectly on Practice Test.
		Study Time: 1 hour
		❏ For sections that still present problems, begin review and reread practice questions.
		❏ **Vocabulary Study:** Chapter VII
		  ❏ Read quandary–whimsical.
		  ❏ Highlight unfamiliar words; divide them into 5 equal groups, and study 1 group each night.
		  ❏ Review all 5 groups for 2 nights.
			Study Time: 1 hour
			❏ Compare your essay to the rubric. Based on the criteria, think about ways you could improve your writing.
			❏ **The Essay:** Chapter VIII
			  ❏ Review transitional words. Consider sentences in your essay that could be improved by the addition of these words and phrases.

7 days before the test	**Study Time:** 1 hour
	❏ **Working with Numbers:** Chapter X
	  ❏ Read sections A–F.
	  ❏ Do practice question 5 in each section.
	❏ **TI-89 Calculator:** Appendix
	  ❏ Do any 3 questions marked with the Calculator icon in the Diagnostic Test, Practice Test, or subject review chapters.
		Study Time: 1 hour
		❏ **Sentence Completions:** Chapter V
		  ❏ Continue to review sections A–B.
		❏ **Critical Reading Passages:** Chapter VI
		  ❏ Continue to review sections A–B.
		❏ **Vocabulary Study:** Chapter VII
		  ❏ Divide all highlighted words into 5 equal groups, and study the first group of words.
			Study Time: 1 hour
			❏ Based on results of the Practice Test, begin to review all targeted areas.
			❏ Divide targeted areas into 4 sections. For first targeted area, do all remaining practice questions.

6 days before the test	**Study Time:** 1 hour
	❏ **Algebra and Functions:** Chapter XI
	  ❏ Read sections A–H.
	  ❏ Do practice question 5 in each section.
	❏ **TI-89 Calculator:** Appendix
	  ❏ Do any 3 questions marked with the Calculator icon in the Diagnostic Test, Practice Test, or subject review chapters.
		Study Time: 1 hour
		❏ **Sentence Completions:** Chapter V
		  ❏ Continue to review sections C–D.
		❏ **Critical Reading Passages:** Chapter VI
		  ❏ Continue to review sections C–D.
		❏ **Vocabulary Study:** Chapter VII
		  ❏ Study the second group of highlighted words.
			Study Time: 1 hour
			Continue to review.
			❏ For second targeted area, do all remaining practice questions.
			❏ Reread your brainstorming for practice essay questions. Think about examples that would further prove your position.

	Mathematics	Critical Reading	Writing

5 days before the test	**Study Time:** 1 hour
	❑ **Geometry:** Chapter XII
	   ❑ Read sections A–I.
	   ❑ Do practice question 6 in each section.
	❑ **TI-89 Calculator:** Appendix
	   ❑ Do any 3 questions marked with the Calculator icon in the Diagnostic Test, Practice Test, or subject review chapters.
		Study Time: 1 hour
		❑ **Critical Reading Passages:** Chapter VI
		   ❑ Continue to review section E.
		❑ **Vocabulary Study:** Chapter VII
		   ❑ Study the third group of highlighted words.
			Study Time: 1 hour
			Continue to review.
			❑ For third targeted area, do all remaining practice questions.

4 days before the test	**Study Time:** 1 hour
	❑ **Probability, Statistics, and Data Analysis:** Chapter XIII
	   ❑ Read sections A–D.
	   ❑ Do practice question 6 in each section.
	❑ **TI-89 Calculator:** Appendix
	   ❑ Do any 3 questions marked with the Calculator icon in the Diagnostic Test, Practice Test, or subject review chapters.
		Study Time: 1 hour
		❑ **Critical Reading Passages:** Chapter VI
		   ❑ Continue to review section F.
		❑ **Vocabulary Study:** Chapter VII
		   ❑ Study the fourth group of highlighted words.
			Study Time: 1 hour
			Continue to review.
			❑ For fourth targeted area, do all remaining practice questions.

3 days before the test	**Study Time:** 1 hour
	❑ **Logic and Problem Solving:** Chapter XIV
	   ❑ Read sections A–C.
	   ❑ Do practice question 6 in each section.
	❑ **TI-89 Calculator:** Appendix
	   ❑ Do any 3 questions marked with the Calculator icon in the Diagnostic Test, Practice Test, or subject review chapters.
		Study Time: 1 hour
		❑ **Critical Reading Passages:** Chapter VI
		   ❑ Continue to review section G.
		❑ **Vocabulary Study:** Chapter VII
		   ❑ Study the last group of highlighted words.
			Study Time: 1 hour
			❑ Do additional practice writing questions at the end of the chapter.
			❑ Review answers. Go back to **Grammar and Usage** (Chapter IX) and review any issues that are still problematic.

2 days before the test	**Study Time:** 1 hour
	❑ **TI-89 Calculator:** Appendix
	   ❑ Redo practice questions 1–10.
		Study Time: 1 hour
		❑ Reread the general strategies for each chapter.
		❑ **Vocabulary Study:** Chapter VII
		   ❑ Review all highlighted words.
			Study Time: 1 hour
			❑ Again review the brainstorming you did for all the sample essay questions. Think of more details you could add to strengthen your evidence.

1 day before the test	❑ Relax. . . . You're well prepared for the test. ❑ Have confidence in your ability to do well.		

continued

	Mathematics	Critical Reading	Writing

Morning of the test	**Reminders:**
	❏ Have a good breakfast;
	❏ Take the following items with you on test day:
	   ❏ Your admission ticket and photo ID
	   ❏ Several #2 pencils and erasers
	   ❏ A calculator with fresh batteries
	   ❏ A watch
	❏ Try to go outside for a few minutes and walk around before the test.
	❏ Most important: Stay calm and confident during the test. Take deep slow breaths if you feel at all nervous. You can do it!		

III. One-Month Cram Plan

One-Month Cram Plan			
	Mathematics	**Critical Reading**	**Writing**

4 weeks before the test	**Study Time:** 2½ hours
	❏ Take **Diagnostic Test** and review answer explanations.
	   ❏ Compare your essay to the rubric and the samples and target areas to improve.
	   ❏ Based on your errors on the Diagnostic Test, identify difficult topics and their corresponding chapters. These chapters are your targeted chapters.		

	Study Time: 2½ hours
	❏ **Working with Numbers:** Chapter X
	   ❏ Read sections A–F.
	   ❏ Do practice question 1 in each section.
	   ❏ For targeted areas, do practice questions 1–2 in each section.
	❏ **Algebra and Functions:** Chapter XI
	   ❏ Read sections A–H.
	   ❏ Do practice question 1 in each section.
	   ❏ For targeted areas, do practice questions 1–2 in each section.
	❏ **Geometry:** Chapter XII
	   ❏ Read sections A–I.
	   ❏ Do practice question 1 in each section.
	   ❏ For targeted areas, do practice questions 1–2 in each section.
	❏ **Probability, Statistics, and Data Analysis:** Chapter XIII
	   ❏ Read sections A–D.
	   ❏ Do practice question 1 in each section.
	   ❏ For targeted areas, do practice questions 1–2 in each section.
	❏ **Logic and Problem Solving:** Chapter XIV
	   ❏ Read sections A–C.
	   ❏ Do practice question 1 in each section.
	   ❏ For targeted areas, do practice questions 1–2 in each section.
	❏ **TI-89 Calculator:** Appendix
	   ❏ Do practice question 1.
		Study Time: 2½ hours
		❏ **Sentence Completions:** Chapter V
		   ❏ Read sections A–B.
		   ❏ Do 3 practice questions in each section.
		   ❏ For targeted areas, do 5 questions in each section.
		❏ **Vocabulary Study:** Chapter VII
		   ❏ Read aberration–extraneous.
		   ❏ Highlight unfamiliar words; divide them into 5 equal groups, and study 1 group each night.
		   ❏ Review all 5 groups for 2 nights.
			Study Time: 2 hours
			❏ **The Essay:** Chapter VIII
			   ❏ Read chapter.
			   ❏ Practice writing 5 sentences using transitional words.
			❏ **Grammar and Usage:** Chapter IX
			   ❏ Read sections A–D.
			   ❏ Do half the practice questions in each section.
			   ❏ For targeted areas, do all the practice questions.

continued

	Mathematics	Critical Reading	Writing

3 weeks before the test	**Study Time:** 2½ hours
	 ❏ **Working with Numbers:** Chapter X
	   ❏ Read sections A–F.
	   ❏ Do practice questions 2–3 in each section.
	 ❏ **Algebra and Functions:** Chapter XI
	   ❏ Read sections A–H.
	   ❏ Do practice questions 2–3 in each section.
	 ❏ **Geometry:** Chapter XII
	   ❏ Read sections A–I.
	   ❏ Do practice questions 2–3 in each section.
	 ❏ **Probability, Statistics, and Data Analysis:** Chapter XIII
	   ❏ Read sections A–D.
	   ❏ Do practice questions 2–3 in each section.
	 ❏ **Logic and Problem Solving:** Chapter XIV
	   ❏ Read sections A–C.
	   ❏ Do practice questions 2–3 in each section.
	 ❏ **TI-89 Calculator:** Appendix
	   ❏ Do practice questions 2–3.
		Study Time: 2½ hours
		 ❏ **Sentence Completions:** Chapter V
		   ❏ Read sections C–D.
		   ❏ Do 3 practice questions in each section.
		   ❏ For targeted areas, do 5 practice questions in each section.
		 ❏ **Critical Reading Passages:** Chapter VI
		   ❏ Read sections A–C.
		   ❏ Do practice questions in each section.
		 ❏ **Vocabulary Study:** Chapter VII
		   ❏ Read facetious–ostracism.
		   ❏ Highlight unfamiliar words; divide them into 5 equal groups, and study 1 group each night.
		   ❏ Review all 5 groups for 2 nights.
			Study Time: 1½ hours
			 ❏ **The Essay:** Chapter VIII
			   ❏ Choose two of the sample essay topics at the end of Chapter VIII. Brainstorm and plan the essay.
			 ❏ **Grammar and Usage:** Chapter IX
			   ❏ Read sections E–H.
			   ❏ Do half the practice questions in each section.
			   ❏ For targeted areas, do all the practice questions.

	Mathematics	Critical Reading	Writing

2 weeks before the test	**Study Time:** 2½ hours
	❑ **Working with Numbers:** Chapter X
	  ❑ Read sections A–F.
	  ❑ Do practice questions 4–5 in each section.
	❑ **Algebra and Functions:** Chapter XI
	  ❑ Read sections A–H.
	  ❑ Do practice questions 4–5 in each section.
	❑ **Geometry:** Chapter XII
	  ❑ Read sections A–I.
	  ❑ Do practice questions 4–5 in each section.
	❑ **Probability, Statistics, and Data Analysis:** Chapter XIII
	  ❑ Read sections A–D.
	  ❑ Do practice questions 4–5 in each section.
	❑ **Logic and Problem Solving:** Chapter XIV
	  ❑ Read sections A–C.
	  ❑ Do practice questions 4–5 in each section.
	❑ **TI-89 Calculator:** Appendix
	  ❑ Do practice questions 4–5.
		Study Time: 2½ hours
		❑ **Critical Reading Passages:** Chapter VI
		  ❑ Read sections D–G.
		  ❑ Do practice questions in each section.
		  ❑ For targeted areas, do additional practice questions at the end of the chapter.
		❑ **Vocabulary Study:** Chapter VII
		  ❑ Read palatial–whimsical.
		  ❑ Highlight unfamiliar words; divide them into 5 equal groups, and study 1 group each night.
		  ❑ Review all 5 groups for 2 nights.
			Study Time: 1 hour
			❑ **The Essay:** Chapter VIII
			  ❑ Choose two of the sample essay topics at the end of Chapter VIII. Brainstorm and plan the essay.
			❑ **Grammar and Usage:** Chapter IX
			  ❑ Read sections I–L.
			  ❑ Do half the practice questions in each section.
			  ❑ For targeted areas, do all the practice questions.

7 days before the test	**Study Time:** 4½ hours ❑ Take **Practice Test** and review answer explanations. ❑ Based on your errors on the Practice Test, identify difficult topics and their corresponding chapters. These chapters are your targeted areas.		

continued

	Mathematics	Critical Reading	Writing

6 days before the test	**Study Time:** 1½ hours
	❑ Based on Practice Test, review topic summaries for all targeted areas.
	❑ Redo those questions that you answered incorrectly on Practice Test.
	❑ **Working with Numbers:** Chapter X
	  ❑ Do practice question 6 in every section.
	❑ **TI-89 Calculator:** Appendix
	  ❑ Do practice question 6.
		Study Time: 1½ hours
		❑ **Sentence Completions:** Chapter V
		  ❑ Continue to review sections A–D.
		❑ **Vocabulary Study:** Chapter VII
		  ❑ Divide all highlighted words into 4 equal groups, and study the first group of words.
			Study Time: 1 hour
			❑ Based on results of the Practice Test, begin to review all targeted areas.
			❑ Divide targeted areas into 4 sections. For first targeted area, do all remaining practice questions.

5 days before the test	**Study Time:** 1 hour
	❑ **Algebra and Functions:** Chapter XI
	  ❑ Do practice question 6 in every section.
	❑ **TI-89 Calculator:** Appendix
	  ❑ Do practice question 7.
		Study Time: 1½ hours
		❑ **Critical Reading Passages:** Chapter VI
		  ❑ Continue to review sections A–C.
		❑ **Vocabulary Study:** Chapter VII
		  ❑ Study the second group of words.
			Study Time: 1 hour
			❑ Based on results of the Practice Test, continue to review all targeted areas.
			❑ For second targeted area, do all remaining practice questions.

4 days before the test	**Study Time:** 1 hour
	❑ **Geometry:** Chapter XII
	  ❑ Do practice question 6 in every section.
	❑ **TI-89 Calculator:** Appendix
	  ❑ Do practice question 8.
		Study Time: 1½ hours
		❑ **Critical Reading Passages:** Chapter VI
		  ❑ Review sections D–G.
		❑ **Vocabulary Study:** Chapter VII
		  ❑ Study the third group of highlighted words.
			Study Time: 1 hour
			Continue to review.
			❑ For third targeted area, do all remaining practice questions.

	Mathematics	**Critical Reading**	**Writing**

3 days before the test	**Study Time:** 1 hour
	❏ **Probability, Statistics, and Data Analysis:** Chapter XIII
	   ❏ Do practice question 6 in every section.
	❏ **TI-89 Calculator:** Appendix
	   ❏ Do practice question 9.
		Study Time: 1 hour
		❏ **Sentence Completions:** Chapter V
		   ❏ Review sections that still need attention.
		❏ **Vocabulary Study:** Chapter VII
		   ❏ Study the last group of highlighted words.
			Study Time: 1 hour
			Continue to review.
			❏ For fourth targeted area, do all remaining practice questions.
			❏ Reread the brainstorming you did for all the sample essay questions.

2 days before the test	**Study Time:** 1 hour
	❏ **Logic and Problem Solving:** Chapter XIV
	   ❏ Do practice question 6 in every section.
	❏ **TI-89 Calculator:** Appendix
	   ❏ Do practice question 10.
		Study Time: 1 hour
		❏ **Critical Reading Passages:** Chapter VI
		   ❏ Review sections that still need attention.
		❏ **Vocabulary Study:** Chapter VII
		   ❏ Review all words.
			Study Time: 1 hour
			Continue to review.
			❏ **Grammar and Usage:** Chapter IX
			   ❏ Do additional practice writing questions at the end of the chapter.
			   ❏ Review your answers.
			❏ Reread the brainstorming you did for all the sample **Essay** questions (Chapter VIII). Think of more details you could add to strengthen your evidence.

1 day before the test	❏ Relax. . . . You're well prepared for the test. ❏ Have confidence in your ability to do well.		

Morning of the test	**Reminders:**
	❏ Have a good breakfast;
	❏ Take the following items with you on test day:
	   ❏ Your admission ticket and photo ID
	   ❏ Several #2 pencils and erasers
	   ❏ A calculator with fresh batteries
	   ❏ A watch
	❏ Try to go outside for a few minutes and walk around before the test.
	❏ Most important: Stay calm and confident during the test. Take deep slow breaths if you feel at all nervous. You can do it!		

IV. One-Week Cram Plan

	One-Week Cram Plan		
	Mathematics	**Critical Reading**	**Writing**
7 days before the test	**Study Time:** 2½ hours ❑ Take **Diagnostic Test** and review answer explanations. ❑ Compare your essay to the rubric and the samples and target areas to improve. ❑ Based on your errors on the Diagnostic Test, identify difficult topics and their corresponding chapters. These chapters are your targeted chapters.		

6 days before the test	**Study Time:** 3 hours
	❑ **Working with Numbers:** Chapter X
	  ❑ Read sections A–F.
	  ❑ Do practice question 1 in each section.
	  ❑ For targeted areas, do practice questions 1–2.
	❑ **Algebra and Functions:** Chapter XI
	  ❑ Read sections A–H.
	  ❑ Do practice question 1 in each section.
	  ❑ For targeted areas, do practice questions 1–2.
	❑ **Geometry:** Chapter XII
	  ❑ Read sections A–I.
	  ❑ Do practice question 1 in each section.
	  ❑ For targeted areas, do practice questions 1–2.
	❑ **Probability, Statistics, and Data Analysis:** Chapter XIII
	  ❑ Read sections A–D.
	  ❑ Do practice question 1 in each section.
	  ❑ For targeted areas, do practice questions 1–2.
	❑ **Logic and Problem Solving:** Chapter XIV
	  ❑ Read sections A–C.
	  ❑ Do practice question 1 in each section.
	  ❑ For targeted areas, do practice questions 1–2.
	❑ **TI-89 Calculator:** Appendix
	  ❑ Do practice questions 1–2.
		Study Time: 3 hours
		❑ **Sentence Completions:** Chapter V
		  ❑ Read sections A–D.
		  ❑ Do 3 practice questions in each section.
		  ❑ For targeted areas, do 5 questions in each section.
		❑ **Vocabulary Study:** Chapter VII
		  ❑ Highlight unfamiliar words; divide them into 3 equal groups.
		  ❑ Review the first group of words.
			Study Time: 2 hours
			❑ **The Essay:** Chapter VIII
			  ❑ Read the chapter.
			❑ **Grammar and Usage:** Chapter IX
			  ❑ Read sections A–C.
			  ❑ For targeted areas, do all the practice questions.

	Mathematics	Critical Reading	Writing

5 days before the test	**Study Time:** 3 hours
	❑ **Working with Numbers:** Chapter X
	  ❑ Read sections A–F.
	  ❑ Do practice question 2 in each section.
	  ❑ For targeted areas, do practice questions 3–4 in each section.
	❑ **Algebra and Functions:** Chapter XI
	  ❑ Read sections A–H.
	  ❑ Do practice question 2 in each section.
	  ❑ For targeted areas, do practice questions 3–4 in each section.
	❑ **Geometry:** Chapter XII
	  ❑ Read sections A–I.
	  ❑ Do practice question 2 in each section.
	  ❑ For targeted areas, do practice questions 3–4 in each section.
	❑ **Probability, Statistics, and Data Analysis:** Chapter XIII
	  ❑ Read sections A–D.
	  ❑ Do practice question 2 in each section.
	  ❑ For targeted areas, do practice questions 3–4 in each section.
	❑ **Logic and Problem Solving:** Chapter XIV
	  ❑ Read sections A–C.
	  ❑ Do practice question 2 in each section.
	  ❑ For targeted areas, do practice questions 3–4 in each section.
	❑ **TI-89 Calculator:** Appendix
	  ❑ Do practice questions 3–4.
		Study Time: 3 hours
		❑ **Critical Reading Passages:** Chapter VI
		  ❑ Read sections A–D.
		  ❑ For targeted areas, do additional practice questions at the end of the Chapter VI.
		❑ **Vocabulary Study:** Chapter VII
		  ❑ Review the second group of words.
			Study Time: 1½ hours
			❑ **The Essay:** Chapter VIII
			  ❑ Look over sample questions. Choose 2 and brainstorm answers.
			❑ **Grammar and Usage:** Chapter IX
			  ❑ Read sections D–F.
			  ❑ For targeted areas, do all the practice questions.

continued

	Mathematics	Critical Reading	Writing

4 days before the test	**Study Time:** 3 hours
	❑ **Working with Numbers:** Chapter X
	    ❑ Read sections A–F.
	    ❑ Do practice questions 3–4 in each section.
	❑ **Algebra and Functions:** Chapter XI
	    ❑ Read sections A–H.
	    ❑ Do practice questions 3–4 in each section.
	❑ **Geometry:** Chapter XII
	    ❑ Read sections A–I.
	    ❑ Do practice questions 3–4 in each section.
	❑ **Probability, Statistics, and Data Analysis:** Chapter XIII
	    ❑ Read sections A–H.
	    ❑ Do practice questions 3–4 in each section.
	❑ **Logic and Problem Solving:** Chapter XIV
	    ❑ Read sections A–C.
	    ❑ Do practice questions 3–4 in each section.
	❑ **TI-89 Calculator:** Appendix
	    ❑ Do practice questions 5–6.
		Study Time: 3 hours
		❑ **Critical Reading Review:** Chapter VI
		    ❑ Read sections E–G.
		    ❑ For targeted areas, do additional practice questions at the end of Chapter VI.
		❑ **Vocabulary Study:** Chapter VII
		    ❑ Review the third group of words.
			Study Time: 1½ hours
			❑ **Grammar and Usage:** Chapter IX
			    ❑ Read sections G–L.
			    ❑ For targeted areas, do all the practice questions.

3 days before the test	**Study Time:** 4½ hours ❑ Take **Practice Test** and review answer explanations. ❑ Based on your errors on the Practice Test, identify difficult topics and their corresponding chapters. These chapters are your targeted areas.		

	Mathematics	Critical Reading	Writing

2 days before the test	**Study Time:** 3 hours
	❑ Based on Practice Test, review topic summaries for all targeted areas.
	❑ Redo those questions that you answered incorrectly on the Practice Test.
	❑ **Working with Numbers:** Chapter X
	   ❑ Read sections A–F.
	   ❑ Do practice question 5 in each section.
	❑ **Algebra and Functions:** Chapter XI
	   ❑ Read sections A–H.
	   ❑ Do practice question 5 in each section.
	❑ **Geometry:** Chapter XII
	   ❑ Read sections A–I.
	   ❑ Do practice question 5 in each section.
	❑ **Probability, Statistics, and Data Analysis:** Chapter XIII
	   ❑ Read sections A–D.
	   ❑ Do practice question 5 in each section.
	❑ **Logic and Problem Solving:** Chapter XIV
	   ❑ Read sections A–C.
	   ❑ Do practice question 5 in each section.
	❑ **TI-89 Calculator:** Appendix
	   ❑ Do practice questions 7–8.
		Study Time: 2 hours
		❑ Based on Practice Test, review chapters that still need attention.
		❑ **Vocabulary Study:** Chapter VII
		   ❑ Review all three groups of highlighted words.
			Study Time: 1 hour
			❑ Based on Practice Test, review chapters that still need attention.
			❑ **The Essay:** Chapter VIII
			   ❑ Brainstorm some topics you know well enough to write about quickly.

continued

	Mathematics	Critical Reading	Writing

1 day before the test	**Study Time:** 2 hours
	❑ **Working with Numbers:** Chapter X
	  ❑ Read sections A–F.
	  ❑ Do practice question 6 in each section.
	❑ **Algebra and Functions:** Chapter XI
	  ❑ Read sections A–H.
	  ❑ Do practice question 6 in each section.
	❑ **Geometry:** Chapter XII
	  ❑ Read sections A–I.
	  ❑ Do practice question 6 in each section.
	❑ **Probability, Statistics, and Data Analysis:** Chapter XIII
	  ❑ Read sections A–D.
	  ❑ Do practice question 6 in each section.
	❑ **Logic and Problem Solving:** Chapter XIV
	  ❑ Read sections A–C.
	  ❑ Do practice question 6 in each section.
	❑ **TI-89 Calculator:** Appendix
	  ❑ Do practice questions 9–10.
		Study Time: 1 hour
		❑ **Vocabulary Study:** Chapter VII
		  ❑ Review all highlighted words.
			Study Time: 30 minutes
			❑ **The Essay:** Chapter VIII
			  ❑ Review the brainstorming you did for all the sample essay questions. Think of more details you could add to strengthen your evidence.

Morning of the test	**Reminders:**
	❑ Have a good breakfast;
	❑ Take the following items with you on test day:
	  ❑ Your admission ticket and photo ID
	  ❑ Several #2 pencils and erasers
	  ❑ A calculator with fresh batteries
	  ❑ A watch
	❑ Try to go outside for a few minutes and walk around before the test.
	❑ Most important: Stay calm and confident during the test. Take deep slow breaths if you feel at all nervous. You can do it!		

V. Sentence Completions

Critical Reading Sections of the SAT

The Critical Reading sections of the test consist of two types of multiple-choice questions: sentence completions and critical reading passages. These questions test your vocabulary and your ability to read critically and analyze carefully. To build your vocabulary, you should become attuned to context clues, those parts of the sentence that help you figure out what a word means. Be curious as you read: look up words you can't define. Having a good vocabulary will be an asset to you in high school, college, and beyond, so you should never think that you are just learning words for the SAT.

Guessing strategy: There is a ¼-point penalty for incorrect answers on the SAT. The purpose of the penalty is to eliminate random guessing. This means that if you have absolutely no idea of the answer, and you can eliminate none of the choices, you should omit the question. However, once you can begin to use process of elimination to narrow your choices, you should consider taking an educated guess. The SAT favors aggressive test-takers.

Here are some strategies for guessing on the Critical Reading sections:

- **Look for familiar roots in the words in the sentence completions.** For example, if you don't know the word *prescience,* but you know *pre-* means "before" and *science* is related to knowledge, you can guess that this word means knowledge beforehand or forethought.

- **Say the unfamiliar vocabulary word out loud.** You may have heard it in context, and saying it may trigger recall.

- **After you've eliminated *one* of the choices, you should guess if you have a hunch about the correct answer. After you've eliminated *two* of the choices, you must guess.** *Remember:* Although you lose no points by omitting, you also gain no points. Statistics show that students who take educated guesses gain points.

- **Always look at the context one more time when guessing between two choices.** Reread the sentence or part of the reading passage. This just may give you enough information to take a more educated guess.

The Least You Need to Know: If you have very limited time to prepare for the test, take the Diagnostic Test and review the answers. Being familiar with the format of each section of the test will be a significant help to you as you take the real SAT. Read through the subject review chapters and focus on the general strategies for each of the Critical Reading sections. Try a few practice questions in each section. Don't try to memorize all the words in the vocabulary chapter, but read through the guessing strategies in each section. Most important, apply logic as you take the test. *Remember:* The SAT is a test of your critical thinking ability.

What Is the Sentence Completion Section?

This part of the Critical Reading section of the test consists of sentences missing one or two words. Your task is to find the best word or words to fill in the blanks. There will be 19 sentence completions on the SAT. In each sentence completion section, the questions gradually get more difficult as you go.

There are four basic types of sentence completion questions:

- One-blank definitional sentences
- Two-blank definitional sentences
- One-blank logic-based sentences
- Two-blank logic-based sentences

Think of a sentence completion question as a word puzzle. You're presented with a sentence that has one or two missing words. You're going to solve this puzzle by becoming a detective and following the context clues to the missing word(s). Every sentence will have a clue or clues that will lead you to the right choice.

Just be a good vocabulary detective and follow these simple steps:

1. **Read the sentence carefully and analyze the sentence structure.**
2. **Find and underline the clue.**
3. **Eliminate incorrect choices (using process of elimination).**
4. **Zero in on the best answer.**

As you read the sentence, pay particular attention to signal words, introductory or transitional words that establish relationships within the sentence.

Here are words that signal a contrast or contradiction:

although	however	rather than
but	in spite of	yet
despite	instead	
even though	nevertheless	

Here are words that signal ideas that are similar:

and	furthermore	likewise
for example	in addition	moreover

Here are words that signal a cause-and-effect relationship:

as a result	hence	thus
because	since	
consequently	therefore	

When you're answering sentence completion questions, follow these strategies:

- **As you read the sentence, think about the word or words you might use to fill in the blanks before you look at the words in the choices.** This thinking will help you narrow down the choices. You may find the exact word you were thinking of or a similar word among the choices.

- **Consider the structure of the sentence.** For example, if there is a clause followed by a colon, the words after the colon are an explanation.

- **Ask yourself: Is the missing word a positive word or a negative word? Is it a praising word or a criticizing word?** Sometimes, with two-blank questions, you can't tell whether the missing words are positive-negative or negative-positive, but as long as you've established that they're opposites, there will only be one choice in the answers that fits.

- **Do not eliminate a word because you think it is the wrong part of speech.** The choices are *always* the correct part of speech. One of the choices may be a word you're accustomed to using as a verb, but in this particular sentence, it's used as a noun. For example, the word *dispatch* is most commonly used as a verb meaning to send off or to transmit. It has been used on several SATs as a noun meaning quickness ("He sent out the package with dispatch").

Very often, in two-blank sentence completions, a fairly easy, familiar word will be paired with a much more difficult word, one whose meaning you may not know. In these cases, consider where you are in terms of level of difficulty: If you're still in the easy or medium range (the first few questions), you can guess the choice with the familiar word that works in the blank. If you're in the more difficult questions (the last two or three on the page), the familiar word is probably a trap. The unfamiliar word in the choice is probably the wrong word for the blank.

A. One-Blank Definitional Sentences

A definitional sentence contains the definition of the missing word or words right in the sentence.

EXAMPLE:

Before Mr. Gomez gets approval to build the new shopping center he designed, he is required to submit a _____, an official summary of his proposed venture.

To answer this question correctly, follow the four steps of the vocabulary detective. When you read and analyze this question, you'll see that it contains a definition of the missing word:

an official summary of a proposed venture

Underline this clue, and think about what the definition means. *An official summary* suggests some sort of document. *A proposed venture* suggests a plan for the future. Here are the choices:

- A.   mediation
- B.   vilification
- C.   standardization
- D.   construction
- E.   prospectus

Now begin to eliminate incorrect choices:

- **Choice A: mediation:** If you don't know the definition of this word (to work with both sides of a dispute to settle a conflict), you might think of medium (middle) or media (means of transmitting information). Not much to do with a proposed venture. Eliminate this choice.
- **Choice B: vilification:** This word should make you think of something vile or a villain. Because this word means a malicious or abusive statement, it, too, is incorrect.
- **Choice C: standardization:** This word might be somewhat tempting, because it sounds like something official, but don't be fooled by SAT tricksters. It simply means the process of making things the same (standard).
- **Choice D: construction:** This is the official "distracter," the wrong answer most likely to attract the attention of the unwary test-taker. Since *construction* is directly related to the topic of the sentence (although it does not mean "an official summary of a proposed venture"), it will distract many students from the right answer.
- **Choice E: prospectus:** Having eliminated the other answer choices, you can zero in on the right answer. The word *prospectus* may be unfamiliar to you, but you'll select it by process of elimination. An alert test-taker will notice that *prospectus* contains the word *prospect*, which is an outlook or likelihood that something will happen in the future.

Practice

Directions: Each of the following sentences has either one or two blanks. Each blank indicates that a word has been left out. Beneath the sentence are five words or sets of words labeled A through E. Choose the word or set of words that, when inserted in the sentence, *best* fits the meaning of the sentence as a whole.

1. The rather pedestrian plot of the film was elevated by its _____ cinematography; the magnificent panoramas of the African veldt were photographed in stunning clarity and with breath-taking beauty.

   A. banal
   B. exquisite
   C. ordinary
   D. abundant
   E. sparse

2. Known as a skillful _____, Uncle Jerry was surrounded by children who loved to hear tales of his travels as a merchant marine.

   A. raconteur
   B. novice
   C. speculator
   D. innovator
   E. arbiter

3. The Sybarites were known for their _____, a lifestyle that focused on the self-indulgent pursuit of pleasure.

   A. pluralism
   B. asceticism
   C. hedonism
   D. spiritualism
   E. recidivism

4. Realizing his original speech was so abstruse and _____ that it would be above the level of most people's understanding, the physicist revised and simplified his comments.

   A. inane
   B. egalitarian
   C. momentous
   D. arcane
   E. sophomoric

5. Ms. Kumock was regarded by her students as _____: she seemed always to know in advance what they were thinking.

   A. brusque
   B. clairvoyant
   C. prudent
   D. serene
   E. predominant

Answers

Note: If you need the definitions of any of the vocabulary words in these questions, see Chapter VII.

1. **B** *Exquisite* fits the definition in the sentence: "breath-taking beauty."

2. **A** A *raconteur* is a story-teller—he would, by definition, attract listeners.

3. **C** *Hedonism* is "the pursuit of pleasure."

4. **D** *Arcane* means "above the level of most people's understanding."

5. **B** *Clairvoyant* means "able to see the future."

B. Two-Blank Definitional Sentences

A two-blank definitional sentence has two missing words and two clues. The first clue will be your hint to the missing word in the first blank, and the second clue will be your hint to the second missing word.

EXAMPLE:

The poetry of George Herbert is surprising in that it is both _____ and _____; his verse humbly expresses his devotional beliefs in images that are often imbued with playful wit.

Again, follow the four steps: Read the sentence and analyze the structure. Remember that in parallel sentences the two clues will provide you with enough information to find the two missing words. Underline the clues. Then use process of elimination to help you narrow your choices.

The clue "humbly expresses his devotional beliefs" will help you find the first missing word, and the second clue, "imbued with playful wit," will lead you to the second word. Now look at the choices:

A. religious . . . pedestrian
B. pious . . . comedic
C. secular . . . mirthful
D. self-effacing . . . trite
E. dogmatic . . . jocular

Begin the process of elimination by eliminating the words that you're familiar with that don't fit the clues. In Choice A, *religious* looks like a good choice for the first blank, but *pedestrian* (dull) does not fit with *playful wit*. Choice C can be eliminated because *secular* contradicts the clue "expresses his devotional beliefs." Choice D *self-effacing* fits nicely with the concept of humbleness, but *trite* does not suggest *playful wit*. In Choice E, *jocular* is a good match for playfulness, but *dogmatic* does not convey the sense of *humble devotion*. That leaves the best answer, Choice B: *pious* is synonymous with humble devotion, while *comedic* fits very well with the concept of *playful wit*.

Practice

Directions: Each of the following sentences has either one or two blanks. Each blank indicates that a word has been left out. Beneath the sentence are five words or sets of words labeled A through E. Choose the word or set of words that, when inserted in the sentence, *best* fits the meaning of the sentence as a whole.

1. Our guide informed us that far from having a docile nature and a sedentary lifestyle, this species of orangutans are _____ and _____.

A. tame . . . isolated
B. savage . . . settled
C. evolved . . . peaceful
D. scientific . . . chaotic
E. ferocious . . . itinerant

2. The discovery of the coelacanth, a fish previously thought extinct, was _____ and _____, startling marine biologists and overturning long-held beliefs.

A. obscure . . . predictable
B. astonishing . . . unanticipated
C. scientific . . . practical
D. irrelevant . . . skeptical
E. effusive . . . emotional

3. Both _____ and _____, Kamal resisted the efforts of others to help him and waited until the last minute to hand in his work.

   A. stubborn . . . efficient
   B. demanding . . . aggressive
   C. obstinate . . . dilatory
   D. intense . . . resistant
   E. dangerous . . . eccentric

4. We often avoid my uncle Oscar because he is both _____ and _____: he talks incessantly and spends extravagantly.

   A. voluminous . . . cantankerous
   B. gregarious . . . vociferous
   C. loquacious . . . odious
   D. garrulous . . . profligate
   E. parsimonious . . . penurious

5. The conductor of the symphony orchestra was famous for being _____ in his public appearances, yet _____ in his private correspondence, for his wildly frenetic performances were in sharp contrast to the measured thoughtfulness of his letters.

   A. agile . . . agitated
   B. diffident . . . quiescent
   C. effervescent . . . imperious
   D. tranquil . . . turbulent
   E. boisterous . . . contemplative

Answers

Note: If you need the definitions of any of the vocabulary words in these questions, see Chapter VII.

1. **E** The phrase *far from* indicates that you're looking for the opposite of *docile* and *sedentary*. *Ferocious* (fierce or savage) is the opposite of *docile* (tame) and *itinerant* (traveling from place to place) is the opposite of *sedentary* (tending to stay in one place).

2. **B** "Startling marine biologists," a clue to look for a word that would indicate surprise, should lead you to *astonishing*. Since this discovery overturned accepted beliefs, it would have been unanticipated.

3. **C** You know that Kamal "resisted the efforts of other to help him," so you're looking for a word that denotes this characteristic: *obstinate* means stubborn. His waiting "until the last minute to hand in his work" tells you he is late or *dilatory*.

4. **D** You're looking for words that mean "talks incessantly" and "spends extravagantly." *Garrulous* is talkative, and *profligate* is wasteful and extravagant.

5. **E** "Wildly frenetic" is the clue to the conductor's public behavior, and "measured thoughtfulness" is the clue to his private habits. *Boisterous* (noisy and rowdy) fits in the first blank, and *contemplative* (calm and thoughtful) fits in the second blank.

C. One-Blank Logic-Based Sentences

The logic-based sentence completion requires you to understand the basic sense of the sentence and the context clues embedded in it. You usually won't find a definition of the missing words, but you will have enough information, if you follow the clues carefully, to find the correct response.

EXAMPLE:

> Although we were able to examine fully-grown adult fruit flies, we were never able to observe them in their _____.

After you've read the sentence carefully, try to locate the context clue and underline it. The context clue in this sentence is *fully-grown adult.* Note that the sentence begins with a signal word, *Although.* Because this is a contrast signal, you know that you're looking for the opposite of *fully-grown adult.* Now look at the choices:

- **A.** dotage
- **B.** maturity
- **C.** incipience
- **D.** aerie
- **E.** habitat

Choice A, *dotage,* is often used to mean "old age." The opposite of *fully-grown adult* is not old age, so you can eliminate Choice A. You can eliminate Choice B for the same reason: *maturity* is too close in meaning to *fully-grown adult.* Choices D and E are the distracters, *aerie* because it is a high nesting place that may suggest a flying insect, and *habitat* because it is a word associated with an examination of living creatures. That leaves Choice C, *incipience.* You may not know the exact definition (it means "in the beginning stage of development"), but it's the only logical choice left.

Practice

Directions: Each of the following sentences has either one or two blanks. Each blank indicates that a word has been left out. Beneath the sentence are five words or sets of words labeled A through E. Choose the word or set of words that, when inserted in the sentence, *best* fits the meaning of the sentence as a whole.

1. Because of Cristen's _____, what could have been a dull weekend in an isolated farmhouse became a delightful two days filled with fun and laughter.

   - **A.** lethargy
   - **B.** shyness
   - **C.** ineptitude
   - **D.** effervescence
   - **E.** tolerance

2. A _____ and sensitive librarian, Mr. Stone had the ability to know exactly which book would suit each one of his fifth-graders.

   - **A.** discerning
   - **B.** caustic
   - **C.** pedantic
   - **D.** venal
   - **E.** libertarian

3. Many urbanites relish weekend getaways in the country, finding their _____ a relief from the frenetic pace of the city.

   A. fundamentalism
   B. obscurity
   C. mutability
   D. tranquility
   E. impermanence

4. Feeling he lacked the _____ needed to become a financial analyst, Manuel sought more advanced training in high-level economic theory.

   A. vacuity
   B. jocosity
   C. frugality
   D. equanimity
   E. perspicacity

5. Ice sculptures, while often quite beautiful and extravagant displays, are necessarily an _____ art form.

   A. evocative
   B. ephemeral
   C. abstemious
   D. idiosyncratic
   E. ascetic

Answers

Note: If you need the definitions of any of the vocabulary words in these questions, see Chapter VII.

1. **D** The logic of the sentences suggests that Cristen's personality must be lively. *Effervescence* means "liveliness" and "enthusiasm."

2. **A** *Discerning* (able to see clearly and insightfully) fits the clue that Mr. Stone knows "exactly which book" to select for his students.

3. **D** *Tranquility* (peacefulness) is the opposite of "the frenetic pace of the city," so it fits the logic of the sentence.

4. **E** *Perspicacity* means "mental sharpness." Since Manuel seeks additional high-level training to become a financial analyst, a job that requires mental keenness, the logic of the sentence should lead you to Choice E.

5. **B** To answer this correctly, you must think about the logic of an ice sculpture. Clearly, an ice sculpture can't last long; thus, it is *ephemeral* (existing only briefly).

D. Two-Blank Logic-Based Sentences

The logic-based sentence completion with two blanks requires you to understand the basic sense of the sentence and the context clues embedded in it. Like the one blank sentence, you usually won't find a definition of the missing words, but you will have enough information, if you follow the clues carefully, to find the pair of words that fits logically. You can also do double elimination: if either of the words in the choices is incorrect, you can eliminate that choice.

EXAMPLE:

Testifying before the FDA, the drug company executive reluctantly admitted that rather than achieving the company's goal of _____ the symptoms of the liver disorder as they had hoped, the new drug unexpectedly _____ them.

A. assuaging . . . alleviated
B. divulging . . . compounded
C. ameliorating . . . exacerbated
D. enervating . . . expunged
E. inundating . . . impeded

First, find the clues in the sentence. Logically, a drug company's goal would be to relieve or get rid of the symptoms of a disorder; after all, that's the purpose of a new drug. You can figure out that the first word will relate to relieving the symptoms. Next, notice that the sentence contains the signal words *rather than;* these words indicate that the goal of relieving the symptoms has been unsuccessful. The word *unexpected* reinforces the idea that this outcome is not the one desired by the company. Now you know the second word will be opposite in meaning to the first word. Use process of elimination to eliminate any of the choices that don't have the meanings you're looking for in the correct order: relieving in the first blank and making worse in the second blank. If you know the definitions of the words, you can eliminate all choices except A and C based on the first word alone. (Use Chapter VII to find the meanings of the words in the choices.) Either *assuaging* or *ameliorating* can mean relieving. Now look at the second words in choice A and C: *alleviating* has the same meaning as *assuaging,* so it doesn't fit the logic of the sentence. The second word in choice C, *exacerbated,* means "made worse," so it's the logical opposite to *ameliorating.*

Practice

Directions: Each of the following sentences has either one or two blanks. Each blank indicates that a word has been left out. Beneath the sentence are five words or sets of words labeled A through E. Choose the word or set of words that, when inserted in the sentence, *best* fits the meaning of the sentence as a whole.

1. Although Eli was reserved by nature, when he stood in front of an audience his habitual _____ was replaced a _____ delivery that made his lectures a delight to attend.

   A. reticence . . . scintillating
   B. leniency . . . strict
   C. sluggishness . . . lethargic
   D. shyness . . . trite
   E. pacifism . . . frenetic

2. Even though Shakespeare's plays were written over 400 years ago, audiences still flock to see them, for their _____ themes make them as _____ today as they were in the Elizabethan Age.

   A. momentary . . . rejuvenating
   B. timeless . . . relevant
   C. dated . . . pertinent
   D. elaborate . . . tangential
   E. eloquent . . . tragic

3. For several days after the avalanche, the deep snow drifts and bitter cold _____ rescue efforts, and hopes of finding any survivors of the climbing party _____.

   A. bolstered . . . diminished
   B. obstructed . . . elevated
   C. jeopardized . . . crystallized
   D. resolved . . . escalated
   E. hindered . . . diminished

4. Despite her normally gregarious nature, when working on her manuscript, the playwright _____ social engagements and lived a life of _____.

   A. flaunted . . . endurance
   B. eschewed . . . asceticism
   C. execrated . . . dissension
   D. subsumed . . . banality
   E. circumscribed . . . acquiescence

5. The student council rejected both the content and the rhetoric of the stringent code of conduct proposed by the faculty advisory committee; they found its restrictions _____ and its tone _____.

   A. plaintive . . . zealous
   B. feckless . . . haphazard
   C. inane . . . laudable
   D. draconian . . . punitive
   E. craven . . . beneficent

Answers

Note: If you need the definitions of any of the vocabulary words in these questions, see Chapter VII.

1. **A** The logic of the sentence sets up an opposition between Eli's usual behavior and his demeanor in front of an audience. The clue that he usually is "reserved" helps you find the word in the first blank that is similar in meaning and tells you to look for a contrasting word in the second blank. *Reticence* is shyness or natural uncommunicativeness. A *scintillating* or sparkling delivery would make his lecture "a delight to attend" and would contrast with his usual quietness.

2. **B** *Even though* signals the logic of contrast. What would contrast with the notion that, although the plays are over 400 years old, people are still going to see them? Certainly, the idea of being *timeless* and still *relevant* would provide the needed contrast.

3. **E** The logic of the sentence suggests that the snow and cold made efforts to rescue the climbers more difficult: *to hinder* is to make more difficult. This difficulty would make the hopes of finding survivors decline: *to diminish* is to become less.

4. **B** The signal word *despite* sets up a contrast between the word *gregarious* (sociable) and the behavior of the playwright when she's working. She would *eschew* (avoid) social engagements and live a restricted and self-denying lifestyle (*asceticism*).

5. **D** The clue word *stringent* (strict) sets up the logic of this sentence in conjunction with the clue that the students rejected the content and the language of the code. *Draconian* rules are overly strict, and *punitive* suggests that the code was meant to punish the students.

VI. Critical Reading Passages

What Are Critical Reading Passages?

The critical reading passages are taken from different content areas—you'll encounter passages from the humanities, social sciences, and natural sciences. Passages are written in a variety of styles; some are purely expository (describing and explaining information), others are narrative in form (telling a story), and others are argumentative (arguing a position). Each SAT contains two sets of paired related readings—one short pair and one long pair.

Each passage is followed by a set of 2 to 13 questions. Most of the questions will fit into the following categories:

- Main purpose
- Central idea
- Extended reasoning
- Line reference (detail and purpose)
- Tone, attitude, and language
- Vocabulary in context
- Synthesis

Here are strategies for successfully completing the SAT critical reading passages:

- **Always read actively.** Focus on what the author is trying to tell you. Think as you read—don't allow your mind to drift. Have a mental dialogue with the text. Sometimes it's helpful to visualize and see the passage enfold in front of your eyes, like a movie.

- **If you're confused by a sentence or a paragraph, don't reread.** The sentence or paragraph may become clearer as you read, or there may not be any questions about that part of the passage. If you have to reread, do so as you answer the questions.

- **Psych yourself up and try to be interested in the passage.** Link the passage in your mind to a familiar topic. This strategy will help you stay focused. You may also want to underline key points in the passage, star them, or jot down a note or two. Just don't get so involved with underlining that you slow down and lose the sense of the passage.

- **Don't allow your personal feelings or your own knowledge about the topic to influence your answers.** Always go back to what is stated in or implied by the text for support for your answer.

- **Always read *all* the choices before you select an answer.** Use process of elimination as you read the choices. If you are sure an answer is wrong, cross out the letter of the choice. If you think it could be right, leave it alone. When you have read all the choices, look again only at the choices that are not crossed out, and evaluate their accuracy. Don't be fooled by an answer that makes a correct statement but does not answer the specific question. A statement may be true based on the information in the passage, but it may still be the wrong answer because it doesn't answer the question you're being asked.

- **Be on the lookout for EXCEPT questions.** For EXCEPT questions, four of the answers will be right. In these questions, you're looking for the *wrong* answer. Circle the word *EXCEPT* in your test booklet so you won't look for answers that are right.
- **Pay particular attention to the ends of the answers.** Many of the choices start out right, but then the last word or phrase is incorrect. These are set up to trick you if you're rushing through the choices.

A. Main Purpose Questions

These critical reading questions ask you to determine the author's main purpose in writing the passage. In other words, why did the author write this piece? What was he trying to accomplish? To answer these questions, you must think about the passage as a whole. Is the author trying to argue a position? Describe a person or a scene? Create a mood? Prove or disprove a theory?

- Sometimes, within a passage an author will have more than one purpose, but for this question, you're only looking for the *main* purpose.
- Use the introductory material (the information in italics just before the passage) to help you figure out why the author wrote this passage.

B. Central Idea Questions

Central idea questions may be posed in several ways: What is the main idea of the passage? With which of the following statements would the author most likely agree? What is the best title for the passage? This passage is primarily concerned with. . . ?

To answer this central idea question, ask yourself this question: If I had to sum up the subject of this passage in one sentence, what would I say? It's often helpful to think about this question as you read the passage, and underline or star the main idea when you think you've come to it.

- Try to follow the author's logic as you read and be alert for the thesis of the passage.
- Pay particular attention to shifts in the passage that are signaled by the words *but, yet,* and *however.* Always circle these words when they start a new paragraph. Sometimes an author will begin a passage by presenting the side of the issue with which she disagrees; then she'll offer a counterargument to the position that has been previously discussed.
- If you're having difficulty finding the main idea of the passage, reread the first sentence in each paragraph. Most will relate to the central idea of the passage.

C. Extended Reasoning Questions

Extended reasoning questions require you to extrapolate; that is, to use critical thinking to go beyond what is directly stated in the passage. You must draw conclusions from what you read. These questions will ask you to *infer* (to draw a conclusion from what the author implies). The question may ask you what the author *suggests* or may ask what you can *assume* from the passage. In a sense, you are "reading between the lines."

- Although the answer will not be directly stated in the passage, always use textual evidence to support your choice.

- Be careful not to allow your own opinions to influence your answer to the question. There will be hints in the passage to guide you to the correct choice.

Practice: Sections A–C

Directions: Carefully read the passage below and answer the questions that follow the passage. Answer the questions based on the content of the passage: both what is stated and what is implied in the passage as well as any introductory material before the passage.

This passage is adapted from a work about travel published in 1814.

In the early period of human history, when voyages and travels were not undertaken from the view of amusement or instruction, or from political or commercial motives, the discovery of adjacent countries was chiefly affected by war, and of distant regions by commerce.

(5) The wars of the Egyptians with the Scythians, mentioned in the pristine pages of history, must have opened faint sources of information concerning the neighboring tribes. Under the Grecian empire of Alexander and his successors, the progress of discovery by war is first marked on the page of history; and science began to attend the banners of victory.

The opulence of nature was now to be disclosed; and Greece was astonished at the miracles of India. The Romans not only inherited the Grecian knowledge, but, extending their arms to the North and (10) West, accumulated discoveries upon regions dimly descried by the Greeks, through the obscurity in which the Phoenicians enveloped their commercial advantages.

1. The primary purpose of this passage is to

   A. criticize a strategy
   B. justify an undertaking
   C. explain a phenomenon
   D. defend an approach
   E. provoke a response

2. The main idea of this passage is

   A. the search for scientific information engendered the desire to travel
   B. the wealth of the western world was mostly derived from looting conquered regions
   C. the systematic conquest of weaker tribes decimated the ancient world
   D. the Greeks were the leaders in the fields of science in the classic world
   E. an increase in knowledge was a corollary of warfare

3. The author suggests that science and warfare

   A. are equally important motivations for nations to undertake exploration
   B. are mutually exclusive
   C. are painful reminders of mankind's desire to destroy that which is unfamiliar
   D. are related in that scientific knowledge is increased by contact predicated on conquest
   E. are obscure historical processes rather than commercial enterprises

Answers: Sections A–C

1. **C** This primary purpose question asks you to think about why the author wrote the passage. Try to eliminate the most obviously incorrect answers first. Is the author criticizing anything? He is not, so cross out Choice A. Is there an undertaking that the author must justify? The author states his points regarding the relationship between war and discovery, but he does not attempt to justify them, so Choice B is incorrect. Choice D is incorrect because the author does not defend; he merely asserts. Choice E is clearly wrong because the author does not try to provoke a response from his reader. That leaves Choice C, which is the correct answer. Don't be misled by the word *phenomenon;* it is used on the SAT to mean any incident, occurrence, or observable fact. In fact, the author is explaining an occurrence in this passage.

2. **E** To find the main idea, try to summarize the passage in a few words. The author is trying to show that exploration and an increase in knowledge were natural consequences of war. As nations conquered other territories, they absorbed the scientific and cultural discoveries of the lands. Notice that each of the incorrect choices has a word or phrase from the passage. If you are not reading carefully, it's easy to be tricked into selecting a choice that "looks" right. Always look beyond the words of an answer to determine its meaning.

3. **D** This inference question asks you to draw a conclusion about the relationship between war and knowledge based on what the author suggests in the passage. He says, "science began to attend the banners of victory" and "The Romans . . . accumulated discoveries." These statements imply that, through conquest, invaders absorbed the knowledge of the conquered territories. Thus, warfare led to an increase in scientific knowledge.

D. Line Reference

Line reference questions refer you to specific lines in the text. There are two types of line reference questions: detail questions and purpose questions.

1. Detail

Detail questions ask you to understand a detail in the passage. Always go back to the text and underline or bracket the lines, but don't be tricked into thinking the answers will always be in those lines. Often, the best clue to the answer will be in the line just *before* the lines referred to; sometimes the best clue will be just *after* the lines referred to. Try to *paraphrase* the lines (put them in your own words).

- Start rereading at least one sentence before the line reference and continue one sentence after.
- Consider every word in the line; sometimes a word that seems unimportant will be the key to the correct answer.

2. Purpose

Purpose questions ask about the author's purpose in using a word or phrase. The question may say, "In line _____ the author refers to _____ in order to . . ." or "The author refers to line _____ in order to make the point that. . . ." Again, go back, underline or bracket the lines, and read the sentence before and after the line reference. Think about *why* the author included this information. What is he trying to achieve here?

- Paraphrase the lines. The lines will be easier to deal with if you understand what they mean.
- Consider the purpose of the entire passage. Usually a detail is included to support the main idea of the passage.

Practice: Section D

Directions: Carefully read the passage below and answer the questions that follow the passage. Answer the questions based on the content of the passage: both what is stated and what is implied in the passage as well as any introductory material before the passage.

The following passage is an excerpt from a 19th-century essay entitled "Self-Reliance."

I read the other day some verses written by an eminent painter which were original and not conventional. The soul always hears an admonition in such lines, let the subject be what it may. The sentiment they instill is of more value than any thought they may contain. To believe your own thought, to believe that what is true for you in your private heart is true for all men, — that is genius. Speak your
(5) latent conviction, and it shall be the universal sense; for the inmost in due time becomes the outmost,—— and our first thought is rendered back to us by the trumpets of the Last Judgment. Familiar as the voice of the mind is to each, the highest merit we ascribe to Moses, Plato, and Milton is, that they set at naught books and traditions, and spoke not what men but what they thought. A man should learn to detect and watch that gleam of light which flashes across his mind from within, more than the lustre of the firmament
(10) of bards and sages. Yet he dismisses without notice his thought, because it is his. In every work of genius we recognize our own rejected thoughts: they come back to us with a certain alienated majesty. Great works of art have no more affecting lesson for us than this. They teach us to abide by our spontaneous impression with good-humored inflexibility then most when the whole cry of voices is on the other side. Else, to-morrow a stranger will say with masterly good sense precisely what we have thought and felt all
(15) the time, and we shall be forced to take with shame our own opinion from another.

1. The author refers to Moses, Plato, and Milton (line 7) in order to

   A. argue that only the ancient sages had real genius
   B. suggest a chronological pattern to the development of thoughtful meditation
   C. refute the notion that these men were individual thinkers rather than reflections of the current thinking of their times
   D. cite examples of men who rejected conventional thought in favor of individual insight
   E. foster the impression that great artists must be men who have been recognized as leaders by their contemporaries

2. In line 9 the phrase *gleam of light* refers to

   A. each person's sense of what is true
   B. verses written by a poet
   C. a divine vision
   D. great works of art
   E. the trumpets of the Last Judgment

Answers: Section D

1. **D** This line reference/purpose question requires that you consider *why* the author mentions these three historical figures. What is his purpose? Choice A is incorrect because the author never says that only sages had genius; in fact, this contradicts his main idea that every person has a spark of genius within. Choice B is there as a trick: it's true that the men are listed in chronological order, but that is unrelated to the author's purpose—he isn't making a point about the historical development of thought. Choice C is the direct opposite of the main point of the passage; the author is not *refuting* (disproving) but advocating the innate value of individual insight. Choice E is incorrect because the author never makes this point. That leaves Choice D, which correctly states the author's purpose in referring to the three men: they are perfect examples of unconventional thinkers who had faith in their own insights.

2. **A** This line reference/detail question asks you to find the idea in the text that is a "gleam of light." The sentence immediately before the line reference mentions "what they thought" (line 8), a reference to the personal ideas of Moses, Plato, and Milton. Earlier, the author discusses "latent conviction" (line 5) and "what is true for you in your private heart is true" (line 4). All of these refer to individual insight, Choice A. Even the title of the passage, "Self-Reliance" (see the introductory note to the passage) supports the sense of relying on one's own sense of what is right and true. Choices B, D, and E, while all mentioned in the passage, are not the correct reference. Choice C is just there to distract you because the passage has a very spiritual message.

E. Tone, Attitude, and Language Questions

Some questions on the test ask you to consider the *tone* of a line or of the whole passage. Other questions ask about the author's *attitude* toward someone or something. If a passage is a narrative (a story), there may be a question about a character's attitude or tone toward someone or something. Be sure you know *whose* attitude you are looking for and toward *whom* or *what*. There may be questions that test your understanding of *rhetoric,* the art of using language to accomplish your purpose.

In addition, you should be able to recognize literal versus metaphorical language. *Literal language* is meant to be taken at face value; it denotes what it means. *Metaphorical language* is not meant to be taken literally. For example, the statement "My pockets are empty" may *literally* denote that there is nothing in the pouches in my pants or skirt; metaphorically, it may mean that I'm broke or poor.

Here are key tone/attitude words used on the SAT, along with their definitions:

- **Indignant:** Angry at unfairness or injustice
- **Objective:** Neutral, impartial
- **Subjective:** Based on personal opinion
- **Whimsical:** Light-hearted, fanciful
- **Comedic, humorous:** Amusing (*Remember:* SAT humor is not always what you would consider funny.)
- **Ironic:** Unexpected, a twist of fate
- **Nostalgic:** Longing for the past
- **Detached:** Neutral, not emotionally or personally involved
- **Resigned:** Sadly accepting

- **Wistful:** Sadly longing
- **Scornful, disdainful, contemptuous:** Disrespectfully critical
- **Equivocal:** Deliberately vague or misleading
- **Ambivalent:** Having mixed feelings, seeing both sides of an issue
- **Cynical:** Pessimistic, expecting the worst from others
- **Witty:** Clever and amusing
- **Didactic:** Instructive or preachy
- **Awe:** Wonder, amazement
- **Derisive, sardonic, sarcastic:** Scornfully mocking
- **Skeptical, incredulous, dubious:** Disbelieving, doubtful
- **Adulatory, laudatory:** Highly praising, worshipping

Pay particular attention to words that modify the tone words: If the choice is *caustically witty,* you know there is a bitter tone to the humor. If the attitude is *unbridled enthusiasm,* you know the author is unrestrained in his positive response. *Veiled hostility* would be implied or indirect hostility.

F. Vocabulary in Context Questions

Vocabulary in context questions ask about the meaning of a word as it is used in the passage. Often, words that have multiple meanings are selected. You must find the appropriate choice for the context. The best technique is to go back to the text, circle the word, and reread the whole sentence. Then replace the circled word with the words in the choices. Select the answer that is most like the original meaning of the sentence.

- **Don't rely on *denotation* (the dictionary meaning of a word) alone.** The correct response often requires you to consider *connotation* (the suggested meaning or implication of a word).
- **Very often, the most common meaning of a word—the one that pops right into your head—is not the correct answer.** Always look at the *context,* the sentences surrounding the word, to help you decide on the best choice.
- **Most of the words will be familiar to you, not like the difficult words from the sentence completion questions.** This is a test of your ability to understand context rather than a test of your vocabulary.

Practice: Sections E–F

Directions: Carefully read the passage below and answer the questions that follow the passage. Answer the questions based on the content of the passage: both what is stated and what is implied in the passage as well as any introductory material before the passage.

The following passage is from the opening chapter of a 20th-century novel written by an American woman.

When Newland Archer opened the door at the back of the club box, the curtain had just gone up on the garden scene. There was no reason why the young man should not have come earlier, for he had dined at seven, alone with his mother and sister, and had lingered afterward over a cigar in the Gothic library with glazed black-walnut bookcases and finial-topped chairs which was the only room in the

(5) house where Mrs. Archer allowed smoking. But, in the first place, New York was a metropolis, and perfectly aware that in metropolises it was "not the thing" to arrive early at the opera; and what was or was not "the thing" played a part as important in Newland Archer's New York as the inscrutable totem terrors that had ruled the destinies of his forefathers thousands of years ago.

The second reason for his delay was a personal one. He had dawdled over his cigar because he was at
(10) heart a dilettante, and thinking over a pleasure to come often gave him a subtler satisfaction than its realization. This was especially the case when the pleasure was a delicate one, as his pleasures mostly were; and on this occasion the moment he looked forward to was so rare and exquisite in quality that— well, if he had timed his arrival in accord with the prima donna's stage-manager he could not have entered the Academy at a more significant moment than just as she was singing: "He loves me—he loves
(15) me not—HE LOVES ME!—" and sprinkling the falling daisy petals with notes as clear as dew.

1. The word *totem* in line 7 most nearly means

    A.   carved
    B.   symbolic
    C.   momentous
    D.   archeological
    E.   horrific

2. The word *realization* in line 11 most nearly means

    A.   epiphany
    B.   understanding
    C.   truthfulness
    D.   idealization
    E.   actuality

3. The author's attitude toward Newland Archer is

    A.   indulgently amused
    B.   scornfully mocking
    C.   markedly hostile
    D.   appropriately adulatory
    E.   anxiously apologetic

Answers: Sections E–F

1. **B** This as a fairly difficult vocabulary-in-context question because the word *totem* is not a particularly familiar word. Most students have probably encountered this word only in association with Native American carved totem poles. However, by using the technique of circling the word, considering the context, and replacing the circled word with the choices, you can use process of elimination to narrow the choices to B and C. Because the context concerns the "right" time to arrive at the opera and the tone of the paragraph is light, the terror is *symbolic* rather than *momentous*.

2. **E** This vocabulary-in-context question is fairly straightforward. In the sentence "He had dawdled over his cigar because he was at heart a dilettante, and thinking over a pleasure to come often gave him a subtler satisfaction than its realization" (lines 9–11), the author sets up a contrast between thinking about a pleasure and actually experiencing the pleasure. Thus, the realization of the pleasure is the actuality of it. None of the other choices will fit the context of the sentence.

3. **A** To understand the author's attitude toward her character, you must look at the language she uses to describe him. There are no harsh or unpleasant adjectives describing Newland Archer in the passage. He arrives late to the opera because it is the "right" thing to do according to the rules of his society; thus, he is somewhat superficial and concerned about appearances. You also learn that most of his pleasures are delicate. True, the author appears to find him a bit self-involved and self-important, but she clearly sees him as likeable. Use process of elimination to eliminate choices B and C because they're too negative. Choice D doesn't allow for the author's obvious awareness of Archer's faults. Eliminate Choice E because the author makes no attempt to apologize for Archer's faults; rather, she seems willing to indulge him and allow herself to be amused by him.

G. Synthesis Questions

There will usually be two paired reading passages on your SAT—one long pair and one short pair. The passages will be on the same topic or related topics. After the two passages, you'll find questions on each passage and questions that ask you to *synthesize* (put the passages together). The passages may oppose each other, be in agreement, or simply parallel one another. Most of the time, it's helpful to read both passages before you answer the questions; however, with the long passages, you may find you'd rather answer the questions that deal only with Passage 1 while it's fresh in your mind before you read Passage 2. Try it both ways in practice and determine which method works best for you.

- As you read, look for the thesis statement that states the position of the author and jot it down next to the passage.

- You'll most likely have to use the information from one passage to interpret some idea in the other passage. Be sure you understand how they relate.

- As you read, think about ways in which the passages oppose one another; also consider what they might agree upon. If the passages take contrasting positions, anything they agree upon will necessarily be very general.

- Recognize that some passages simply present an overview or survey of a topic and do not take a pro or con position.

Practice: Section G

Directions: Carefully read the passages below and answer the questions that follow each passage. The questions after the pair of related passages may ask you about the relationship between the passages. Answer the questions based on the content of the passages: both what is stated and what is implied in the passages as well as any introductory material before each passage.

Passage 1

On every worker's desk in every worker's cubicle in every major corporation in the United States, there sits a computer. To many of us, it is inconceivable that having a computer was once considered a luxury. Now we cannot imagine doing business without data programs, e-mails, video conferencing, and the Internet. Along with this boon in technology, however, has arisen a rather surprising issue: privacy
(5) in the workplace. With easy access to the Internet, many workers cannot resist the temptation to send personal e-mails, do some Internet browsing, and maybe even shop a bit on company time. Concerned by this use of company technology and waste of employee time, corporations are fighting back by installing monitoring devices. In 1986, Congress passed the Electronic Communications Privacy Act, which gave employers the right to monitor electronic communications in the workplace. Now companies
(10) can be sure all the "work" employees are doing on their computers is truly work related.

Passage 2

I love my job. I get to sit on an ergonomically designed chair in my own little private cubicle with a brand-new state-of-the-art computer on my sleek and shiny desk. The work is not too demanding; my responsibility is to check the financial records of the local stores. These tend to come into the central office in waves: there are peaks and troughs. During a peak, I am swamped and work nonstop to keep up.
(5) But, then come the troughs . . . a blissful hour or so of inactivity. While I wait for the next batch of receipts to come in, I catch up on my e-mails and even do some of my holiday shopping. This is such a great timesaver for me. Since I can't afford my own computer yet, I can keep up with friends and family while I'm at my desk. But, recently, some of my colleagues have heard rumors of corporate snooping. They say the company is going to install monitoring devices to make sure we use our computers only for
(10) company business. I can't believe they would invade our privacy like that! I love this company and am a very loyal employee. If the rumor proves true, I can't imagine I will feel the same way about going to work each day.

1. The author of Passage 1 repeats the word *every* (line 1) in order to

   A. indicate the value of up-to-date equipment
   B. underscore the ubiquity of computers
   C. disparage modern society's reliance on technology
   D. comment on the accuracy of machines versus human calculations
   E. praise the worker's ability to adapt to new tools

2. The author of Passage 1 would most likely respond to the last sentence of Passage 2 by

   A. suggesting that computers have dramatically improved the productivity and accuracy of workers
   B. noting that some companies have given their employees laptops to take home with them
   C. observing that company loyalty should be based on brand loyalty
   D. arguing that work time is just that: time to work
   E. asserting that companies can't afford to monitor all employees

3. Unlike Passage 1, Passage 2 makes use of

   A. statistical evidence
   B. technological terminology
   C. anecdote
   D. historical evidence
   E. investigative techniques

4. The authors of both passages would agree that

   A. corporations should prevent employees from using technology for non-work-related activities
   B. monitoring the use of computers is an invasion of an employee's right to privacy
   C. technology has engendered unforeseen personal rights issues
   D. good business practices demand the involvement of employees in policy decision-making
   E. Internet use has become a danger to privacy

5. The two passages differ most in their

   A. knowledge of the technical aspects of modern technology
   B. attitude toward the use of time in a work environment
   C. opinion of the value of Internet shopping
   D. sense of the importance of employee loyalty
   E. respect for the role of the government in fostering good business practices

Answers: Section G

1. **B** The author repeats the word *every* to emphasize the point that computers are found everywhere in the work environment. This question is a fairly straightforward reading question, but it does test your vocabulary. You're expected to know that to *underscore* is to emphasize and that *ubiquity* means "present everywhere." Choice A is incorrect because the author doesn't mention the value or importance of computers, just that they're present. He is not disparaging (Choice C) or praising (Choice E). Choice D is never referred to in the passage.

2. **D** Choices A, B, and C are off topic; these issues are only tangentially related to the topics discussed in the passages. Choice E is wrong because the cost of monitoring the employees is not mentioned in either passage. In the last sentence of Passage 2, the author implies that his attitude toward his job is based on his ability to use his "free time" for personal tasks. On the other hand, the author of Passage 1 clearly states, "Now companies can be sure all the 'work' employees are doing on their computers is truly work related." The authors differ in their attitudes about what constitutes the proper use of time and equipment in the office.

3. **C** Neither passage contains statistical or historical evidence, so choices A and D are incorrect. Choice B is wrong because technological terminology is limited to references to the Internet and computers in both passages. There is no mention of investigative techniques in Passage 2. Because Passage 2 is a personal narrative, it can be considered an *anecdote* (a personal story).

4. **C** Because these passages disagree on choices A and B, neither can be correct. Neither passage really discusses Choice D, and although Choice E has some language from the passages, nowhere is this topic addressed. Choice C is correct. Passage 1 indicates that personal use of the computer during work has raised "surprising" privacy issues, and the author of Passage 2 "can't believe" the company would monitor his use of the computer. Thus, this issue is an unforeseen one.

5. **B** The passages reveal a clear difference in attitude toward employee use of time and equipment in the work environment. Passage 1 is sympathetic to the corporation that wants to be sure "all the 'work' employees are doing on their computers is truly work-related." Passage 2 sees nothing wrong with using "downtime" to accomplish personal tasks on the company computer. Choices A, C, D, and E are not relevant to the content of the two passages.

Additional Practice

Directions: Carefully read the passage below and answer the questions that follow the passage. Answer the questions based on the content of the passage: both what is stated and what is implied in the passage as well as any introductory material before the passage.

The following passage is adapted from a letter written by George Washington in 1790.

The reflection on the days of difficulty and danger which are past is rendered the more sweet, from a consciousness that they are succeeded by days of uncommon prosperity and security. If we have wisdom to make the best use of the advantages with which we are now favored, we cannot fail, under the just administration of a good Government, to become a great and happy people. The Citizens of the United
(5)   States of America have a right to applaud themselves for having given to mankind examples of an

enlarged and liberal policy: a policy worthy of imitation. All possess alike liberty of conscience and immunities of citizenship. It is now no more that toleration is spoken of, as if it was by the indulgence of one class of people, that another enjoyed the exercise of their inherent national gifts. For happily the Government of the United States, which gives to bigotry no sanction, to persecution no assistance
(10) requires only that they who live under its protection should demean themselves as good citizens, in giving it on all occasions their effectual support. It would be inconsistent with the frankness of my character not to avow that I am pleased with your favorable opinion of my Administration, and fervent wishes for my felicity.

1. According to Washington, "reflection on the days of difficulty and danger which are past is rendered the more sweet" (line 1) because

   A. these days follow times of peaceful coexistence with other nations

   B. the development of a new nation is in danger

   C. of awareness that they have led to a period of safety and richness

   D. pleasant days spent thinking about the past are so rare in a world of turmoil

   E. analyzing events in the past yields no value for the present

2. Which of the following statements would most undermine Washington's assertion that "All possess alike liberty of conscience and immunities of citizenship" (lines 6–7)?

   A. The Declaration of Independence adopted in 1776 states "All men are created equal."

   B. Before the adoption of the Fourteenth Amendment, citizens of the states were automatically considered citizens of the United States.

   C. The Expatriation Act states "the right of expatriation is a natural and inherent right of all people, indispensable to the enjoyment of the rights of life, liberty, and the pursuit of happiness."

   D. Slavery continued to exist in the United States until the institution was ended by the sufficient states' ratification of the Thirteenth Amendment on December 18, 1865.

   E. New York State passed laws allowing married women to own property separate from their husbands.

3. In the context of the passage, the statement "It is now no more . . . national gifts" (lines 7–8) suggests

   A. at one time, some groups believed they had the inherent right to extend to or withhold privileges from other groups

   B. some citizens are more indulgent than others in their interpretation of their natural rights

   C. all citizens have the inalienable right to enjoy the natural resources of this great nation

   D. this nation is founded on principles of toleration of diversity and belief in individual freedom

   E. assumptions about the foundation of democratic ideals are no longer viable

4. The word *exercise* (line 8) most nearly means

   A. vigorous activity
   B. training
   C. goal
   D. stretching
   E. use

5. The word *sanction* (line 9) most nearly means

   A. veto
   B. consent
   C. restriction
   D. injunction
   E. action

6. In the last sentence of the passage, Washington

   A. implies that he is not usually a frank man

   B. fears that he must admit to an inconsistency of character

   C. admits that he relishes the admiration of his correspondent

   D. wishes that he could be happier with his administration

   E. promises to defend the rights of all citizens, regardless of whether they agree with him

Answers to Additional Practice

1. **C** In this line reference/detail question, Washington states that thinking about the past, a time when this nation faced a time of danger, is "sweet." It is sweet because this time has been succeeded (followed) by a time that is safe and secure, "a consciousness that they [past days] are succeeded by days of prosperity and security." Choice A confuses the time sequence (peaceful days follow dangerous days, not the other way around). There is no evidence to support Choice B. There is no mention of the rarity or value of time to think, so choices D and E are incorrect.

2. **D** Remember that *to undermine* means "to weaken." First consider what the line reference means, and try paraphrasing it. Washington asserts that "All possess alike" the rights and privileges of citizenship. Choices A and B are supported by Washington's comments, so eliminate these two. Choice C refers to the Expatriation Act, so it is off topic. Although Choice E could be interpreted as contradictory to Washington, it is too vague and gives no specific date for this law. Choice D, which clearly states that slavery was legal until 1865, specifically contradicts Washington's assertion that "All" had rights.

3. **A** This extended reasoning question asks you to understand a rather difficult sentence and then consider what it suggests. First, paraphrase the sentence: "It is now no more that toleration is spoken of, as if it was by the indulgence of one class of people, that another enjoyed the exercise of their inherent national gifts." You might come up with something like this: "We no longer think that one class of people has the right to 'tolerate' another, as if it were their natural right to grant privileges on their whim to other groups." Once you have the paraphrase, you can more easily see that Washington suggests that, at one time, this attitude was the popular thought. Choice A states this clearly. Choices B, C, and D all use words from Washington's assertion, but they don't convey the correct thought. One of the tricks of the SAT writers is to use specific words from the passages in the answers to mislead you into choosing the incorrect response. Be sure you understand the *meaning* of an answer. Don't pick it because some of the words are correct.

4. **E** This vocabulary-in-context question is not a difficult one if you follow the substitution method. First, circle the word *exercise* in the text. Next, read the context. Finally, substitute all the words in the choices for the circled word. You'll recognize that *exercise* does not refer to vigorous activity, training, or stretching in this context, so you can eliminate choices A, B, and D, respectively. Although national gifts may be a goal (Choice C), it does not fit in this context as well as "use of their inherent national gifts" does. Choice E is the most logical fit for this sentence.

5. **B** This vocabulary-in-context question is more difficult, but you can still get the correct answer if you follow the substitution method. First, circle the word *sanction* and consider the context: "the Government of the United States, which gives to bigotry no sanction." Because Washington has been praising the fundamental belief in equality in the new nation, you know you're looking for a word that indicates that the government does not approve of *bigotry* (prejudice or intolerance). Because the word *no* precedes the word *sanction,* you need a positive word to convey the correct meaning. Choices A, C, and D are all negative words, so you can eliminate them. Choice E does not give the meaning of approval. *Consent* (Choice B) conveys the meaning of approval and fits the context of the sentence.

6. **C** This is a straight reading comprehension question. Again, it tests your ability to paraphrase. Think about what Washington is saying in the last sentence. Put it in your own words. He states that he is "pleased with your favorable opinion of my Administration," so you know he feels good about the positive feedback he has received. Choices A, B, and D try to trick you by using specific words from the line. Choice E is a statement that may be true, but it isn't the right answer to the question. (Remember to be alert to the true but wrong choices.) Choice C correctly interprets Washington's feelings.

VII. Vocabulary Study

aberration: An abnormality

abet: To aid in the commission (usually of a crime)

abrasive: Rough; coarse

abscond: To depart suddenly and secretly

abstemious: Characterized by self-denial or abstinence

abstruse: Difficult to understand

acquiesce: To comply; to agree; to submit

acumen: Quickness of intellectual insight

admonition: Gentle scolding or warning

affable: Good-natured; easy to approach

agile: Able to move quickly (physically or mentally)

alacrity: Cheerful willingness or promptness

alleviate: To relieve; to make less hard to bear

aloof: Reserved; distant

altruism: Unselfishness; charitableness

amalgamate: To mix or blend together

ambiguous: Having a double meaning

ameliorate: To relieve; to make better

amiable: Friendly

animosity: Hatred

apocryphal: Of doubtful authority or authenticity

apparition: Ghostly sight

appease: To soothe

approbation: Approval

arboreal: Pertaining to trees

arcane: Difficult to understand; known to only a few

ardor: Passion

articulate: Eloquent; able to express oneself well

ascetic: One who practices self-denial and excessive abstinence

ascribe: To assign as a quality or attribute

asperity: Harshness; roughness

assiduous: Unceasing; persistent

assuage: To relieve

astute: Keen in discernment

audacious: Bold; fearless

auspicious: Favorable

austere: Severely simple; strict; harsh

authoritarian: Demanding; despotic

avarice: Greed

baleful: Malignant

banal: Commonplace; trite

bellicose: Warlike

belligerent: Displaying a warlike spirit

benefactor: One who does kindly and charitable acts

benevolence: An act of kindness or generosity

benign: Good and kind

berate: To scold severely

bewilder: To confuse

blithe: Carefree; joyous

boisterous: Lively; rowdy; overexcited

bolster: To support

bombast: Pompous or inflated language

boorish: Rude

brevity: Briefness

burnish: To make brilliant or shining

cacophony: A disagreeable or discordant sound

cajole: To convince by flattering speech

callow: Young and inexperienced

calumny: Slander

candid: Straightforward; honest

cantankerous: Grouchy; irritable

capacious: Roomy

capitulate: To surrender

castigate: To punish

caustic: Sarcastic and severe

censure: To criticize severely

chagrin: Embarrassment or dismay

chicanery: The use of trickery to deceive

circumstantial: Based on inference rather than conclusive proof

cloying: Excessively sweet

coerce: To force

cogent: Strongly persuasive

collusion: A secret agreement for a wrongful purpose

comedic: Amusing

compendious: Concise

compound: To combine; to intensify

comprehensive: All-inclusive; broad in scope

compromise: Meet halfway; expose to danger or disgrace

compunction: Uneasiness caused by guilt or remorse

conciliatory: Tending to reconcile

concord: Harmony

conflagration: A great fire

congeal: To coagulate

congenial: Agreeable; friendly

connoisseur: An expert judge of art, especially one with thorough knowledge and sound judgment

console: To comfort

conspicuous: Clearly visible

constrict: To bind

contemplative: Calm and thoughtful

contrite: Remorseful

copious: Plentiful

corroboration: Confirmation

credulous: Easily deceived

cupidity: Greed

curtail: To cut off; to cut short

dearth: Scarcity

deleterious: Hurtful

denounce: To condemn; to criticize harshly

deplete: To reduce; to lessen

depraved: Wicked; morally corrupt

deride: To ridicule

derivative: Coming from some origin; not original

desiccant: A drying agent

detrimental: Harmful

deter: To frighten away

diatribe: A bitter or malicious criticism

didactic: Pertaining to teaching

diffidence: Shyness; lack of self-confidence

dilatory: Tending to cause delay

dilettante: One who dabbles in many different activities

discern: To distinguish; to see clearly

disconsolate: Hopelessly sad

dissemble: To hide by putting on a false appearance

disseminate: To scatter; to distribute

dissent: Disagreement

divulge: To tell something previously private or secret

dogmatic: Stubbornly opinionated; making assertions without evidence

draconian: Very harsh or severe

dubious: Doubtful; skeptical; questionable

duplicity: Deceitfulness; dishonesty

ebullient: Showing enthusiasm

eclectic: Coming from a variety of sources

effervescent: Bubbly; enthusiastic

effrontery: Boldness; audacity

egalitarian: Believing in equality

elucidate: To clarify

elusive: Tending to escape

embellish: To add decoration

embezzle: To misappropriate secretly

encumbrance: A burden

enervate: To weaken

engender: To produce

enigma: A riddle or puzzle

enmity: Hatred

equable: Equal; serene

equanimity: Calmness; composure

equivocate: To be deliberately vague or misleading

eradicate: To destroy thoroughly

erratic: Irregular

erroneous: Incorrect

erudite: Scholarly; very learned

eschew: To avoid

euphonious: Pleasant sounding

evanescent: Existing briefly; ephemeral; fleeting

evoke: To call or summon forth

exacerbate: To make worse

exculpate: To free from blame

execrate: To detest or hate

expedient: Useful; advantageous

explicate: To explain; to clarify

explicit: Clear; unambiguous

expropriate: To deprive of possession

expunge: To erase; to remove from a record

extant: Still existing and known

extenuate: To make less severe

extinct: No longer in existence

extol: To praise in the highest terms

extraneous: Irrelevant

facetious: Amusing

facile: Easy

fallacious: Illogical

fatuous: Idiotic; stupid

fervid: Intense; passionate

flamboyant: Flashy; showy

flaunt: To show off

flippant: Frivolous; inappropriate lack of seriousness

flout: To treat with contempt

frivolity: Silly and trivial behavior or activities

frugal: Economical

garrulous: Talkative; chatty

gentility: Refinement; courtesy

germane: Relevant

gregarious: Sociable; outgoing

guile: Duplicity

gullible: Credulous

harangue: A tirade

harbinger: First sign; messenger

hedonism: Pursuit of pleasure

heed: Pay attention to

heinous: Odiously sinful

heresy: An opinion or doctrine that opposes accepted beliefs or principles

histrionic: Overly dramatic

hybrid: Cross breed; mixture

hypocrisy: Extreme insincerity

iconoclasm: A challenge to or overturning of traditional beliefs, customs, or values

idiosyncrasy: A habit peculiar to an individual; a quirk

ignoble: Low in character or purpose

ignominious: Shameful

illicit: Unlawful

illusory: Deceptive; misleading

immaculate: Clean; without blemish

imminent: About to occur

immutable: Unchangeable

impassive: Unmoved by or not exhibiting feeling

impecunious: Having no money

impede: To block; to obstruct

imperious: Insisting on obedience; arrogant

imperturbable: Calm

impervious: Impenetrable

impetuous: Impulsive

implacable: Incapable of being pacified

implicate: To hint or suggest involvement

implicit: Implied

impromptu: Anything done or said on the spur of the moment

improvident: Lacking foresight or thrift

impugn: To oppose or attack

impute: To attribute

inadvertent: Accidental

inane: Silly

incessant: Unceasing

inchoate: In the early stages; unformed

incipient: Initial; beginning of development

incisive: Sharp; perceptive

incite: To rouse to a particular action

incongruous: Unsuitable for the time, place, or occasion

inculcate: To teach by frequent repetition

indelible: Permanent; unable to be removed

indigence: Poverty

indigenous: Native

indignant: Angry at unfairness

indolence: Laziness

indomitable: Unconquerable

indulgent: Yielding to the desires of oneself or those under one's care

ineffable: Unable to be expressed in words

ineluctable: Impossible to avoid

inept: Not fit or suitable

inevitable: Unavoidable

inexorable: Unrelenting

ingenuous: Candid, frank, or open in character

inimical: Adverse

innocuous: Harmless

inscrutable: Impenetrably mysterious or profound

insinuate: To imply

insipid: Tasteless

instigate: To start; to cause trouble

insurrection: Active resistance to authority

intransigent: Unyielding

intrepid: Fearless and bold

introspection: The act of observing and analyzing one's own thoughts and feelings

inundate: To flood

inure: To harden or toughen by use or exposure

inveterate: Habitual

invidious: Showing or feeling envy

invincible: Unable to be conquered, subdued, or overcome

iota: Small or insignificant amount

irascible: Prone to anger

irate: Moved to anger

ire: Anger

irksome: Annoying

irrefutable: Certain; undeniable

irresolution: Indecisiveness

itinerant: Wandering

jocular: Inclined to joke

jovial: Merry

judicious: Prudent

lackadaisical: Listless

languid: Relaxed

lascivious: Lustful

lassitude: Lack of vitality or energy

laudable: Praiseworthy

legacy: A bequest

licentious: Immoral

listless: Inattentive

lithe: Supple

loquacious: Talkative

lugubrious: Indicating sorrow; mournful

lustrous: Shining

malevolence: Ill will

malign: To speak evil of; to slander

malleable: Pliant

maudlin: Foolishly and tearfully sentimental

melancholy: Sad

mendacious: Untrue

mendicant: A beggar

mesmerize: To hypnotize

meticulous: Careful; painstaking; fussy

mettle: Courage

microcosm: The world or universe on a small scale

mien: The external appearance or manner of a person

mirth: Laughter; happiness

miser: A stingy person

misnomer: A name wrongly or mistakenly applied

modicum: A small amount

mollify: To soothe

momentous: Highly significant

mordant: Sarcastically biting

moribund: On the point of dying

morose: Gloomy

multifarious: Having great diversity or variety

mundane: Worldly; ordinary

munificent: Extraordinarily generous

myriad: A large indefinite number

mystical: Spiritual; magical

nadir: The lowest point

nefarious: Wicked or evil

negligent: Careless

neophyte: A beginner

noisome: Very offensive, particularly to the sense of smell

nondescript: Having no distinguishing characteristics

noxious: Hurtful

obfuscate: To confuse; to make unnecessarily complicated

objective: Impartial; neutral

obscure: Hard to understand; indistinct; not known

obsequious: Showing a servile readiness; slavish obedience

obstreperous: Boisterous

obtrude: To push oneself on others

obviate: To clear away or prevent

odious: Hateful

officious: Meddling in what is not one's concern

ominous: Threatening

onerous: Burdensome or oppressive

onus: A burden or responsibility

opportunist: One who takes advantage of something, especially in a devious way

opprobrium: Shame; disgrace

ostentation: A showy display

ostracism: Exclusion from society

palatial: Magnificent; palace-like

panacea: A cure-all

paragon: A model of excellence

pariah: A social outcast

parsimonious: Cheap; stingy

partisan: Showing partiality to a party or one side of an issue

pathos: The quality that arouses emotion or sympathy

paucity: Scarcity; lack

pedantic: Too concerned with correct rules and accuracy; plodding

pedestrian: Dull; ordinary; humdrum

penchant: A strong liking

penurious: Excessively cheap or stingy

peremptory: Authoritative; dictatorial

perfidy: Treachery; traitorousness

perfunctory: Just going through the motions; mechanical

peripheral: Tangential; unimportant; minor

perjury: Lying under oath

permeate: To pervade

pernicious: Harmful; poisonous

perspicacity: Sharp insightfulness or discernment

perturbation: Mental excitement or confusion

petulant: Childish irritability

pervasive: Widespread

phlegmatic: Sluggish; lacking energy

pious: Religious

placate: To calm or appease

platitude: A written or spoken statement that is dull or commonplace

plethora: Excess; abundance

poignant: Emotionally painful

pluralism: Different groups with different beliefs existing within one society

ponderous: Unusually weighty or forcible

portent: Anything that indicates what is to happen; an omen or sign

pragmatic: Practical

precarious: Perilous; risky; unstable

preclude: To prevent

precocious: Advanced for one's age

predominate: To be chief in importance

premature: Coming too soon

presage: To foretell

prescience: Knowledge of events before they take place

prevalent: Widespread

prevaricate: To avoid giving an honest answer; to be deliberately misleading

primordial: Existing at the beginning of time

pristine: Pure; unspoiled

probity: Virtue; integrity

proclivity: A natural inclination

procrastination: Delay

prodigal: Wasteful; extravagant

prodigious: Immense

profligacy: Extremely wasteful; having low moral standards

profound: Showing great perception; having deep meaning

profuse: Produced or displayed in overabundance

prolix: Wordy

prosaic: Unimaginative

provident: Providing for the future

prudence: Caution

puerile: Childish

pugnacious: Quarrelsome

punctilious: Strictly observant of the rules prescribed by law or custom

quandary: A puzzling predicament

quibble: A trivial objection

quiescence: Being quiet, still, or at rest; inactive

quixotic: Chivalrous or romantic to a ridiculous or extravagant degree

quotidian: Of an everyday character; ordinary

ramify: To divide or subdivide into branches or subdivisions

recalcitrant: Stubbornly resistant

recant: To withdraw formally one's belief (in something previously believed or maintained)

recidivism: The tendency to relapse into crime

recluse: One who lives in retirement or seclusion

recondite: Understood by only a select few; arcane; esoteric

recuperate: To recover

relegate: To demote

renovate: To restore

repast: A meal

repudiate: To refuse to have anything to do with; to reject

repulsive: Grossly offensive

resilience: The ability to bounce back, cope, or adapt

respite: Interval of rest

reticent: Reserved; unwilling to communicate

revelatory: Revealing an emotion or quality

revere: To respect highly; to worship

ritual: Established pattern of behavior, often ceremonial

sagacious: Wise and perceptive

salutary: Beneficial

sanction: To approve authoritatively

sanguine: Cheerfully confident; optimistic

sardonic: Scornfully or bitterly sarcastic

satiate: To satisfy fully the appetite or desire of

scintillating: Dazzling; sparkling

scrupulous: Precise; having moral integrity

secular: Nonreligious

sedulous: Diligent; persistent

self-effacing: Modest; humble

shrewd: Characterized by skill at understanding and profiting by circumstances

sluggard: A person habitually lazy or idle

solace: Comfort

solvent: Having sufficient funds

somnolent: Sleepy

sophomoric: Immature

soporific: Causing sleep

sordid: Filthy; morally degraded

sparse: Thinly spread

specious: Something that has the appearance of truth but is actually false

spurious: Not genuine

squalid: Dirty and/or poverty-stricken

stanch: To stop the flowing of; to check

stingy: Cheap; unwilling to spend money

subsume: To include in something larger

subterfuge: A deceitful maneuver

subterranean: Underground

subtle: Slight; understated

succinct: Concise

sumptuous: Rich; costly

supercilious: Haughty; arrogant

superfluous: More than is needed

suppress: To prevent from being disclosed or published

sybarite: One who loves luxuries

sycophant: A servile flatterer

tacit: Without words; unspoken

taciturn: Quiet; untalkative

tedious: Boring; monotonous

temerity: Boldness; nerve

terse: Brief; concise

timorous: Lacking courage

torpid: Dull; sluggish

tractable: Easily led or controlled

tranquil: Calm; peaceful

transitory: Existing for a short time only

trepidation: Fear

trite: Made commonplace by frequent repetition

truculence: Ferocity

turbid: In a state of turmoil; muddled

turbulent: Moving violently

turgid: Swollen

ubiquitous: Being present everywhere

unctuous: Insincerely earnest

undermine: To subvert in an underhand way; to weaken

undulate: To move like a wave or in waves

upbraid: To scold

vapid: Dull; uninteresting

vehement: Very eager or urgent

venal: Mercenary; open to corruption

venial: Forgivable; pardonable

veracity: Truthfulness

verbose: Wordy

vestige: A remaining trace of something gone

vigilant: Alert and watchful

vitiate: To corrupt

vitriolic: Bitter; spiteful

vociferous: Forcefully loud

volatile: Unstable; explosive

voluble: Talkative

voluminous: Large; long; prolific

whimsical: Fanciful; light-hearted; quirky

VIII. The Essay

The SAT always starts with the essay question. You have 25 minutes to read, think, plan, write a first draft, and proofread. In the answer booklet, you'll find lined paper; you must write only on this paper, and you must stay within the black margins. Be sure to write legibly because your essay is being read quickly by a reader unfamiliar with your handwriting. The essay counts as one-third of your writing score.

The essay question is set up as follows:

1. **First you are asked to think about a *prompt,* a few sentences stating an issue, such as the following:**

   Most people spend their lives trying to be successful. To achieve this goal, some have tried to create a formula for a successful life. According to British statesman Benjamin Disraeli, "One secret of success in life is for a man to be ready for his opportunity when it comes."

2. **Next, you are asked a question, such as:**

   What do you think is the way to achieve success in life?

3. **Then, you're given instructions, such as:**

   Your task is to plan and write an essay in response to the question. You should state your position on the issue and develop your point of view. Using examples from your reading, your own experiences and observations, your studies, or current events, support your position with evidence and examples.

Approach to the Essay: Thinking

Thinking is the first (and often most important) step. As you read the prompt, think about the issue for 2 to 3 minutes. What is your definition of success? What criteria would you use to evaluate a successful life? Who do you think of when you think of a successful person? Why do these people come to mind? To be successful, does a person have to be rich? Happy? Respected? Admired?

The answer to these questions will be your position. It will state your point of view in response to the question.

Note: You don't have to take only one side of an issue. Sometimes an issue is complex, and under some conditions, you would agree while under other conditions, you would disagree. That is an acceptable response as long as you state clearly what the conditions are.

Approach to the Essay: Planning

It's helpful to begin your planning by spending 2 to 3 minutes writing a *thesis sentence,* a one-sentence assertion that presents the position that your examples will prove. If you still aren't sure exactly where you stand on the issue, do some brainstorming first: Think of all the examples, reasons, and ideas that will support each side, and then determine on which side your argument will be stronger.

You may decide to qualify the argument. Qualifying statements limit the argument. For example, if you qualify the sample essay question, your thesis might state:

I would define success as a sense of satisfaction with my daily life, but to achieve this goal, I will need to have enough money to live comfortably.

This thesis sets up an argument that success is measured by satisfaction with life, but it qualifies that position by stating that money is also a factor.

When you know your position, begin to plan your essay. List your thoughts on the question page in your test booklet. These notes can be very brief—just ideas for the examples you'll use to support your position.

Always write from strength. Some students assume that because the graders are English teachers, literary essays will impress them. Not true. Writing about *The Scarlet Letter* is not necessarily better than writing about your basketball team. What is important is choosing an appropriate example, one that you know well, to support your thesis. Avoid hypothetical examples or very broad generalizations—the strength of your essay is in the specific details.

Don't feel that you have to use multiple examples in your essay. Some very good essays present one fully developed example, while others give two or three examples. The number of examples depends on how much you know about the issue and what you think is the most effective evidence to support your opinion.

There is no magic number of paragraphs that you must write. As you begin a new topic, start a new paragraph.

Approach to the Essay: Writing

Spend 16 to 18 minutes writing the essay.

State Your Thesis Clearly in the Introductory Paragraph

Having an original opening paragraph, one that will grab the attention of your reader, is always an advantage. However, in a timed writing, you don't need a long introductory paragraph. Get to the point quickly, so you have time to develop your argument. Make sure you establish your position and set up the development of examples.

Develop Your Examples

In the topic sentence of your first body paragraph, state the example or reason that you'll develop. Then explain the example or reason so the reader understands why it supports your thesis. Try to give specific details. If you're using a personal experience, use sensory details: What did you see? How did you feel? Were there sounds, smells, or tastes involved? If you're using a historical example, describe the time period, the specific events—the more names, dates, and places that prove your point, the more effective your evidence.

If your knowledge is sketchy, choose a better example. Don't write about Mother Teresa unless you know a lot about her.

Organize Coherently

As you develop your examples, be sure to use transitional phrases. Transitional words and phrases link ideas and indicate the relationship of ideas within a sentence, a paragraph, or a passage. They are essential tools for a writer who wants to achieve a clear and logical flow of ideas. (See the following table for examples of transitional words and phrases.)

These words and phrases are the key to coherence, and graders are trained to spot them. When you begin a new paragraph, use a phrase like, "*Another* path to success lies in . . ." or "Close friendships *also* enrich a successful life." Use transitional phrases within the paragraph as well to help your ideas flow logically.

Important Transitional Words and Phrases	
Words Used to Indicate an Example	**Words Used to Show a Result**
For example	Consequently
For instance	Hence
Specifically	Accordingly
	Therefore
Words Used to Indicate a Reason	**Words Used to Indicate More Information**
As	Besides
Because	In addition
Since	Moreover
Due to	Furthermore
Words Used to Contrast	**Words Used to Show Similarity**
Although	Another
But	Similarly
However	Likewise
In contrast	Also
Nevertheless	Again
Whereas	In the same way
While	Too
Yet	Equally
On the other hand	
Still	
Despite	
Words Used to Establish Time Relationships	**Words Used for Emphasis**
Before	Then
During	Then again
After	Once
At last	At the same time
At this point	Indeed
Later	Clearly
Soon	To be sure
Next	Without doubt
Until	Assuredly
Recently	

Use Active Verbs

To make your writing lively rather than flat, avoid state of being verbs (forms of the verb *to be*) and weak passive sentences. Also, avoid phrases like *I believe* and *I think,* as well as clichés.

Weak: I think people who are looking for the goose that laid the golden egg are foolish.

Strong: Successful people seek challenge rather than expect easy triumph.

Weak: I believe that a lot of time is lost by people who just sit around like couch potatoes and wait for some good things to happen to them.

Strong: People who are not proactive waste time.

Vary Your Sentence Structure

Most students have a tendency to write simple and compound sentences that follow the subject-verb pattern. Because you'll have very little time to revise your essay, be aware of sentence structure as you write.

- Start a sentence with a participial phrase:

  Instead of: I search for the type of friends who will support me in all my efforts.

  Write: Searching for supportive friendships, I seek like-minded achievers.

- Start with a subordinate clause:

  When I seek friends, I search for supportive individuals.

- Start with an adverb:

  Consistently, I seek friendships with supportive individuals who share my goals.

Proofread

Try to allow 2 to 3 minutes to read over your essay. Be sure your writing is legible. If you see a mistake, change it by crossing out neatly or erasing carefully. You may insert a word or phrase above the line with a caret (^). *Remember:* Do not write outside the black lines.

After you finish the essay, take a deep breath, let it out slowly, and psych yourself up for the rest of the test.

Sample Essay Topics

1. Our society places a strong emphasis on winning, on being the first, on being the best. The implication is that if we lose a competition, we have failed. Yet, sometimes defeat teaches valuable lessons, lessons about ourselves or about life.

    Can we learn more from defeat than from victory? Plan and write an essay in which you develop your point of view on this question. Be sure to support your position with reasons and examples taken from personal experience, observation, reading, or studies.

2. The latest trend in an effort to improve education in this country is frequent standardized testing. Beginning as early as kindergarten, children are tested on their reading, writing, and math skills to make sure they are achieving standard goals. Yet some educators believe this testing does more harm than good and puts undue pressure on children.

   Is standardized testing an effective way to determine the success of our educational programs? Plan and write an essay in which you develop your point of view on this question. Be sure to support your position with reasons and examples taken from personal experience, observation, reading, or studies.

3. Often we are sure that we are approaching a situation in the right way. We think we know just what has to be done and how to do it. Then, an alternative is presented, and we must make a decision whether to stay with what has worked in the past or try a new plan.

   Is it better to stick with the familiar or to take a chance on a new approach? Plan and write an essay in which you develop your point of view on this question. Be sure to support your position with reasons and examples taken from personal experience, observation, reading, or studies.

4. Most philosophers believe freedom means independence from the rule of others. Yet, in a democratic society, laws limit our self-rule. Thus, in order to live in a free society, one must agree to give up some freedoms.

   Is it possible to live peacefully with others and not limit freedom? Plan and write an essay in which you develop your point of view on this question. Be sure to support your position with reasons and examples taken from personal experience, observation, reading, or studies.

IX. Grammar and Usage

When you're working on the Writing portion of the SAT, the acronym PRIMPED CATS can help you answer the questions correctly. Each letter stands for a grammatical error you'll encounter on the SAT Writing test. Remember this acronym, and you're well on your way to SAT Writing success.

P: Pronoun errors

R: Redundancy

I: Idioms

M: Modification

P: Parallelism

E: Errors in adjective/adverb confusion

D: Diction

C: Comparisons

A: Agreement

T: Tense

S: Sentence structure

A. Types of Multiple-Choice Grammar Questions

There are three types of questions that will test your ability to recognize and correct errors in grammar and usage:

- Sentence corrections
- Find the error
- Paragraph correction

1. Sentence corrections

Sentence corrections present you with a sentence with an underlined portion; sometimes the whole sentence is underlined. Your task is to figure out whether the underlined part is correct. If you think it is correct, you'll pick Choice A. (Choice A is always the same as the sentence in the question.) If something seems wrong, read choices B, C, D, and E to find the correct revision.

EXAMPLE:

Each of the students <u>involved in the research program brought their science project</u> to the fair.

- A. involved in the research program brought their science project
- B. involved into the research program brought his or her science project
- C. involving in the research program brought his or her science project

    D.   being involved in the research program brought their science project

    E.   involved in the research program brought his or her science project

The correct answer is E.

You can eliminate Choice A because the sentence has a pronoun antecedent agreement error. The pronoun *Each* is singular and must take the singular pronoun *his or her*. Choice B corrects the pronoun error, but has an idiom error, "involved into." Choices C and D both use the incorrect verb forms, *involving* and *being involved*.

2. Find the error

In find-the-error questions, you must identify the underlined part of the sentence that contains an error or select "No error."

EXAMPLE:

The <u>most delicious</u> chocolate <u>is made</u> from cacao beans <u>that are</u> first roasted, then ground, and then
       A   B   C
<u>you mix it</u> with cocoa butter. <u>No error.</u>
   D   E

The correct answer is D.

The underlined portion *you mix it* lacks parallelism and has a pronoun agreement error. Underlined Choice D should be *mixed*.

3. Paragraph correction

In this section, you're presented with a draft of an essay that needs revision. Questions after the essay will ask you about organization, coherence, and revision or combination of sentences.

EXAMPLE:

(1) Making chocolate from beans is a rather complicated but rewarding experience. (2) Although not good for the inexperienced or impatient cook. (3) There are many tedious steps before you have an edible finished product.

The best way to combine sentence 1 and sentence 2 is

    A.   Making chocolate from beans is a rather complicated but rewarding experience; not a good one for the inexperienced or impatient cook.

    B.   Making chocolate from beans is a rather complicated but rewarding experience; though a problem for the inexperienced or impatient cook.

    C.   Making chocolate from beans is a rather complicated but rewarding experience, inexperienced or impatient cooks will have a problem

    D.   Making chocolate from beans is a rather complicated but rewarding experience if you are an inexperienced or impatient cook.

    E.   Making chocolate from beans is a rather complicated but rewarding experience, but it is not for the inexperienced or impatient cook.

The correct answer is E.

Choices A and B use the semicolon incorrectly because the second clause is not a main clause. Choice C is a run-on sentence, and choice D changes the sense of the sentence.

Practice

1. Although my mother asked Eli and I to go to the mall with her, we were too involved with homework to leave.

    A.   Although my mother asked Eli and I to go to the mall with her, we

    B.   Although my mother asked Eli and me to go to the mall with her, us

    C.   Although my mother asked Eli and I to go to the mall with her; we

    D.   Although my mother asked Eli and me to go to the mall with her, him and me

    E.   Although my mother asked Eli and me to go to the mall with her, we

2. When we campaigned for class officers in the weeks before the election, no one will suspect that Juliet will win.

    A.   no one will suspect that Juliet will win.

    B.   no one suspected that Juliet will win.

    C.   no one suspected that Juliet would win.

    D.   no one was suspecting that Juliet will win.

    E.   no one will suspect that Juliet would win.

3. Sure that his performance was better than the singers, Clay felt confident that he would get the lead in the musical.

    A.   Sure that his performance was better than the singers,

    B.   Sure that his performance was the best of the singers,

    C.   Feeling sure that his performance was better than those of the singers,

    D.   Sure that his performance was better than that of the other singers,

    E.   Being sure that his performance was better than the singers,

4. <u>Although dead for twenty-six years, jazz great Thelonious Monk's music is still played everywhere jazz fans gather.</u>

    A. Although dead for twenty-six years, jazz great Thelonious Monk's music is still played everywhere jazz fans gather.

    B. Although dead for twenty-six years, jazz great Thelonious Monk and his music is still played everywhere jazz fans gather.

    C. Although Thelonious Monk has been dead for twenty-six years, his great jazz music is still played everywhere jazz fans gather.

    D. Although dead for twenty-six years, and jazz great Thelonious Monk's music is still played everywhere jazz fans gather.

    E. Even though he is dead for twenty-six years, jazz great Thelonious Monk's music is still played everywhere jazz fans gather.

5. Every summer vacation, my family and best friend's family <u>go either camping in one of the national parks or to visit national monuments.</u>

    A. go either camping in one of the national parks or visiting national monuments.

    B. either camp in one of the national parks or visit national monuments.

    C. are going either to camp in one of the national parks or visiting national monuments.

    D. either camping in one of the national parks or visiting national monuments.

    E. was going either camping in one of the national parks or visiting national monuments.

6. In her job <u>as an operator</u> for the police department hot line, Tamika discovered <u>it was difficult</u> to get
                  A   B

    people to <u>speak calm</u> and slowly <u>in an emergency</u>. <u>No error.</u>
                C   D   E

7. <u>Flying into</u> the <u>hurricane-damaged area</u> of <u>Costa Rica is</u> the leaders <u>of the</u> United Nations Disaster
     A   B   C   D

    Relief Agency. <u>No error.</u>
                 E

8. The Department of Motor Vehicles <u>has compiled</u> statistics <u>that show</u> the average age that teenagers
                                  A   B

    <u>apply for</u> a driver's license <u>rose</u> dramatically since 1980. <u>No error.</u>
      C   D   E

9. <u>Before he addressed</u> his employees honestly, the CEO felt <u>it important</u> to put in <u>prospective</u> the
          A   B   C

    downturn <u>in profits</u> that might lead to plant closings. <u>No error.</u>
            D   E

10. <u>To prepare</u> for the 2014 Olympics, the Russian <u>city of</u> Sochi has developed a new ski resort, built
      A   B

    modern condominiums, and <u>has just finished transforming</u> the waterfront <u>area into</u> a glamorous rec-
                                      C   D

    reation spot. <u>No error.</u>
               E

Answers

1. **E** Choices A and C incorrectly use the nominative pronoun *I* instead of the objective pronoun *me*. Choice B incorrectly changes the nominative pronoun *we* to the objective pronoun *us*. Choice D incorrectly changes the nominative pronoun *we* to the objective pronouns *him* and *me*.

2. **C** The first clause is in the past tense, so the second clause must be consistent. *Juliet will win* must be changed to *Julie would win*. Choice E incorrectly changes the tense of *suspect* to *will suspect*. Only Choice C has all consistent tenses.

3. **D** The sentence has an illogical comparison of *performance* to *singers* as do choices B and E. Choice C uses the plural pronoun *those* instead of the singular pronoun *that* to refer to Clay's performance

4. **C** The sentence has vague modification as the introductory phrase modifies Monk's music rather than Monk. Choice B has a subject-verb agreement error ("Monk and his music *is*"). Choice D is not a complete sentence. Choice E has a tense error ("is dead") in the first clause.

5. **B** Parallelism is needed after the correlative pronouns *either . . . or*. *Camping* is not parallel to *to visit*. Choice C is not parallel and Choice D has no helping verb for *camping* and *visiting*. Choice E has an agreement error: *was going*.

6. **C** The adjective *calm* must be changed to the adverb *calmly* to modify the verb *speak*.

7. **C** The subject *leaders* (which comes after the verb) needs a plural verb *are* rather than the singular *is*.

8. **D** The past-tense *rose* should be the present participle *has risen* to show that the change in age has taken place over time (since 1980).

9. **C** The word *prospective* is incorrectly used in place of the word *perspective*.

10. **C** *Has just finished transforming* is not parallel to *developed* and *built*. It should be changed to *transformed*.

B. Pronoun Errors

1. Pronoun antecedent agreement errors

Pronouns are words that are used to replace nouns. The noun that the pronoun replaces is called the *antecedent*. Usually, but not always, the antecedent comes before the pronoun.

A pronoun must agree with its antecedent in gender and number. If the antecedent of a pronoun is singular, the pronoun must be singular; if the antecedent is plural, the pronoun must be plural. If the antecedent is feminine, the pronoun must be feminine; if the antecedent in masculine, the pronoun must be masculine. For example:

> Debbie brought her laptop to the Math Challenge.

Debbie is the feminine singular antecedent for the feminine singular pronoun *her*.

> The *students* brought *their* laptops to the Math Challenge.

Students is the plural antecedent for the plural pronoun *their*.

If the antecedent refers to both genders, the phrase *his or her* is acceptable to avoid sexist language. When this phrasing is repeated several times in a sentence or paragraph, it may become awkward, though; you can avoid the problem by changing the sentence to the plural form:

Awkward: Each student put his or her laptop on his or her desk.

Better: The students put their laptops on their desks.

When indefinite pronouns are antecedents, determine whether they are singular or plural. Here are some singular indefinite pronouns:

each	one	no one	someone
either	everyone	nobody	somebody
neither	everybody	anyone	anybody

Here are some examples:

Each of the boys on the team took his trophy home.

Everyone chooses his or her favorite novel.

Exceptions: Sometimes, with *everyone* and *everybody,* the sense of the sentence is compromised when the singular pronoun is used. In these cases, the plural form is acceptable.

Awkward: Everyone in the crowd stood and applauded when he or she saw the float.

Better: Everyone in the crowd stood and applauded when they saw the float.

Here are some plural indefinite pronouns:

several	few	both	many

Here are some indefinite pronouns that are either singular or plural, depending on how they're used:

some	most	any
all	none	

For example:

Some of the play has lost *its* meaning.	singular in meaning
Some of the houses have lost *their* roofs.	plural in meaning

Two or more singular antecedents joined by *or* or *nor* take the singular pronoun:

Either Marlee or Olivia will bring her car to the football game.

Neither Louie nor Jaxon has taken his road test.

Every pronoun must clearly refer to a specific antecedent. To avoid vague pronoun reference, be sure you can pinpoint the antecedent of the pronoun.

Vague: In the newspaper it says that more young people voted this year than last year. (The pronoun *it* has no antecedent.)

Better: The article in the *Tribune* states that more young people voted this year than last year.

Vague: Jessica wants to be a doctor because it is so rewarding. (The pronoun *it* has no antecedent.)

Better: Jessica wants to be a doctor because the work is so rewarding.

Vague: Barbara came late to every meeting, which annoyed her supervisor. (The word *which* is a vague pronoun because it has no antecedent.)

Better: Barbara came late to every meeting, a habit that annoyed her supervisor.

Or even better: Barbara's chronic lateness annoyed her supervisor.

Vague: Students are coming to school on time, bringing their books to class, and taking notes regularly. This helps the school receive federal funds. (*This* is a vague pronoun because it has no antecedent.)

Better: Students are coming to school on time, bringing their books to class, and taking notes regularly. The improved attendance helps the school receive federal funds.

2. Pronoun case errors

If you've ever wondered whether to write *I* or *me,* you've encountered a pronoun case problem. Pronouns change their form depending on how they're used. The different forms of the pronouns are called *cases.* Pronouns have three cases:

- **Nominative:** The nominative case of pronouns is used when the pronoun is the subject or the predicate nominative.
- **Objective:** The objective case is used when the pronoun is the object of a verb or the object of a preposition.
- **Possessive:** The possessive case is used to indicate possession.

Nominative	Objective	Possessive
I	me	my, mine
we	us	our, ours
you	you	your, yours
he	him	his
she	her	her, hers
it	it	its
they	them	their, theirs
who	whom	whose

First, look at the whole sentence and determine what role the pronoun plays in the sentence. Is it the subject? Then use the nominative case. Is it an object of a verb or the object of a preposition? Then choose the objective case. Is the pronoun showing ownership? Then use the possessive case.

Nominative case:

- The pronoun as subject:
  - *He* and *I* want to be lab partners in chemistry.

- Judy and *she* went shopping for decorations for the prom.
- *Who* is going to be class president next year?

■ The pronoun as *predicate nominative* (a word in the predicate part of the sentence that is linked to the subject):

- The winners must have been *they*.
- The team captains are Sophie and *she*.

Objective case:

■ The pronoun as *object of a verb* (direct object or indirect object):

- Alexis gave *her* the gift. (*Her* is the indirect object of the verb *gave*.)
- Hayley invited Juan and *him* to the dance. (*Juan* and *him* are the direct objects of the verb *invited*.)

■ The pronoun as object of a preposition:

- The head of the committee wanted to share the responsibility with *them*. (*Them* is the object of the preposition *with*.)
- To *whom* should I address the letter of recommendation? (*Whom* is the object of the preposition *to*.)

Possessive case:

■ Use the possessive case to show ownership and before a *gerund* (*-ing* form of a verb used as a noun):

- The director appreciates *your* being prompt for all rehearsals. (*Your* is the possessive pronoun used before the gerund *being*.)
- *His* quick thinking saved the day. (*His* is the possessive pronoun used before the gerund *thinking*.)

Practice

Directions: Select the correct pronoun.

1. This birthday present is from Cindy and (I, me).

2. The Intel Corporation awarded Julia and (she, her) the prize.

3. No one objected to (he, him, his) bringing a date to the prom.

4. Neither the seniors nor (us, we) have won the play contest.

5. Neither of these journals has all (its, their) entries.

6. Each of the participants presented (his or her, their) experiments to the panel.

7. Joe and Mark brought (his, their) calculators to the exam.

8. It is silly to let this disagreement come between you and (she, her).

9. I can't wait to find out if the champion is (her, she).

10. (Who, Whom) do you think should lead the group?

Answers

1. **me** The pronoun *I* is incorrect because the nominative pronoun is used for the subject or the predicate nominative. In this sentence, the pronoun *me* is the object of the preposition *from*.

2. **her** The pronoun *she* is incorrect because the nominative form is used for the subject or the predicate nominative. In this sentence, the pronoun *her* is the object of the verb *awarded*.

3. **his** The pronoun *he* is incorrect because the nominative form is used for the subject or the predicate nominative. The pronoun *him* is incorrect because the objective form is used for an object of a verb or an object of a preposition. The pronoun *his* is correct because the possessive pronoun is used before a gerund (the *-ing* form of a verb used as a noun).

4. **we** The pronoun *us* is incorrect because the objective form is used for an object of a verb or an object of a preposition The pronoun *we* is correct because the nominative pronoun is used for the subject or the predicate nominative. In this sentence, *we* is part of the compound subject *the seniors and we*.

5. **its** The pronoun *neither* (the antecedent) is singular. The singular pronoun *its*, not the plural pronoun *their*, must be used to refer to a singular antecedent.

6. **his or her** The pronoun *each* (the antecedent) is singular. The singular pronouns *his or her*, not the plural pronoun *their*, must be used to refer to a singular antecedent.

7. **their** The compound subject *Joe and Mark* (the antecedents) is plural. The plural pronoun *their*, not the singular pronoun *his*, must be used to refer to a plural antecedent.

8. **her** The pronoun *she* is incorrect because the nominative pronoun is used for the subject or the predicate nominative. In this sentence, the pronoun *her* is the object of the preposition *between*.

9. **she** The pronoun *her* is incorrect because the objective form is used for an object of a verb or an object of a preposition. The pronoun *she* is correct because the nominative pronoun is used for the predicate nominative.

10. **Who** The pronoun *whom* is incorrect because the objective form is used for an object of a verb or an object of a preposition. The pronoun *who* is correct because the nominative pronoun is used for the subject. In this sentence, *who* is the subject of the verb *should lead*.

C. Redundancy

In standard written English, conciseness is a goal. It is best to express your ideas in as few well-chosen words as possible. Always be alert for such repetitive and wordy expressions as:

true fact	extreme in degree	due to the fact that
important essentials	large in size	ten years in age
two equal halves	round in shape	problem that needs a solution
consensus of opinion	close proximity	
unexpected surprise	new innovations	
various different	the future to come	

For example:

At the present time, the problem the community is currently facing must be addressed.

At first reading, you may think the sentence is grammatically correct. You'd be almost right. However, if you reread the sentence from the beginning, you'll see the phrase *At the present time.* This phrase makes the word *currently* redundant. You'll have to find a choice that eliminates this redundancy.

Practice

Directions: Rewrite the following sentence to avoid redundancies and wordiness.

1. By associating and connecting together, the two teams were able to come up with a new innovation.

2. We chose a sign that was large in size due to the fact that we hoped every person and all people would be able to see it.

3. Every year the teachers do an annual review of their classroom supplies.

4. I told you the reason why you should take the SAT is because it is a good test.

5. Larry will tell you the honest truth about his past experience.

6. It is the consensus of opinion that we should advance forward and join together to solve the problems that need solutions.

Answers

Your answers might be slightly different. It isn't important as long as you eliminate the redundant expressions.

1. **By connecting, the two teams were able to come up with an innovation.** The words *associating* and *connecting* mean essentially the same thing, as do the words *new* and *innovation*. The sentence will be more concise if these unnecessary words are eliminated.

2. **We chose a large sign so everyone could see it.** The expression *large in size* is redundant; *large* obviously refers to size. *Due to the fact that* is another wordy expression as is *every person and all people.*

3. **The teachers do an annual review of their classroom supplies.** *Annual* means "every year" so it is redundant to write both.

4. **I told you to take the SAT because it is a good test.** *The reason why . . . is because* is a wordy expression.

5. **Larry will tell you the truth about his experiences.** The truth is by definition honest; it does not need to be qualified. In this sentence, the word *experience* does not need to be preceded by *past;* that point is implied by the sentence.

6. **The consensus is that together we can advance and solve problems.** The word *consensus* means "agreement of opinion," so opinion is unnecessary. An advance is always forward and problems always need solutions. Aim for conciseness and eliminate these unnecessary words.

D. Idioms

Idioms are expressions or verb phrases that are used in English. The problem arises when the incorrect preposition is used with a verb. Unfortunately, there are no rules—you just need to know what is accepted as correct. Usually, you can trust your ears—go with what sounds right.

Here are some common idioms:

abide by	conform to	opinion of
agree to (something)	consists of	participate in
agree with (someone)	depend on	prefer to
apply for	differ from	preoccupied with
approve of	discriminate against	prohibited from
argue about (something)	escape from	protect from
argue with (someone)	in contrast to	relevant to
arrived at	insensitive to	subscribe to
believe in	insight into	succeeded in
capable of	insist upon	
comment on	method of	
complain about	object to	

Practice

Directions: Correct the idiom errors in the following sentences.

1. Ignacio proved that he was capable to rebuild the engine on the '62 Chevy.

2. While I was reading *Macbeth,* I was amazed that Shakespeare had such insight on ambitious leaders who ruthlessly seize power.

3. Alex tried to get his mother's attention, but she was preoccupied on the complicated recipe she was preparing.

4. Contrasting with the ornate style of Gothic architecture, modern geometric buildings have clean lines and sharp edges.

5. Because my dad is such a great cook, my family prefers eating at home rather than eating in restaurants.

Answers

1. Ignacio proved that he was <u>capable of rebuilding</u> the engine on the '62 Chevy.

2. While I was reading *Macbeth,* I was amazed that Shakespeare had such <u>insight into</u> ambitious leaders who ruthlessly seize power.

3. Alex tried to get his mother's attention, but she was <u>preoccupied with</u> the complicated recipe she was preparing.

4. <u>In contrast to</u> ornate Gothic architecture, modern geometric buildings have clean lines and sharp edges.

5. Because my dad is such a great cook, my family <u>prefers</u> eating at home <u>to</u> eating in restaurants.

E. Modification

1. Misplaced modifiers

Modifiers are words, phrases, or clauses that describe, change, or specify other parts of a sentence. Modifiers are often participial phrases. For example:

> *Riding on the bus,* we read the article in the paper.

Riding on the bus describes *we.*

> As I turned the corner, I heard my dog *barking loudly.*

Barking loudly describes *dog.*

Sometimes modifiers are infinitive phrases:

> *To understand English grammar,* students must practice writing and speaking correctly.

To understand English grammar modifies *students.*

In English, changes in word order (syntax) lead to changes in meaning. A modifier that is misplaced can cause confusion. For example:

- **Maria spotted an orange cat sitting on a bench eating a sandwich.** In this example, the cat is sitting and eating.
- **Sitting on a bench eating a sandwich, Maria spotted an orange cat.** Here, Maria is sitting and eating.
- **Sitting on a bench, Maria spotted an orange cat eating a sandwich.** Maria is sitting and the cat is eating.

To avoid confusion, you should always place modifying phrases and clauses as close as possible to the words they modify.

2. Dangling modifiers

Dangling modifiers have no word or phrase to modify. For example, the following sentence is confusing:

> Standing on the bridge overlooking the city, the buildings look like children's toys.

Who is standing? Certainly not the buildings. To correct dangling modifiers, you must add the missing words or revise the sentence. You might revise this sentence to be:

> Standing on the bridge overlooking the city, George thought the buildings looked like children's toys.

Or:

> As George stood on bridge overlooking the city, the buildings looked like children's toys.

Practice

Directions: Revise the following sentences to correct the modification errors:

1. Athena found her cellphone walking home from practice.

2. To order safely from the Internet, your credit card should be protected.

3. Looking up at the sky, the eclipse was both magnificent and frightening.

4. While working out in the gym, my leg muscle cramped.

5. Ashley wore her new bag over her shoulder, which she had just purchased at the mall.

6. Perhaps best known for convincing her husband to murder the king, Lady Macbeth's rampant ambition became uncontrollable.

Answers

Your answers may vary, but be sure all modification confusion is corrected.

1. **Walking home from practice, Athena found her cellphone.** The original sentence implies that the cellphone was walking home from practice.

2. **To order safely from the Internet, you should be sure your credit card is protected.** The original sentence implies that the credit card was ordering from the Internet.

3. **Looking up the sky, we discovered the eclipse was both magnificent and frightening.** The original sentence implies that the eclipse was looking up at the sky.

4. **While I was working out in the gym, my leg muscle cramped.** The original sentence implies that the leg muscle was working out in the gym.

5. **Ashley wore her new bag, which she had just purchased at the mall, over her shoulder.** The original sentence implies that Ashley had purchased her shoulder at the mall rather than her new bag.

6. **Perhaps best known for convincing her husband to murder the king, Lady Macbeth allowed her rampant ambition to become uncontrollable.** The original sentence implies that Lady Macbeth's ambition was best known, rather than Lady Macbeth herself.

F. Parallelism

Parallel ideas should be in the same grammatical form.

When you join ideas using conjunctions, nouns should be joined with nouns, prepositional phrases joined with prepositional phrases, and clauses joined with clauses.

	Unparallel	Parallel
Nouns	Martin Luther King, Jr., was honored for his courage, faith, and he had a willingness to stick to his beliefs.	Martin Luther King, Jr., was honored for his courage, faith, and perseverance.
Verb phrases	I like to ski, to hike, and swimming.	I like to ski, to hike, and to swim. I like skiing, hiking, and swimming.
Prepositional phrases	We left the party early because of the inclement weather, and it was late.	We left the party because of the inclement weather and the lateness of the hour.
Clauses	Hamlet found it difficult to believe that his father had died of natural causes and in the innocence of his uncle.	Hamlet found it difficult to believe that his father had died of natural causes and that his uncle was innocent.

Correlative conjunctions (such as *both . . . and, either . . . or, neither . . . nor,* and *not only . . . but also*), which always occur in pairs, can be tricky: Be sure what comes after the first conjunction is parallel to what comes after the second conjunction.

Unparallel: The car wash *not only* did a great job on my car, *but also* on my brother's.

Parallel: The car wash did a great job *not only* on my car, *but also* on my brother's.

Unparallel: The general had *neither* the support of his troops *nor* did he have the loyalty of his officers.

Parallel: The general had *neither* the support of his troops *nor* the loyalty of his officers.

Practice

Directions: Revise the following sentence to correct the errors in parallelism.

1. Julius Caesar could not be sure that he had the support of the common people or if the other senators would stand by him.

2. Brutus was ambitious, gullible, and he thought a lot about his own motives.

3. I either want to do my English research paper on Ernest Hemingway or F. Scott Fitzgerald.

4. Galileo not only believed that the Earth was round but also that it rotated around the sun.

5. Those who try skydiving both know the thrill of weightlessness and the excitement of flying.

Answers

Your answers may vary slightly.

1. **Julius Caesar could not be sure that he had the support of the common people or the other senators.**

2. **Brutus was ambitious, gullible, and introspective.**

3. **I want to do my English research paper on either Ernest Hemingway or F. Scott Fitzgerald.**

4. **Galileo believed not only that the Earth was round but also that it rotated around the sun.**

5. **Those who try skydiving know both the thrill of weightlessness and the excitement of flying.**

G. Errors with Adjectives and Adverbs

1. Comparisons

Use the comparative form of the adjective to compare *two* nouns or pronouns. The comparative form is formed in two ways:

- **One-syllable adjectives:** Add -*er*. (This ending is also used for some two-syllable adjectives.) For example:
  - Of the two boys, Troy is the younger.
  - Samantha is the funnier of the two sisters.
- **Most two syllable adjectives:** Put the word *more* in front of word. For example:
  - My computer is more efficient than Herb's.

Use the superlative form of the adjective to compare *three or more* nouns or pronouns. The superlative form is formed in two ways:

- **One-syllable adjectives:** Add -*est*. (This ending is also used for some two-syllable adjectives.) For example:
  - Amy is the youngest girl in the class
  - The happiest teacher in the district is Sarah.
- **Most two syllable adjectives:** Put the word *most* in front of word. For example:
  - Dina won the award for the most cautious driver.

Here are some irregular comparison forms:

	Comparative	Superlative
good	better	best
bad	worse	worst
little	less or lesser	least
much	more	most
far	farther or further	farther or furthest

Some adjectives, such as the following, are absolute values and cannot be intensified with *more* or *most:*

complete	round	totally
correct	square	unique
perfect	superior	
preferable	supreme	

2. Adjective/adverb confusion

Use an adjective to modify a noun or a pronoun, and use an adverb to modify a verb, an adjective, or another adverb.

Incorrect: In the short story "The Minister's Black Veil," the main character walks about the town heavy-veiled. (This sentence uses the adjective *heavy* instead of the adverb *heavily.*)

Correct: In the short story "The Minister's Black Veil," the main character walks about the town heavily veiled.

Practice

Directions: Correct the errors in the following sentences:

1. Of the jaguar and the hyena, the jaguar is the fastest.

2. When she won the lottery, my neighbor was the most happiest woman in town.

3. The fire chief was impressed by how speedy we all exited the building during the fire drill.

4. I thought the stuffed animal I bought for my little sister was more cuter than then one she has on her bed.

5. When we measured all ten basketball players, Jamal was the taller.

6. Among all the pottery on display, Russell's was the most unique.

Answers

1. **Of the jaguar and the hyena, the jaguar is the <u>faster</u>.** When you're comparing two things, use the comparative form (in this case, *faster*) rather than the superlative form (in this case, *fastest*).

2. **When she won the lottery, my neighbor was the <u>happiest</u> woman in town.** Don't modify the superlative form of an adjective (in this case, *happiest*) with *most*.

3. **The fire chief was impressed by how <u>speedily</u> we all exited the building during the fire drill.** Use an adverb (in this case, *speedily*) rather than an adjective (in this case, *speedy*) to modify a verb (in this case, *exited*).

4. **I thought the stuffed animal I bought for my little sister was <u>cuter</u> than then one she has on her bed.** Don't modify the comparative form of an adjective (in this case, *cuter*) with *more*.

5. **When we measured all ten basketball players, Jamal was the <u>tallest</u>.** When you're comparing three or more things, use the superlative form (in this case, *fastest*).

6. **Among all the pottery on display, Russell's was <u>unique</u>.** The word *unique* is an absolute and should not be modified with *more* or *most*.

H. Diction

Diction means "word choice." A diction error occurs when a word is used incorrectly or inappropriately.

On the SAT, diction errors often occur with words that look alike such as *refer/infer, prospective/perspective, formally/formerly, defensible/defensive,* or *reliable/reliant.* Be alert and careful as you read the sentences.

Here are some commonly misused words:

- *among/between:* Use *between* for two people or things ("between my brother and me"). Use *among* for three or more ("among all my friends").

- *fewer/less:* Use *fewer* for anything you can count ("fewer times at bat"). Use *less* for whole quantities (less pain).

- *amount/number:* Use *amount* for whole quantities ("amount of homework"). Use *number* for things you can count ("number of math problems").

Practice

1. The choice for the lead in the play is (between, among) Ella and Sophie.

2. The Battle of the Classes will be (between, among) all four grades in the high school.

3. Because of budget cuts, (less, fewer) awards will be given to athletes this year.

4. When he was accused of plagiarism, the student became quite (defensible, defensive), claiming his work was completely original.

5. A large (amount, number) of students attended the pep rally on the football field.

6. From the (perspective, prospective) of an incoming freshman, the high school may seem overwhelming.

Answers

1. **between** Use *between* to refer to two people or things.

2. **among** Use *among* to refer to more than two people or things.

3. **fewer** *Fewer* refers to a number of individual things. (You can count awards.)

4. **defensive** You're defensive when you try to avoid or deflect criticism. *Defensible* means capable of being explained or protected from attack.

5. **number** Number refers to individual things (such as students) that can be counted.

6. **perspective** *Perspective* refers to one's viewpoint or outlook; *prospective* refers to something likely to occur.

I. Comparisons

1. Illogical comparisons

Use the word *other* or the word *else* to compare one thing or person to the rest of the group.

> Illogical comparison: Our debate team won more prizes than any team. (This is illogical because your team is a team.)
>
> Logical comparison: Our debate team won more prizes than any *other* team.

2. Unbalanced comparisons

Comparisons must be balanced and parallel. Use the words *than* or *as* to balance the sentence.

> Unbalanced: The mathletes won as many points if not more than their opponents.
>
> Balanced: The mathletes won *as* many points *as*, if not more *than*, their opponents.

3. Faulty comparisons

You must compare like things—apples to apples, not apples to oranges.

> Faulty: After tasting all the exotic dishes at the ethnic food fair, I found I like the foods from India better than China. (In this sentence, you're comparing *foods* to *China*.)
>
> Correct: After tasting all the exotic dishes at the ethnic food fair, I found I like the foods from India better than the foods (or those) from China. (Here you're comparing *foods* to *foods*.)

> Faulty: Our track star was more dominant than the previous years. (This sentence compares the *track star* to *years*.)
>
> Correct: Our track star was more dominant than those in previous years. (Here you're comparing *star* to *those*, which is a pronoun referring to *track stars*.)

Practice

Directions: Correct the comparison errors in the following sentences.

1. The music of Rascal Flats is as good as Sugarland.

2. Rachel felt her poetry was better than any student in the writing class.

3. My car is cleaner than any car in the parking lot.

4. It was clear that the flowers from the local garden shop were fresher than the florist.

5. The movie *Diehard 3* was as suspenseful, if not more suspenseful than the prequel.

6. The Spanish restaurant on South Street is better than any restaurant in town.

Answers

1. **The music of Rascal Flats is as good as <u>that of</u> Sugarland.**

2. **Rachel felt her poetry was better than <u>that of</u> any student in the writing class.**

3. **My car is cleaner than any <u>other</u> car in the parking lot.**

4. **It was clear that the flowers from the local garden shop were fresher than <u>those</u> from the florist.**

5. **The movie *Diehard 3* was as suspenseful <u>as</u>, if not more suspenseful than, the prequel.**

6. **The Spanish restaurant on South Street is better than any <u>other</u> restaurant in town.**

J. Agreement

1. Agreement of subject and verb

A verb must agree with its subject in number. A singular subject takes the singular form of a verb; a plural subject takes the plural form of the verb.

Singular: My **answer agrees** with yours.   one answer

Plural: My **answers agree** with yours.   more than one answer

Note: While most nouns form the plural by adding the letter *s*, most verbs in their plural form do not end in the letter *s*.

Phrases may intervene between the subject and the verb. In most cases, ignore the intervening phrase:

My answers **on the test** agree with yours.

On the test is a prepositional phrase.

Intervening prepositional phrases do not affect agreement of subject and verb, so the best approach is to cross out or bracket intervening phrases. This will avoid confusion.

Note: The subject of a sentence is *never* part of a prepositional phrase.

The sleeping **cabin** with a bathroom and two beds **is** available.

The sleeping **cabin** [with a bathroom and two beds] **is** available.

Be sure to find the subject and match it with the verb:

Studying for final exams helps me do well on the test.

Bracket the intervening phrases:

Studying [for final exams] **helps** me do well on the test.

Studying is the singular subject; *helps* is the singular form of the verb.

Sometimes multiple phrases intervene:

The photographs of the family taken in the field beyond the house show a group of smiling people of all ages.

Follow the same procedure and reread the entire sentence bracketing the phrases:

The **photographs** [of the family taken in the field beyond the house] **show** a group of smiling people of all ages.

Photographs is the plural subject; *show* is the plural form of the verb.

Intervening parenthetical or explanatory phrases also do not affect agreement of subject and verb, so the best approach is to cross out or bracket intervening phrases. This will avoid confusion.

Example 1: My cousin, along with ten of her closest friends, volunteers in a hospital.

Bracket the intervening phrase or phrases and match the subject with the verb:

My **cousin**, [along with ten of her closest friends,] **volunteers** in a hospital.

Example 2: Our chapter of DECA, like all the others chapters in the surrounding districts, attends the state competition.

Our **chapter** [of DECA,] [like all the others chapters][in the surrounding districts,] **attends** the state competition.

Example 3: Julius Caesar, accompanied by many of the deceitful senators, was approached by a soothsayer who warned him of danger.

Julius Caesar, [accompanied by many of the deceitful senators] **was** approached by a soothsayer who warned him of danger.

2. Agreement problems with indefinite pronouns

Singular indefinite pronouns take the singular form of the verb; plural indefinite pronouns take the plural form of the verb.

> *Each* of the games on the computer *requires* skillful manipulation.   singular
> *Both* of the games on the computer *require* skillful manipulation.   plural

Singular subjects joined by the correlative conjunctions *either . . . or* and *neither . . . nor* are singular.

> Either the *novel* or the *play is* acceptable.

Plural subjects joined by these correlative conjunctions are plural.

> Neither the *trees* nor the *bushes were* damaged by the fire.

When one subject is singular and one subject is plural, the verb agrees with the closer subject:

> Neither the *parents* nor the little *girl is* afraid of spiders.
> Either the *coach* or my *parents are driving* to the game.

3. Agreement problems with inverted sentences

These sentences will be tricky because you'll encounter the verb before the subject. Again, the key to success is to find the subject, wherever it is in the sentence.

Note: The words *here* and *there* are never subjects.

> Two months before the hurricane there **were** warning **signs.**

The plural subject *signs* agrees with the plural form of the verb *were*.

> There **are** many **problems** with the economy today.

The plural subject *problems* agrees with the plural form of the verb *are*.

Be sure to read the whole sentence through to find the subject:

> Onto the field **march** the **band** and **the color guard.**

The plural subject *band* and *color guard* agrees with the plural form of the verb *march*.

> Over the trees **flies** a small **bird.**

The singular subject *bird* agrees with singular form of the verb *flies*.

4. Noun agreement

Use a singular noun to refer to a singular noun and a plural noun to refer to a plural noun. Sounds logical, right? Yet, problems do arise:

> People who wish to be a teacher should apply here.

This sentence is incorrect because the plural noun *people* requires the plural noun *teachers* to be logical.

> Correct: **People** who wish to be **teachers** should apply here.
>
> Incorrect: Tourists with a visa must sign in at Passport Control.
>
> Correct: **Tourists** with **visas** must sign in at Passport Control.

Practice

Directions: Select the best word in the following sentences.

1. Into every life (come, comes) some issues that perplex us.

2. A carton of books (is, are) ready to be opened and stacked on the shelves.

3. Neither the cats nor the dog (is, are) in the house.

4. Each of the sentences on the bulletin boards (is, are) written by a student.

5. (Does, Do) either of the maps show the Himalayan Mountains?

6. One of the puzzling aspects of the physics equations (is, are) the vector analysis.

Answers

1. **come** The subject of the verb *come* is the plural noun *issues*.

2. **is** The subject of the verb *is* is the singular noun *carton*.

3. **is** With two subjects joined by *neither . . . nor,* use the subject closer to the verb *(the dog is)*.

4. **is** The singular indefinite pronoun *each* is the subject of the verb *is*.

5. **Does** The subject of the verb *does show* is the singular indefinite pronoun *either*.

6. **is** The subject of the verb *is* is the singular indefinite pronoun *one*.

K. Tense

Verbs tell the action or state of being in a sentence. They are also the time words, the principal indicators of tense. As you read, be aware of the tense of the passage and note any inconsistencies.

The six tenses in English are

- **Present:** Action taking place in the present
- **Past:** Action that has already taken place in the past
- **Future:** Action that will take place in the future
- **Present perfect:** Action that began in the past and continues into the present
- **Past perfect:** Action that began in the past and was completed before some other action
- **Future perfect:** Action completed in the future, before some other action in the future

Present Tense

	Singular	Plural
First person	I walk.	We walk.
Second person	You walk.	You walk.
Third person	He/she/it walks.	They walk.

Past Tense

	Singular	Plural
First person	I walked.	We walked.
Second person	You walked.	You walked.
Third person	He/she/it walked.	They walked.

Future Tense

	Singular	Plural
First person	I will walk.	We will walk.
Second person	You will walk.	You will walk.
Third person	He/she/it will walk.	They will walk.

Present Perfect Tense

	Singular	Plural
First person	I have walked.	We have walked.
Second person	You have walked.	You have walked.
Third person	He/she/it has walked.	They have walked.

Past Perfect Tense

	Singular	Plural
First person	I had walked.	We had walked.
Second person	You had walked.	You had walked.
Third person	He/she/it had walked.	They had walked.

Future Perfect Tense		
	Singular	**Plural**
First person	I will have walked.	We will have walked.
Second person	You will have walked.	You will have walked.
Third person	He/she/it will have walked.	They will have walked.

Perfect tenses are always formed by using *have, has,* or *had* plus the past participle form of the verb. You also have the option of using the progressive form *(-ing)* in each tense to show ongoing action:

- Present progressive: I am walking.
- Past progressive: I was walking.
- Future progressive: I will be walking.
- Present perfect progressive: I have been walking.
- Past perfect progressive: I had been walking.
- Future perfect progressive: I will have been walking.

The present participle is the *-ing* form of the verb. In the case of the verb *to walk,* it's *walking.* (These *-ing* forms cannot be verbs alone; they need a helping verb.)

The past participle is the *-ed, -d, -t, -en,* or *-n* form of the verb. In the case of the verb *to walk,* it's *walked.*

Many verbs have irregular forms:

Present	Past	Past Participle
arise	arose	(have) arisen
become	became	(have) become
bring	brought	(have) brought
catch	caught	(have) caught
do	did	(have) done
drink	drank	(have) drunk
drive	drove	(have) driven
eat	ate	(have) eaten
fall	fell	(have) fallen
fly	flew	(have) flown
lend	lent	(have) lent
ring	rang	(have) rung
sing	sang	(have) sung
swim	swam	(have) swum
write	wrote	(have) written

Often verbs occur in verb phrases with a helping verb and a main verb. Some verbs like *do, have,* and *be* can be both main verbs and helping verbs:

> Roberto will **do** his homework.   main verb
> Roberto and Anna **do need** to practice their duet.   helping verb

Watch for sentences that have illogical shifts in tense or use incorrect verb forms.

> Illogical shift: He **searched** for signs of deer when he **notices** the tracks.
> Correct: He **is searching** for signs of deer when he **notices** the tracks.   present
> Or: He **was searching** for signs of deer when he **noticed** the tracks.   past

Check the tense of the context to determine whether the sentence should be in the present or past.

> Incorrect verb form: We were shocked that he **had drank** all the water in the canteen.
> Correct: We were shocked that he **had drunk** all the water in the canteen.

Practice

Directions: Write the correct form of the italicized verb in the blank.

1. I was pleased to discover that I had _____ a mile. *swim*

2. By the next meet, I will have _____ my own record. *beat*

3. When I woke up, I found that two inches of snow had _____. *fall*

4. At last week's meeting, I _____ a presentation. *give*

5. Joan _____ her dog to school yesterday. *bring*

6. After the bell has _____, we can leave for the beach. *ring*

Answers

1. **swum** To show action that took place before past action, use the past perfect tense.

2. **beaten** To show action that began in the present and continues into the future, use the future perfect tense.

3. **fallen** To show action that took place before past action, use the past perfect tense.

4. **gave** This is the simple past tense.

5. **brought** This is the simple past tense.

6. **rung** Use the present perfect tense to indicate an action that occurs at an indefinite time in the past.

L. Sentence Structure

1. Run-on sentences

Two or more complete thoughts joined in one sentence without proper punctuation constitutes a run-on sentence:

> The lecture was on the life cycle of the frog it seemed to go on for hours.

The run-on can be corrected in several ways:

- **Break the sentence up into separate sentences:** The lecture was on the life cycle of the frog. It seemed to go on for hours.
- **Join the main clauses with semicolons:** The lecture was on the life cycle of the frog; it seemed to go on for hours.
- **Change one or more of the main clauses to subordinate clauses:** Because the lecture was on the life cycle of the frog, it seemed to go on for hours.
- **Use a comma and a conjunction:** The lecture was on the life cycle of the frog, and it seemed to go on for hours.
- **Use the semicolon and a conjunctive adverb:** The lecture was on the life cycle of the frog; consequently, it seemed to go on for hours.

The most common run-on occurs when a comma joins two sentences (in what's known as a comma splice):

> Serena really likes Aaron, she thinks he can help her achieve her goals.

Correct the comma splice by any one of the run-on correction methods:

> Serena really likes Aaron; she thinks he can help her achieve her goals.

2. Sentence fragments

Most sentence fragments are phrases or subordinate clauses.

> Being interested in setting up a charity auction.   participial phrase
> To be interested in setting up a charity auction.   infinitive phrase
> Since we are all interested in setting up a charity auction.   subordinate clause

To avoid fragments, remember:

- A sentence must have subject and a verb and express a complete thought.
- No word ending in *-ing* can stand alone as a verb without a helping verb (except one-syllable verbs like *sing* and *ring*).

Practice

Directions: Correct the following sentences.

1. Raghav being the highest scoring quarterback on the football team.

2. Many people think dogs make the best pets, cats are affectionate, too.

3. Hoping to fill all the seats in the auditorium for the school musical.

4. Pearl loves to go Florida, she has so many friends and relatives to visit there.

5. Not only did the class picnic get rained out on Saturday, but cancelled forever.

6. The TV show *Lost* is filmed in Hawaii, the lucky cast gets to live there.

Answers

Answers may vary.

1. **Raghav has been the highest scoring quarterback on the football team.**

2. **Many people think dogs make the best pets, but cats are affectionate, too.**

3. **We are hoping to fill all the seats in the auditorium for the school musical.**

4. **Pearl loves to go Florida because she has so many friends and relatives to visit there.**

5. **Not only did the class picnic get rained out on Saturday, but it was also cancelled forever.**

6. **The TV show *Lost* is filmed in Hawaii; the lucky cast gets to live there.**

X. Working with Numbers

A. Fractions and Decimals

Fractions and decimals are common questions on the SAT. Many of these questions require you to identify the correct numerical value of a given point on a number line in either decimal or fraction form. For example:

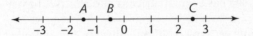

The approximate numerical values of points A, B, and C on the number line above are –1.5, –0.5, and 2.5, respectively.

Many questions also require you to determine a correct inequality involving x, x^2, and x^3 when a numerical value of x is given. For example:

- When $x < -1$, $x^3 < x < x^2$. (For example, if $x = -2$, then $x^2 = 4$ and $x^3 = -8$.)
- When $-1 < x < 0$, $x < x^3 < x^2$. (For example, if $x = -\frac{1}{2}$, then $x^2 = \frac{1}{4}$ and $x^3 = -\frac{1}{8}$.)
- When $0 < x < 1$, $x^3 < x^2 < x$. (For example, if $x = \frac{1}{2}$, then $x^2 = \frac{1}{4}$ and $x^3 = \frac{1}{8}$.)
- When $x > 1$, $x < x^2 < x^3$. (For example, if $x = 2$, then $x^2 = 4$ and $x^3 = 8$.)

For the purpose of comparing x, x^2, and x^3, there are four intervals on a number line from which a number can be selected.

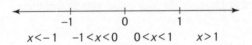

The order of the inequality involving x, x^2, and x^3 depends on from which of the four intervals the value of x is selected. Memorizing the order of the inequality in relation to the intervals on a number line is difficult. Your best bet is to simply substitute a numerical value into x, x^2, and x^3, and compare the results. Use your calculator if you find it helpful.

Practice

1. In the accompanying diagram, five points, *A*, *B*, *C*, *D*, and *E*, are on a number line in the positions indicated. Which point has *m* as its coordinate if $m < m^3 < m^2$?

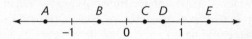

 A. *A*
 B. *B*
 C. *C*
 D. *D*
 E. *E*

2. If $b < -1 < a < 0$, which of the following has the smallest value?

 A. $-b^3$
 B. $-b$
 C. ab
 D. $-a^2$
 E. a^3

3. On the number line below, *a*, *b*, *c*, *d*, and *e* are equally spaced between –2 and 1. Which of the following fractions has the greatest value?

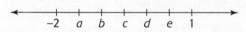

 A. $\dfrac{1}{a}$

 B. $\dfrac{1}{b}$

 C. $\dfrac{1}{c}$

 D. $\dfrac{1}{c+d}$

 E. $\dfrac{1}{e}$

4. As part of the high school physical fitness program, each of the 180 students in a school was required to sign up for exactly one activity: soccer, baseball, table tennis, or volleyball. If half the students signed up for soccer, one-third signed up for baseball, and, of the remaining students, twice as many signed up for volleyball as signed up for table tennis, how many students signed up for table tennis?

 A. 5
 B. 10
 C. 15
 D. 20
 E. 30

5. Janet opened a full 32-ounce container of juice and poured 14 ounces into her glass. Karen drank two-thirds of what Janet left in the container. How many ounces of juice were still in the container after Karen drank her juice?

6. What is the numerical value of $\dfrac{\frac{1}{2}+\frac{1}{3}}{\frac{1}{6}}$?

Answers

1. **B** To find the correct answer, select values for A, B, C, D, and E in the indicated intervals and see which one produces a true statement when substituted in $m < m^3 < m^2$. If $A = -10$, then $m < m^3 < m^2$ becomes $-10 < -1{,}000 < 100$; this isn't true, so m is not the coordinate of A. If $B = -0.5$, then $m < m^3 < m^2$ becomes $-0.5 < -0.125 < 0.25$; this is true, so m could be the coordinate of B. If $C = 0.5$, then $m < m^3 < m^2$ becomes $0.5 < 0.125 < 0.25$; this isn't true, so m is not the coordinate of C. Because C and D are in the same interval (they're both greater than 0 and less than 1), the relationships are the same and m could not be the coordinates of D. If $E = 3$, then $m < m^3 < m^2$ becomes $3 < 27 < 9$; this isn't true, so m is not the coordinate of E. The only point that could have m as its coordinate is B. *(See Appendix on Working with Inequalities.)*

2. **D** You can either consider each choice or select a variety of values and substitute. If you consider each choice:

   - Choice A: Because b is less than -1, b^3 is also less than -1 and $-b^3$ is greater than 1.
   - Choice B: Because b is less than -1, $-b$ is greater than 1.
   - Choice C: Because a and b are both negative, their product is positive and ab is positive.
   - Choice D: Because a^2 is always positive, $-a^2$ is negative.
   - Choice E: Because a is negative, a^3 is negative.

   Negative numbers are smaller than positive numbers, so you can eliminate choices A, B, and C. To compare a^3 with $-a^2$, you need to substitute a number for a to see which is smaller. For example, if $a = -0.5$, then $a^3 = -0.125$ and $-a^2 = -0.25$. So, $-a^2 < a^3$. The smallest value is $-a^2$.

   If you substitute values, you might let $b = -10$ and $a = -0.5$. Then $-b^3 = 1{,}000$, $-b = 10$, $ab = 5$, $-a^2 = -0.25$, and $a^3 = -0.125$. The smallest value is -0.25, which is $-a^2$.

3. **E** The length of the segment from -2 to 1 is 3. Because the interval from -2 to 1 has been divided into six equal segments, each segment is 0.5 in length and $a = -1.5$, $b = -1$, $c = -0.5$, $d = 0$, and $e = 0.5$. Because a, b, and c are negative and $d = 0$, choices A, B, C, and D will all be negative. Because e is positive, only the value of Choice E is positive. The greatest value must be $\frac{1}{e}$.

4. **B** Half of the students signed up for soccer, so that's $\frac{1}{2}(180) = 90$ students. One-third of the students signed up for baseball, so that's $\frac{1}{3}(180) = 60$ students. The $180 - (90 + 60) = 180 - 150 = 30$ remaining students signed up for table tennis or volleyball. Of the 30 remaining students, twice as many signed up for volleyball as signed up for table tennis. Let x be the number of students who signed up for table tennis and $2x$ be the number of students who signed up for volleyball, so $x + 2x = 30$, $3x = 30$, and $x = 10$.

5. **6 ounces** Janet left $32 - 14 = 18$ ounces of juice in the container. Karen drank $\frac{2}{3}(18) = 12$ ounces of juice. The number of ounces of juice still in the in the container after Karen drank was $18 - 12 = 6$ ounces.

6. **5** $\dfrac{\frac{1}{2} + \frac{1}{3}}{\frac{1}{6}} = \dfrac{\frac{3}{6} + \frac{2}{6}}{\frac{1}{6}} = \dfrac{\frac{5}{6}}{\frac{1}{6}} = \frac{5}{6}\left(\frac{6}{1}\right) = 5.$

B. Percent and Proportions

A *percent* is the ratio of a number to 100. When you have to find the percent of a number, always express the given percent as either an equivalent fraction or a decimal. For example, write 5% as 0.05 or $\frac{5}{100}$, and $n\%$ as $0.01n$ or $\frac{n}{100}$.

A proportion is an equation that states that two ratios are equal. For example, $\frac{2}{3} = \frac{10}{15}$ or 3:6 = 4:8. When setting up a proportion, make sure that you use the same unit of measurement for the corresponding quantities and write the ratios in the same order. For example, given the question "If 5 pens cost 60¢, how much will 2 dozen pens cost at the same rate?", you should express 2 dozen pens as 24 pens and use the proportion $\frac{5}{60} = \frac{24}{x}$, where x represents the cost of 24 pens. Notice that the order of the proportion is $\frac{5 \text{ pens}}{\text{cost of 5 pens}} = \frac{24 \text{ pens}}{\text{cost of 24 pens}}$. You could also use other equivalent proportions such as $\frac{5 \text{ pens}}{24 \text{ pens}} = \frac{\text{cost of 5 pens}}{\text{cost of 24 pens}}$.

Practice

1. If n is a positive number, which of the following represents $2n\%$ of 150?

   A. $3n$
   B. $30n$
   C. $60n$
   D. $75n$
   E. $300n$

2. The graph below shows how John's salary was determined in 2008. If John earned a total of $18,000 in overtime pay in 2008, how much did he receive as bonuses?

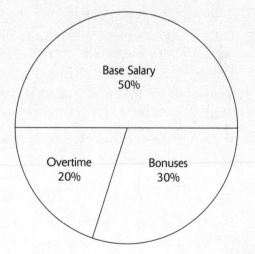

   A. $6,000
   B. $9,000
   C. $27,000
   D. $54,000
   E. $90,000

3. Given a number such that $\frac{2}{5}$ of the number is 30, what is $\frac{1}{3}$ of the number?

A. 4
B. 10
C. 12
D. 25
E. 75

4. On a blueprint for an office building, 6 inches represents 45 feet. Using this scale, how many inches on the blueprint will represent 30 feet?

A. 1.5
B. 2
C. 2.5
D. 3
E. 4

5. Erica and Niki were the only candidates running for president of the senior class. When the votes were tallied, the ratio of the number of votes that Erica received to the number of votes that Niki received was 3 to 2. If 60 students voted for Erica, how many students voted in the election?

6. Two rounds of auditions were being held to select 40 students for a new chorus that was being formed. In the first round of auditions, 30 students were selected, 80% of whom were girls. If the 25% of the members of the chorus had to be boys, how many boys had to be selected in the second round of auditions?

Answers

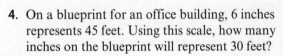

1. A Because $2n\%$ is $\frac{2n}{100}$, then $2n\%$ of 150 is equivalent to $\frac{2n}{100}(150) = 3n$.

2. C Let x be John's annual salary. Because the overtime pay was 20% of John's salary, $0.2x = 18{,}000$ and $x = 90{,}000$. The bonuses were 30% of John's salary, so $0.3x = 0.3(90{,}000) = 27{,}000$. Thus, John's bonuses for 2008 were $27,000.

You can also do this problem by setting up a proportion to find the bonuses. Let y be the bonuses. Then $\frac{0.2}{18{,}000} = \frac{0.3}{y}$, $0.2y = (0.3)(18{,}000)$, and $y = 27{,}000$.

3. D Let x be the number. Since $\frac{2}{5}$ of the number is 30, you have $\frac{2}{5}x = 30$ or $x = 75$. Thus, $\frac{1}{3}$ of the number is $\frac{1}{3}(75) = 25$.

You can also do this problem by using a proportion: $\frac{\frac{2}{5}}{30} = \frac{\frac{1}{3}}{x}$. Thus, $\frac{2}{5}x = \frac{1}{3}(30)$, or $x = 25$.

4. E To find the number of inches on the blueprint, x, use the proportion $\frac{6}{45} = \frac{x}{30}$. Then $45x = 6(30)$ and $x = 4$.

Notice that you do not have to convert inches to feet. When you set up a proportion, corresponding quantities must have the same unit of measurement. In this problem, you're comparing inches on the blueprint to height measured in feet. Both blueprint numbers are in the same units (inches), and both heights are in the same units (feet), so the proportion may be set up without converting. If the height of one building were given in feet and the height of the other building were given in inches, you would have to convert both to feet or both to inches before the proportion could be set up.

5. **100** To find the number of votes that Niki received, x, solve the proportion $\frac{3}{2} = \frac{60}{x}$ or $x = 40$. Because 60 students voted for Niki and 40 voted for Erica, the number of students who voted is $60 + 40 = 100$.

6. **4** If 25% of the 40 chorus members must be boys, there must be a total of $0.25(40) = 10$ boys selected. In the first round, because 80% of the 30 students were girls, 20% of the 30 students were boys and 20% of 30 is $0.20(30) = 6$. Because 10 boys are needed and 6 were already selected in the first round, in the second round the number of boys selected must be $10 - 6 = 4$.

C. Real Numbers

As you prepare for the SAT, you will find that many questions test your understanding of the properties of real numbers—specifically, the properties of prime numbers, multiplication by zero, and odd and even integers. Here is a summary of some of these properties:

Primes

- A prime number is a positive integer greater than 1, whose only positive factors are itself and 1.
- Prime numbers are 2, 3, 5, 7, 11, 13, . . .
- 1 is not a prime number.
- 2 is the only even prime number.

Zero

- 0 is the only number that is neither positive nor negative.
- 0 is an even number.
- If $ab = 0$, then $a = 0$ or $b = 0$ (or both a and b equal 0).

Even/Odd

- *even + even = even* and *(even)(even) = even*
- *odd + odd = even* and *(odd)(odd) = odd*
- *even + odd = odd (even)(odd) = even*

Use substitution to determine if an algebraic expression is even or odd.

Integers

- Since the set of integers is $\{. . . , -2, -1, 0, 1, 2, . . .\}$, if a question asks for integral values only, be sure to eliminate numbers that are not integers such as $\frac{1}{2}$, 2.5, or $\sqrt{7}$.

Practice

1. Which of the following is not a factor of 72?

   A. 8
   B. 16
   C. 24
   D. 36
   E. 72

2. If n is a positive integer, which of the following expressions always represents an odd integer?

   A. $n + 5$
   B. $2n - 4$
   C. $3n + 3$
   D. $6n + 3$
   E. $n^2 + 1$

3. If n and k are both prime numbers, which of the following is *not* a possible value of nk?

   A. 10
   B. 13
   C. 33
   D. 35
   E. 49

4. If $x^2y = 16$ and $xyz = 0$, which of the following must be true:

   A. $x > 0$
   B. $y < 0$
   C. $y = 0$
   D. $z < 0$
   E. $z = 0$

5. What is the smallest three-digit number that has both 5 and 13 as factors?

6. If all of the integers greater than or equal to 500 and less than or equal to 600 were written on a list, how many times would the digit 5 appear?

Answers

1. **B** A number is a factor of 72 if the remainder is zero when 72 is divided by the number. If you divide 72 by 8 or 24 or 36 or 72, the remainder is zero. If you divide 72 by 16, the remainder is not zero. Thus, 16 is not a factor of 72. Alternatively, 72 can be factored as a product of primes—72 = (2)(2)(2)(3)(3)—and 16 can be factored as a product of primes—16 = (2)(2)(2)(2). Because 16 has four factors of 2, and 72 has only 3 factors of 2, 16 cannot be a factor of 72.

2. **D** Test each choice by substituting values for n. Because even/odd results are influenced by whether the number substituted is even or odd, you must use an even number and an odd number when you test. When you substitute 4 for n, $n + 5 = 9$, $2n - 4 = 4$, $3n + 3 = 15$, $6n + 3 = 27$, $n^2 + 1 = 17$. All these results are odd except for Choice B, so you can eliminate Choice B. When you substitute 3 for n in the remaining choices, $n + 5 = 8$, $3n + 3 = 12$, $n^2 + 1 = 10$, and $6n + 3 = 21$. The only expression that represents an odd integer is $6n + 3$.

3. **B** Each choice, except for Choice B, may be expressed as a product of two prime numbers: $10 = 5 \times 2$, $33 = 3 \times 11$, $35 = 7 \times 5$, $49 = 7 \times 7$. Choice B, 13, can never be expressed as a product of primes because 13 is a prime number (it has only 1 and itself as factors and 1 is not a prime number).

4. **E** Because $xyz = 0$, at least one of the variables x, y, or z must be 0. If either $x = 0$ or $y = 0$, the product x^2y would have to equal 0. Because $x^2y = 16$, which implies that neither x nor y are equal to 0, the factor that equals zero must be z.

5. **130** Because $13 \times 5 = 65$ and 65 is a two-digit number, you need to try the next common multiple. The next common multiple is $13 \times 5 \times 2 = 130$. The smallest three-digit number is 130.

6. **120** From 500 to 600, the digit 5 is used 100 times as the hundreds digit, 10 times as the tens digit, and 10 times as the units digit. The number of times the digit 5 would appear is $100 + 10 + 10 = 120$.

D. Divisibility and Remainders

An SAT question on divisibility and remainders often requires you to find the remainder when an algebraic expression is divided by a given number. For example, you might be asked the remainder when $2n + 6$ is divided by 3, given that the remainder of n divided by 3 is 1. The strategy here is to substitute a number for n so that when n is divided by 3, the remainder is 1. Notice that there are many numbers that satisfy this requirement (4, 7, 10, and so on). You could select any of these numbers. For example, if you pick 4 for n, then $2n + 6 = 2(4) + 6 = 14$. Therefore, the remainder of 14 divided by 3 is 2. Problem solved. This approach works because remainders repeat in cycles when integers that form an arithmetic sequence are divided by an integer.

Practice

1. If n is any integer that has a remainder of 2 when divided by 5, what is the remainder when $3n - 1$ is divided by 5?

   A. 0
   B. 1
   C. 2
   D. 3
   E. 4

2. Ms. Chen has 12 dozen pencils in a box. If she gives each of the 24 students in her class 5 pencils, how many pencils will be left in the box?

   A. 0
   B. 1
   C. 2
   D. 12
   E. 24

3. If a positive integer, n, is divisible by 2, 5, and 6, which of the following must also be divisible by 2, 5, and 6?

   A. $n + 10$
   B. $n + 12$
   C. $n + 13$
   D. $n^2 - 13$
   E. $2n + 30$

4. If k is an integer and 3 is the remainder when k is divided by 5, how many values for k are possible when $0 < k < 100$?

   A. 10
   B. 19
   C. 20
   D. 23
   E. 40

135

5. If n is an even integer and 4 is the remainder when n is divided by 5, what digit is n's units digit?

6. Mr. Cohen bought a box of individually wrapped chocolates and decided to give the chocolates to his students. If he gave each student 2 pieces of chocolate, 25 pieces would be left in the box. If he gave each student 3 pieces, 5 pieces would be left in the box. How many students are in Mr. Cohen's class?

Answers

1. **A** To solve this problem, choose a value for n that has a remainder of 2 when divided by 5. Substitute this value in $3n - 1$ and find the remainder when the result is divided by 5. Because the remainder is 2 when 7 is divided by 5, use $n = 7$. If $n = 7$, then $3n - 1 = 3(7) - 1 = 20$. Because the remainder is 0 when 20 is divided by 5, the value of the remainder when $3n - 1$ is divided by 5 is 0.

2. **E** There are $12 \times 12 = 144$ pencils in the box. If Ms. Chen will give $5 \times 24 = 120$ pencils to her students. The number of pencils that remain in the box will be $144 - 120 = 24$.

3. **E** A possible value for n is 30, because the remainder is 0 when 30 is divided by 2, by 5, and by 6. When you evaluate the choices, substitute 30 for n, and you have $n + 10 = 40$, $n + 12 = 42$, $n + 13 = 43$, $n^2 - 13 = 887$, and $2n + 30 = 90$. Only Choice E produces an answer that is divisible by 2, 5, and 6. Thus, $2n + 30$ is divisible by 2, 5, and 6.

   You could also use a different approach based on the fact that if n is divisible by 2, 5, and 6, then n is a multiple of 2, 5, and 6, and if two numbers are divisible by 2, 5, and 6, then their sum is also divisible by 2, 5, and 6. Because 10, 12, and 13 are not divisible by 2, 5, and 6, choices A, B, C, and D are eliminated. For Choice E, you know that 30 is a multiple of 2, 5, and 6, and that $2n$ is a multiple of 2, 5, and 6 because n is a multiple of 2, 5, and 6. So the sum $2n + 30$ is a multiple of 2, 5, and 6. The expression that is divisible by 2, 5, and 6 is $2n + 30$.

4. **C** To solve this problem, list the possible integers for k and look for a pattern. The smallest value for k is 3; some of the other values are 8, 13, 18, 23, 28, 33, and 38. The remainder will be 3 when the units digit is 3 or 8. Between 0 and 100, there are ten integers with 3 as the units digit and ten integers with 8 as the units digit. The number of possible values for k is $10 + 10 = 20$.

5. **4** Some possible values of n are 4, 9, 14, 19, 24, and 29. You can see from this list that the units digit for n could be either 4 or 9. Because n is an even integer, the units digit is 4.

6. **20** If x is number of students in Mr. Cohen's class and y is the number of pieces of chocolate in the box, then $2x + 25 = y$ and $3x + 5 = y$ or $2x + 25 = 3x + 5$ and $x = 20$. The number of students in Mr. Cohen's class is 20.

E. Patterns and Sequences

Two common types of sequences on the SAT are

- **Arithmetic sequences:** An arithmetic sequence is a sequence whose consecutive terms have a common difference. For example, in the sequence 3, 5, 7, 9, . . . , the common difference is 2.
- **Geometric sequences:** A geometric sequence is a sequence such that the ratios of consecutive terms are the same. For example, in the sequence 2, 6, 18, 54, . . . , the ratio is 3.

Below is a summary of formulas for finding the nth term and the sum of the first n terms for both arithmetic and geometric sequences.

	n**th term**	**Sum of the first n terms**
Arithmetic sequences	$a_n = a_1 + (n-1)d$ a_1 = first term d = common difference	$S_n = (a_1 + a_n)\left(\dfrac{n}{2}\right)$ or $S_n = \left(\dfrac{n}{2}\right)\left[2a_1 + (n-1)d\right]$
Geometric sequences	$a_n = a_1 r^{(n-1)}$ a_1 = first term r = common ratio	$S_n = \dfrac{a_1 - a_1(r)^n}{1-r}$

When working with a pattern, always determine what is being repeated. The repeating unit may be a block of numbers, a group of algebraic expressions, or a geometric figure. This information will help you determine other properties of the given pattern.

Practice

1. If the number of bacteria in a Petri dish doubled every hour and if, at noon, there were 800 bacteria in the Petri dish, how many bacteria were in the Petri dish at 8 a.m. that day?

   A. 25
   B. 50
   C. 100
   D. 200
   E. 400

2. If the kth term of a sequence is defined as $5k - 1$, what is the value of the smallest term greater than 100?

   A. 20
   B. 21
   C. 104
   D. 109
   E. 504

3. If the first term of a sequence is 2 and each successive term is found by multiplying the preceding term by –3, what is the sum of the fourth and fifth terms?

   A. –216
   B. –108
   C. 108
   D. 162
   E. 216

4. At Mary's high school, classes meet for 40 minutes and the time between classes is 10 minutes. If Mary's first-period class begins at 8 a.m. and she is scheduled for a total of seven consecutive classes, what time does her seventh-period class end?

   A. 12:40 p.m.
   B. 12:50 p.m.
   C. 1:40 p.m.
   D. 1:50 p.m.
   E. 2:00 p.m.

5. $1^2, 2^2, 3^2, 4^2, \ldots$

   The first four terms of a sequence are shown above. If the sum of the first n terms is greater than 100, what is the smallest value of n?

6. The diagram below shows a pattern of squares connected by line segments. The side of each square is 1cm long and each connecting line segment is 4cm long. If the pattern stops at the nth square and the sum of the perimeters of the squares plus the sum of the lengths of the connecting line segments is 124cm, what is the value of n?

Answers

1. **B** You can solve this problem by setting up a table or by using the formula for finding a term of a geometric sequence. To solve by setting up a table, count back in time from noon to 8 a.m. in one-hour increments. Start with 800 and then take half of the number of bacteria as you count back in time.

Noon	11 a.m.	10 a.m.	9 a.m.	8 a.m.
800	400	200	100	50

From the table you can see that at 8 a.m., the number of bacteria was 50.

To solve using the formula for finding a term of a geometric sequence, start with $a_n = a_1 r^{(n-1)}$. Because the number of bacteria doubles every hour, $r = 2$. If the first term, a_1, is the number of bacteria in the dish at 8 a.m., then the fifth term is 800, the number of bacteria in the dish at noon. Thus, $800 = a_1(2^{5-1}) =$ or $a_1 (2^4) = 16a_1$ and $a_1 = 50$. At 8 a.m., the number of bacteria was 50.

2. **C** Because the value of the kth term is $5k - 1$, solve $5k - 1 > 100$ and you have $5k > 101$ or $k > 20.2$. You know that k has to be an integer and the smallest integer greater than 20.2 is 21, so $k = 21$ and $5k - 1 = 104$, which is the smallest term greater than 100.

3. **C** This is a geometric sequence, so using the formula $a_n = a_1 r^{(n-1)}$ you have the fourth term $a_4 = (2)(-3)^{(4-1)} = 2(-3)^3 = -54$ and the fifth term $a_5 = 2(-3)^{(5-1)} = 162$. The sum of the fourth and fifth terms is $162 + (-54) = 108$.

4. **C** Because each class lasts for 40 minutes, seven classes meet for $7 \times 40 = 280$ minutes. Between the first and seventh periods, the six ten-minute intervals require 60 minutes. The total time is $280 + 60 = 340$ minutes, or 5 hours and 40 minutes. Because first period begins at 8 a.m., seventh period ends at 1:40 p.m.

5. **7** To find when the sum will be greater than 100, start adding the terms: $1^2 + 2^2 = 5$, $1^2 + 2^2 + 3^2 = 14$, and so on. When you reach $1^2 + 2^2 + 3^2 + 4^2 + 5^2 + 6^2 = 96$, and $1^2 + 2^2 + 3^2 + 4^2 + 5^2 + 6^2 + 7^2 = 140$, you know that the first time the sum is greater than 100 occurs when $n = 7$. The smallest value of n is 7.

6. **16** The figure is made up of repeating units, where each unit is made up of a square with perimeter of 4cm and a connecting segment on the right with length 4cm, so the length of each repeating unit is 8cm. The total length is 124cm, so $124 \div 8 = 15.5$, so there are 15 repeating units with half a unit (4cm) left over. These remaining 4cm form the next square, which is the 16th square. The pattern ends at the 16th square. The value of n is 16.

F. Sets

Questions involving sets on the SAT can often be solved using Venn diagrams. A Venn diagram is a diagram using overlapping circles to show relationships among given sets. For example, if A is the set {2, 4, 6, 8, 10} and B is the set {1, 2, 3, 4, 5}, then the relationship between Set A and Set B can be shown using a Venn diagram as illustrated below.

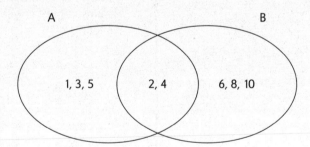

If a Venn diagram has multiple overlapping regions, try outlining the circles in different colors or markings to help you identify the regions.

If you're listing elements in order to identify the elements that two sets have in common, you can save time if you first list the elements that belong to the smaller set and then identify which of those elements are also in the larger set. For example, given that Set A contains all the prime numbers less than 10 and Set B contains all positive even integers less than 100, list all the elements of Set A, {2, 3, 5, 7}, and notice that 2 is an element of both sets.

Practice

1. If A is the set of odd integers less than 24 and B is the set of prime numbers less than 20, how many numbers are common to both sets?

   A. 7
   B. 8
   C. 9
   D. 10
   E. 12

2. The distribution of the elements in sets A, B, and C is shown in the accompanying Venn diagram. The numbers and variables in the regions are the numbers of elements in those regions. If there are exactly ten elements that are in both Set B and Set C, what is the value of x?

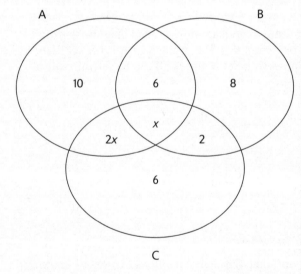

   A. 2
   B. 4
   C. 6
   D. 8
   E. 10

3. Each of the 24 students in Mr. Martin's class plays tennis, soccer, or both. If 4 students play both sports and 8 play only tennis, how many students play only soccer?

   A. 12
   B. 14
   C. 16
   D. 18
   E. 20

4. When x is a member of Set A, the value of $\sqrt{x^2} + x$ is also a member of Set A. Which of the following could be Set A?

   A. $\{-2, 1\}$
   B. $\{-1, 0\}$
   C. $\{-1, 0, 1\}$
   D. $\{0, 1\}$
   E. $\{0, 1, 2\}$

5. There are 30 cups of coffee on a table. If 16 have milk added, 14 have sugar added, and 10 have both milk and sugar added, how many cups of coffee have neither milk nor sugar?

6. In a music class with 20 students, each student plays only the violin, plays only the cello, or plays both. If 4 students play both the violin and the cello and, of all the students in the class, twice as many play the violin as play the cello, how many students play only the cello?

Answers

1. **A** Because Set B has fewer elements than Set A, list the elements in Set B and see how many elements in Set B are odd integers. The elements in Set B are {2, 3, 5, 7, 11, 13, 17, 19}. The elements in Set A that are odd integers less than 24 are {3, 5, 7, 11, 13, 15, 17, 19, 23}. The number of common elements is 7.

2. **D** Because the Venn diagram shows that $x + 2$ elements are in both Set B and Set C, $x + 2 = 10$ or $x = 8$.

3. **A**

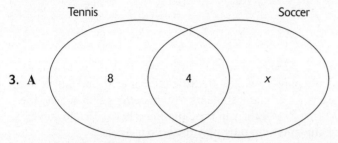

Because 4 students play in both sports and 8 students play only tennis, the number of students who only play soccer is $24 - (8 + 4) = 24 - 12 = 12$.

4. **B** Substituting gives the results listed in the following table.

x	-2	-1	0	1	2
$\sqrt{x^2} + x$	0	0	0	2	4

Of the choices, the only set that satisfies the condition is {−1,0}.

5. **10**

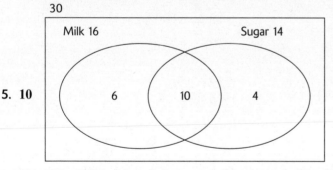

Use a Venn diagram to help you see that there are $16 - 10 = 6$ cups with only milk added and $14 - 10 = 4$ cups with only sugar added. Because there are $6 + 10 + 4 = 20$ cups of coffee with milk, sugar, or both, the number of cups of coffee with neither milk nor sugar is $30 - 20 = 10$.

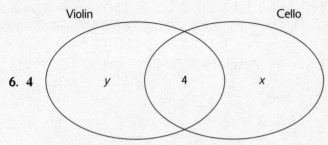

6. 4

Set up a Venn diagram with x representing the number of students who only play the cello and y representing the number of students who only play the violin. Because there are 20 students in the class, $x + y + 4 = 20$ or $x + y = 16$. Because twice as many students who play the violin as play the cello, $y + 4 = 2(x + 4)$ or $y = 2x + 4$. Substitute $2x + 4$ for y in the equation $x + y = 16$ and solve to find that $x = 4$ and $y = 12$. The number of students who only play the cello is 4.

XI. Algebra and Functions

A. Algebraic Expressions

When you're working with algebraic expressions, you need to follow the rules for order of operations. These rules of operation are sometimes referred to as PEMDAS:

- **P:** Parentheses—for example, $3(4 + 6) = 3(10) = 30$
- **E:** Exponents—for example, $5(3)^2 = 5(9) = 45$
- **M:** Multiplication—for example, $3 + 2(4) = 3 + 8 = 11$
- **D:** Division—for example, $40 \div 2 \times 5 = 20 \times 5 = 100$ (***Note:*** Division and multiplication are done from left to right.)
- **A:** Addition—for example, $4 + 6 - 3 = 10 - 3 = 7$
- **S:** Subtraction—for example, $10 - 2 + 3 = 8 + 3 = 11$. (***Note:*** Addition and subtraction are done from left to right.)

Practice

1. If you hire Mary's Car Service to drive you across town, you will be charged $10 plus an additional $2, for each $\frac{1}{4}$ of a mile. Which of the following represents the total number of dollars that you would be charged if the trip is n miles?

   A. $2n$
   B. $10 + 2n$
   C. $10 + 4n$
   D. $10 + 8n$
   E. $12n$

2. If Janet is n years old, Karen is 2 years younger than Janet, and Mary is 4 years more than twice Janet's age, which of the following represents how many years older Mary is than Karen?

   A. 2
   B. $n - 2$
   C. n
   D. $n + 2$
   E. $n + 6$

3. If Marissa drove for h hours at an average rate of m miles per hour and then she drove for k hours at an average rate of n miles per hour, what is the total distance, in miles, that she had driven?

  A. $m + n$

  B. $\dfrac{m+n}{h+k}$

  C. $\dfrac{m}{h} + \dfrac{n}{k}$

  D. $(h + k)(m + n)$

  E. $mh + nk$

4. If x and y are positive integers, $x > y$ and $x + y = 7$, which of the following could be a value of $x^2 - y^2$?

  A. 14

  B. 35

  C. 45

  D. 48

  E. 49

5. Points A, B, C, and D lie on the same line. If B is the midpoint of $\overline{AC}$, C is the midpoint of $\overline{BD}$, and $AD = 12k$, what is the length of $\overline{BD}$ in terms of k?

6. If a and b are constants and $x(ax + b) = 4x^2 + 2ax$ is true for all values of x, what is the value of $a + b$?

Answers

1. **D** Because you're charged $2 for each quarter mile, the charge for each mile is 4($2) = $8 and the charge for n miles would be $8n$. The total charge, in dollars, is $10 + 8n$.

2. **E** Because Janet's age is n, Karen's age is $(n - 2)$ and Mary's age is $2n + 4$. Since Mary is older than Karen, the difference in their ages is $(2n + 4) - (n - 2)$, which is equivalent to $2n + 4 - n + 2$ or $(n + 6)$.

3. **E** Because Distance = Rate × Time, when Marrissa drove for h hours at an average of m miles per hour, the distance was mh miles. Similarly, when she drove for k hours at an average rate of n miles per hour, the distance was nk miles. The total distance, in miles, is $mh + nk$.

4. **B** Because x and y are positive integers and $x + y = 7$, the possible values of x and y are:

x	1	2	3	4	5	6
y	6	5	4	3	2	1

Since $x > y$, you have (4,3), (5,2), and (6,1). Substituting these x and y values in $x^2 - y^2$, you have $x^2 - y^2 = 7$, 21, or 35. Of the given choices, the one that is a possible value of $x^2 - y^2$ is 35.

5. **8k**

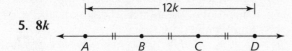

B is the midpoint of $\overline{AC}$, so $AB = BC$. *C* is the midpoint of $\overline{BD}$, so $BC = CD$. Since $AB = BC$ and $BC = CD$, you know that $AB = BC = CD$. Because $AB + BC + BD = AD$ and $AD = 12k$, each segment is $4k$ in length and $BC + CD = 4k + 4k = 8k$ and $BD = 8k$.

6. **12** Because you're trying to find the value of $a + b$, not the value of x, you need to try to isolate a and b. If you start by removing parentheses, you find that $ax^2 + bx = 4x^2 + 2ax$. You have two terms on the left side, one term with x^2 and one term with x. Because the right side also has exactly two terms, one term with x^2 and one term with x, you can match the terms to find that $ax^2 = 4x^2$ and $bx = 2ax$. Because $ax^2 = 4x^2$, you have $a = 4$, and because $bx = 2ax$, you have $b = 2a = 2(4) = 8$. The value of $a + b$ is $4 + 8 = 12$.

B. Equations

On the SAT, you'll be tested on solving equations—linear, quadratic, absolute value, and radical equations. Keep in mind the following when you're solving equations:

- When you're given an equation, the solution to the equation is often not the answer to the question.
  - Sometimes you must do an additional substitution to answer the question.
  - Sometimes, instead of solving the equation for a value, you change the equation to match an expression that can be used to find the answer to the question. (See question 3 in the following "Practice" section.)
- Quadratic equations in the SAT usually can be solved by factoring.
- When you have to solve an equation that has the variable under the radical sign, usually you'll have to first isolate the radical on one side of the equation and then raise both sides to a power. Because this process can create an extraneous answer, be sure to check that the answers satisfy the original equation.
- Usually, you'll be able to save time if you use a graphing calculator to solve equations.

Practice

1. If $a > b$ and $ay - by = 4$, what is the value of y when $(a - b)^2 = 4$?

   A. 0
   B. 1
   C. 2
   D. 4
   E. 8

2. If x is a real number, how many values of x satisfy the equation $(x + 10)^2 = 25$?

   A. 0
   B. 1
   C. 2
   D. 3
   E. 4

3. If $2x + 3y = 10$, what is the value of $4x + 6y$?

A. 15
B. 20
C. 30
D. 40
E. 60

5. For which positive number is 16 times the cube root of the number the same as the number?

4. If $(a - 1)(b + 2)(c - 3) = 0$, what is the smallest value for $a^2 + b^2 + c^2$?

A. 0
B. 1
C. 4
D. 9
E. 14

6. If a and b are positive integers such that $a < b$ and $7a + 11b = 243$, what is the value of $b - a$?

Answer

1. **C** Since $(a - b)^2 = 4$, you know that $(a - b) = \pm 2$. Because $a > b$, you know $a - b > 0$ and $a - b = 2$. To find y when $a - b = 2$, express $ay - by = 4$ in the factored form $y(a - b) = 4$ and substitute 2 for $(a - b)$. Then $(y)(2) = 4$ and $y = 2$.

2. **C** Instead of multiplying $(x + 10)(x + 10)$ and then factoring to solve the quadratic equation $x^2 + 20x + 75 = 0$, keep the equation in its original form and find the square root of both sides. Thus $(x + 10) = \pm 5$. Solving the equations $x + 10 = 5$ and $x + 10 = -5$, you have $x = -5$ or $x = -15$. Therefore, there are two values of x satisfying the given equation.

3. **B** The question did not ask for the individual values of x and y, but instead the value of $4x + 6y$. Notice that $4x + 6y = 2(2x + 3y)$. Multiply both sides of the equation $2x + 3y = 10$ by 2 and you have $2(2x + 3y) = 20$. Thus, $4x + 6y = 20$.

4. **B** In order for $(a - 1)(b + 2)(c - 3)$ to have a value of 0, only one of the following three conditions must be met: $a = 1$, $b = -2$, or $c = 3$. If you let $a = 1$ and then choose to let $b = 0$ and $c = 0$, the product of $(a - 1)(b + 2)(c - 3)$ will be 0, and the value of $a^2 + b^2 + c^2$ will be the smallest value possible or $(1)^2 + (0)^2 + (0)^2 = 1$.

5. $x = 64$ If x is the number, then $16\left(\sqrt[3]{x}\right) = x$. Cubing both sides, you have $4{,}096x = x^3$ or $x^3 - 4{,}096x = 0$. Factoring the equation $x^3 - 4{,}096x = 0$, you have $x(x^2 - 4{,}096) = 0$. Thus $x = 0$ or $x = \pm\sqrt{4{,}096} = \pm 64$. Since x is a positive number, $x = 64$.

6. **9** Since $7a + 11b = 243$ is one equation with two variables, you may either guess until you find an integral pair that satisfies the equation and have $b > a$, or you may use a graphing calculator.

To solve using the graphing calculator, express $7a + 11b = 243$ as $7x + 11y = 243$. Solve for y to find that $y = \dfrac{243 - 7x}{11}$ Enter this equation into your calculator and go to the Table function to find the integral pairs (30,3), (19,10), and (8,17). Only the pair (8,17) has $y > x$, the equivalent of $b > a$. Thus, $b - a = 17 - 8 = 9$.

C. Inequalities

Solving inequalities is part of the SAT. In general, you can solve a simple inequality the same way you would solve an equation, except when multiplying or dividing an inequality by a negative number. If you multiply or divide both sides of an inequality by a negative quantity, the direction of the inequality sign is reversed.

Also, a common question on the SAT involves the order of x, x^2, and x^3, where x is a real number.

The four intervals where the order of x, x^2, and x^3 changes are when:

- **x is less than –1:** In this case, $x^3 < x < x^2$.
- **x is between –1 and 0:** In this case, $x < x^3 < x^2$.
- **x is between 0 and 1:** In this case, $x^3 < x^2 < x$.
- **x > 1:** In this case, $x < x^2 < x^3$.

Practice

1. If $\frac{1}{6} < \frac{3}{n} < \frac{1}{4}$, how many integral values of n are possible?

   A. 1
   B. 3
   C. 5
   D. 6
   E. 7

2. Five years ago, Mary was at least 3 more than twice Karen's age. If k represents Karen's age now and m represents Mary's age now, which of the following describes the relationship of their ages 5 years ago?

   A. $m > 2k + 3$
   B. $m > 2k - 3$
   C. $m + 5 > 2(k + 5) - 3$
   D. $m - 5 \leq 2(k + 5) + 3$
   E. $m - 5 \geq 2(k - 5) + 3$

3. If a and b are positive integers and $(a - b)^2 = 36$, which of the following must be true?

   A. $a^2 + b^2 < 36$
   B. $a^2 + b^2 > 36$
   C. $a^2 + b^2 = 36$
   D. $a^2 - b^2 = 36$
   E. $a - b = 6$

4. Given that $x^2 - y^2 < 12$ and $x + y > 10$, if x and y are positive integers and $x > y$, what is the value of y?

   A. 3
   B. 4
   C. 5
   D. 6
   E. 8

5. If x is a real number and $x < x^3 < x^2$, what is one possible value of x?

6. If $h \geq k \geq 0$ and $(h + k)(h + k) \leq 36$, what is the largest possible value for k?

Answers

1. **C** The inequalities $\frac{1}{6} < \frac{3}{n} < \frac{1}{4}$ is equivalent to $\frac{1}{6} < \frac{3}{n}$ and $\frac{3}{n} < \frac{1}{4}$. Solving $\frac{1}{6} < \frac{3}{n}$ you have $n < 18$. Similarly, solving $\frac{3}{n} < \frac{1}{4}$, we have $12 < n$ or $n > 12$. Since $n > 12$ and $n < 18$, n must be 13, 14, 15, 16, or 17. There are 5 integral values for n.

2. **E** Five years ago, Mary's age was $m - 5$ and Karen's age was $k - 5$. If five years ago Mary had been 3 years more than twice Karen's age, the relationship of their ages would have been described as $m - 5 = 2(k - 5) + 3$. Since five years ago, Mary was at least 3 years more than twice Karen's age, the equation becomes an inequality instead: $m - 5 \geq 2(k - 5) + 3$.

	Current Age	Age 5 Years Ago
Mary	m	$m - 5$
Karen	k	$k - 5$

3. **B** Since $(a - b)^2 = a^2 - 2ab + b^2$, you know that $a^2 - 2ab + b^2 = 36$ or $a^2 + b^2 = 36 + 2ab$. Because a and b are positive integers, $2ab$ is positive. Thus, $a^2 + b^2 > 36$.

4. **C** Factor $x^2 - y^2$ as $(x + y)(x - y)$ and rewrite $x^2 - y^2 < 12$ as $(x + y)(x - y) < 12$. Since $x + y > 10$, let $x + y = 11$. Note that if you let $x + y = 12$ or 13 or more, the inequality $(x + y)(x - y) < 12$ will not work. Now $(x + y)(x - y) < 12$ becomes $(11)(x - y) < 12$. The only possible integer value for $x - y$ is 1. Solve the simultaneous equations $x + y = 11$ and $x - y = 1$ by adding the 2 equations. You have $2x = 12$ or $x = 6$. Thus, $y = 5$.

5. **Any number between −1 and 0**

Let $x = -\frac{1}{2}$. Then $x^2 = \frac{1}{4}$ and $x^3 = -\frac{1}{8}$. The inequality is satisfied. In fact, if you let x be equal to any value between −1 and 0—in other words, $-1 < x < 0$—the inequality will hold. In general, when comparing the value of a power of x such as $x^2, x^3, x^4, \ldots$, you should examine values from four intervals: $(-\infty, -1)$, $(-1, 0)$, $(0, 1)$, and $(1, \infty)$. In this case, for the inequality $x < x^3 < x^2$, the interval is $(-1, 0)$.

6. **3** Since $h \geq k$, the largest possible value for k is h. Substituting h for k, you have $(h + h)(h + h) \leq 36$, or $4h^2 \leq 36$. Solve for h and you have $h^2 \leq 9$ or $-3 \leq h \leq 3$. Since $h \geq 0$, $-3 \leq h \leq 3$ is equivalent to $h \leq 3$. Since $k = h$, the largest possible value for k is 3.

D. Absolute Values

When solving problems involving absolute values on the SAT, it is helpful to remember the following:

- The absolute value of a number is never negative. It's either positive or zero. For example, $|-3| = 3$, $|3| = 3$, and $|0| = 0$.
- The definition of the absolute value of a number is : $|x| = \begin{cases} x, \text{ if } x \geq 0 \\ -x, \text{ if } x < 0 \end{cases}$
- There are three common types of questions involving absolute value:
  - If $|x| = a$, $a > 0$, then solve the two equations $x = a$ and $x = -a$.
  - If $|x| > a$, $a > 0$, then solve the two inequalities $x < -a$ or $x > a$.
  - If $|x| < a$, $a > 0$, then solve the two inequalities $x > -a$ and $x < a$ or solve $-a < x < a$.

Practice

1. $10 - |n + 2| = 4$

   If n is a negative number, what is the value of n?

   A. -2
   B. -6
   C. -8
   D. -10
   E. -16

2. If $\left|\dfrac{k}{3} - 4\right| = \dfrac{k}{3} - 4$, what is the smallest possible value for k?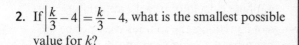

   A. -12
   B. 8
   C. 0
   D. 12
   E. 15

3. If a and b are nonzero numbers and $|a + b| = |a| + |b|$, then which of the following must be true?

   A. $a = b$
   B. $ab > 0$
   C. $ab < 0$
   D. $a > b$
   E. $b > a$

4. In the xy-plane, which of the following points lies on the graph of the equation $-2|x| + y = 2$?

   A. $(-3,8)$
   B. $(-1,0)$
   C. $(0,-2)$
   D. $(4,-1)$
   E. $(6,-2)$

5. If n satisfies both of the equations below, what is the value of n?

   $|2n - 4| = 10$

   $|3 - 2n| = 11$

6. If x is a negative integer, and $\left|\dfrac{x}{2} - 1\right| < 2$, what is the value of x?

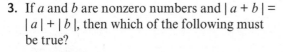

Answers

1. **C** The inequality is equivalent to $6 = |n + 2|$. Then $n + 2 = 6$ or $n + 2 = -6$ and you have $n = 4$ or $n = -8$. Since n is a negative number, $n = -8$.

2. **D** The absolute value of a quantity must be greater than or equal to 0. Since $\left|\frac{k}{3} - 4\right| = \frac{k}{3} - 4$, you have $\frac{k}{3} - 4 \geq 0$. Solve the inequality; you have $\frac{k}{3} \geq 4$ or $k \geq 12$. Thus, the smallest value for k is 12.

3. **B** The equation $|a + b| = |a| + |b|$ is true only when both a and b are positive or both are negative. For example, $|3 + 4| = |3| + |4|$, and $|-3 - 4| = |-3| + |-4|$. If a and b have different signs, the equation is false—for example, $|-3 + 4| \neq |-3| + |4|$. Therefore, the choice that must be true is $ab > 0$.

4. **A** If a point lies on the graph of an equation, then the coordinates of the point satisfy the equation. Substitute the coordinates of each point in the five choices, into the equation and check. In Choice A, using $x = -3$ and $y = 8$, you have $-2|-3| + 8 = 2$ or $-6 + 8 = 2$, or $2 = 2$. Thus, the coordinates satisfy the equation. The point that is on the graph is $(-3,8)$.

5. **7** Solve $|2n - 4| = 10$, and you have $2n - 4 = 10$ or $3 - 2n = 9$, which gives you $n = 7$ or $n = -3$. Solve $|3 - 2n| = 11$, and you have $3 - 2n = 11$ or $3 - 2n = -11$, which gives you $n = -4$ or $n = 7$. Therefore, the value of n that satisfies both equations is 7.

6. **-1** The inequality $\left|\frac{x}{2} - 1\right| < 2$ is equivalent to $-2 < \left(\frac{x}{2} - 1\right) < 2$. Adding 1 to all three parts, we have $-1 < \frac{x}{2} < 3$. Multiplying by 2, we have $-2 < x < 6$. Since x is a negative integer, $x = -1$.

E. Systems of Equations

On the SAT, you may be asked to solve a system of two or more equations. If so, keep in mind the following:

- Most systems of equations can be solved by using a graphing calculator (see the appendix).
- Read the question carefully. When you solve a system of equations, the solution may not be the answer to the question. You may have to substitute the value of a variable in another expression to find the answer to the question.
- Applying the multiplication property of 0, if $xyz = 0$ and $xy \neq 0$, then you have $z = 0$.
- When you're solving a system of equations, if one equation has variables x and y and another has x^2 and y^2, substituting (usually the preferred method for solving) can lead to very complicated equations. Instead of using substitution, begin by factoring the equations. Often, this produces an expression with x and y that matches part of the other equation and can make the problem easier to solve.

Practice

1. If $2a - 2b = 5$ and $a^2 - b^2 = 10$, what is the value of $a + b$?

   A. 4
   B. 5
   C. 10
   D. 20
   E. 100

2. If $4a - 5b = 20$ and $b = 4$, what is the value of $2b + 5a$?

   A. −42
   B. 0
   C. 8
   D. 30
   E. 58

3. If a, b, c, and d are positive integers and $a = 2b$, $b = 3c$, and $2a = cd$, what is the value of d?

   A. 1
   B. 3
   C. 6
   D. 12
   E. Cannot be determined

4. If $a > 0$, $c > 0$, and $a^2b = 9$ and $bc^2 = 25$, what is the value of abc?

   A. 15
   B. 25
   C. 45
   D. 75
   E. 225

5. At the beginning of the school year, Caitlin paid $22 for 4 pens and 3 notebooks. Two months later, she decided to buy 6 more of the same pens and 5 more of the same notebooks before the price changed. If she spent $35 on these additional pens and notebooks, what was the cost, in dollars, of one notebook?

6. If $a - b + c = 60$ and $3a + 2b + 3c = 240$, what is the value of $a + c$?

Answers

1. **A** Because one equation has a and b while the other has a^2 and b^2, begin by factoring. Since $(a - b)(a + b) = 10$ and $2(a - b) = 5$ or $(a - b) = \frac{5}{2}$, you know that $\frac{5}{2}(a + b) = 10$ or $(a + b) = 4$.

2. **E** Since $b = 4$ and $4a - 5b = 20$, you know that $4a - 5(4) = 20$ or $4a = 40$ or $a = 10$. Because $a = 10$ and $b = 4$, $2b + 5a = 2(4) + 5(10)$ or 58.

3. **D** Since you have to find the value of d, begin by working with the equation that has d as a variable, $2a = cd$. Solve $2a = cd$ for d, you have $d = \frac{2a}{c}$. If you knew the values of a and c, you could find the value of d. Since $b = 3c$, solving for c, you have $c = \frac{b}{3}$. Substituting

   $a = 2b$ and $c = \frac{b}{3}$ in $d = \frac{2a}{c}$, you have $d = \frac{2(2b)}{\frac{b}{3}} = (4b)\left(\frac{3}{b}\right) = 12$.

   Another approach is to begin with $a = 2b$ and substitute $3c$ for b and obtain $a = 6c$. Then the equation $2a = cd$ becomes $2(6c) = cd$, which gives $12c = cd$ and then you get $d = 12$.

4. A When you multiply the equations $a^2b = 9$ and $bc^2 = 25$, you have $(a^2b)(bc^2) = (9)(25)$ or $a^2b^2c^2 = 225$ and $abc = \pm15$. Because $a > 0$ and $c > 0$ and $a^2b > 0$, you know that $b > 0$. Thus, $abc = 15$.

5. 4 Let p be the price of a pen and n be the price of a notebook, then $4p + 3n = 22$ and $6p + 5n = 35$. To solve for n, multiply the first equation by -3 and the second by 2 to find that $-12p - 9n = -66$. Add $12p + 10n = 70$, and you get $n = 4$. The number of dollars that one notebook cost was 4.

6. 72 Since you're trying to find an expression that involves a and c, try to eliminate b from the system. This can be accomplished if you multiply $a - b + c = 60$ by 2 and then add the equations as follows:

$$2a - 2b + 2c = 120$$
$$\underline{3a + 2b + 3c = 240}$$
$$5a \qquad + 5c = 360$$

Since $5a + 5c = 360$, dividing both sides of the equation by 5, you have $a + c$ is 72.

F. Exponents

If a and b are integers:

- $(x^a)(x^b) = x^{a+b}$. For example, $(x^3)(x^4) = x^7$.
- $\dfrac{x^a}{x^b} = x^{a-b}$. For example, $\dfrac{x^{10}}{x^4} = x^6$.
- $(ax^b)^n = a^n(x^{bn})$. For example, $(2x^5)^3 = (2)^3(x^5)^3 = 8x^{15}$.
- $x^0 = 1$, $x \neq 0$. For example, $(-4)^0 = 1$ but $-4^0 = -1$.
- $x^{-n} = \dfrac{1}{x^n}$, $x \neq 0$. For example, $3^{-2} = \dfrac{1}{3^2}$.
- $x^{\frac{a}{b}} = \left(\sqrt[b]{x}\right)^a$ or $\sqrt[b]{x^a}$, if $\sqrt[b]{x}$ exists. For example, $8^{\frac{2}{3}} = \left(\sqrt[3]{8}\right)^2$ or $\sqrt[3]{8^2} = 4$.

When you're solving questions involving exponents, keep these tips in mind:

- Remember that the base does not change when you're multiplying powers of the same base or raising a power to a power—for example, $(7^3)(7^2) = (7)^5$ and $(7^3)^2 = 7^6$.

- When you're trying to find the value of an exponent in an equation, one way to solve the problem is to try to express each side of the equation as a single power. If the base of the power is the same on both sides of the equation, set the exponents equal.

Practice

1. If $3^n + 3^n + 3^n = 9^6$, what is the value of n?

   A. 2
   B. 3
   C. 4
   D. 11
   E. 12

2. If $(2x^2)^3 = 8x^n$ for all values of x, what is the value of n?

   A. 3
   B. 4
   C. 5
   D. 6
   E. 7

3. If $a > 2$ and $a^5 = p$ and $a^3 = q$, which of the following is equivalent to a^{-7}?

   A. $2p - q$

   B. $q^2 + 1$

   C. $q^2 - 1$

   D. $\dfrac{p^2}{q}$

   E. $\dfrac{q}{p^2}$

4. If $5^4(5^a) = 5^{20}$, what is the value of a?

   A. 5

   B. 6

   C. 10

   D. 16

   E. 80

5. If $n^a = 5$ and $n^b = 25$, what is the value of $n^{2a + b}$?

6. If x is a positive integer, $x^a = \dfrac{x^4}{x^b}$ and $x^a = x^2(x^b)$, what is the value of b?

Answers

1. **D** Since you're trying to find an exponent, express each side as a power with the same base and then set the exponents equal. Since $3^n + 3^n + 3^n = 3(3^n) = (3^1)(3^n) = 3^{n+1}$ and since $9^6 = (3^2)^6 = 3^{12}$, you know that $3^{n+1} = 3^{12}$ and $n + 1 = 12$ or $n = 11$.

2. **D** Since you're trying to find an exponent, express each side as a power with the same base and set the exponents equal. Since $(2x^2)^3 = 2^3(x^2)^3 = 8x^6$ and $(2x^2)^3 = 8x^n$, you know that $8x^6 = 8x^n$ or $n = 6$.

3. **E** Substitute a^5 for p and a^3 for q in each expression and examine the results:

- Choice A: $2a^5 - a^3$
- Choice B: $(a^3)^2 + 1 = a^6 + 1$
- Choice C: $(a^3)^2 - 1 = a^6 - 1$
- Choice D: $\dfrac{\left(a^5\right)^2}{a^3} = a^7$
- Choice E: $\dfrac{a^3}{\left(a^5\right)^2} = \dfrac{a^3}{a^{10}} = a^{-7}$

Then a^{-7} is equivalent to Choice E $\dfrac{q}{p^2}$. Another way to solve this problem is as follows: Since $a^5 = p$ and $a^3 = q$, you have $\dfrac{a^5}{a^3} = a^2 = \dfrac{p}{q}$. Then $a^7 = a^5\left(a^2\right) = (p)\,\dfrac{p}{q} = \dfrac{p^2}{q}$. Thus, $a^{-7} = \dfrac{1}{a^7} = \dfrac{1}{\dfrac{p^2}{q}} = \dfrac{q}{p^2}$.

4. **D** You're trying to find an exponent, so express each side as a power with the same base and set the exponents equal. Since $5^4(5^a) = 5^{4+a}$ and $5^4(5^a) = 5^{20}$, you know that $5^{4+a} = 5^{20}$ and $4 + a = 20$ or $a = 16$.

5. **625** Since $n^{2a+b} = n^{2a}(n^b) = (n^a)^2(n^b)$ and $n^a = 5$ and $n^b = 25$, you know that $n^{2a} = (5)^2 = (25)$. The value of n^{2a+b} is $(25)(25) = 625$.

6. **b = 1** You're trying to find an exponent, so express each side as a power with the same base and set the exponents equal. Since $x^a = \dfrac{x^4}{x^b}$ and $\dfrac{x^4}{x^b} = x^{4-b}$, you know that $x^a = x^{4-b}$ and $a = 4 - b$. Since $x^a = x^2(x^b)$ and $x^2(x^b) = x^{2+b}$, you know that $x^a = x^{2+b}$ and $a = 2 + b$. Solving the system $a = 4 - b$ and $a = 2 + b$, you have $4 - b = 2 + b$, or $b = 1$.

G. Direct and Inverse Variation

On the SAT, you'll be tested on direct and inverse variation. Here are the key rules to remember:

- When two quantities x and y are directly proportional, then:
  - $y = kx$ or $\dfrac{y}{x} = k$, $x \neq 0$, for some constant k, with $k \neq 0$.
  - As x increases, y increases, for $k > 0$.
  - The graph is a line whose slope is k and the y-intercept is 0.
  - If (x_1, y_1) and (x_2, y_2) are points on the graph, then $\dfrac{x_1}{y_1} = \dfrac{x_2}{y_2}$.
- When two quantities x and y are inversely proportional, then:
  - $y = \dfrac{k}{x}$ or $xy = k$ for some constant k, with $k \neq 0$.
  - As x increases, y decreases, for $k > 0$.
  - The graph is a hyperbola.
  - If (x_1, y_1) and (x_2, y_2) are points on the graph, then $(x_1)(y_1) = (x_2)(y_2)$.

Practice

1. If m and n are inversely proportional and $n = 6$ when $m = 4$, what is the value of m when $n = 12$?

   A. −2
   B. 2
   C. 8
   D. 14
   E. 18

2. If $y = f(x)$ and y is directly proportional to x, which of the following could be the graph of $f(x)$?

   A.
   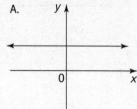

   B.
   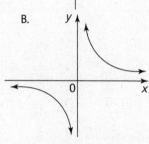

   C.
   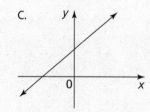

   D.
   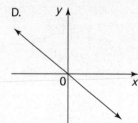

   E.
   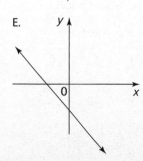

3. Some of the values of p and q are shown in the accompanying table. If p is directly proportional to q, what is the value of k?

p	4	6	10
q	6	k	15

   A. 6
   B. 8
   C. 9
   D. 10
   E. 12

4. Given a function $y = f(x)$ such that y is inversely proportional to x, which of the following could be $f(x)$?

A.

x	y
2	4
3	6
4	8

B.

x	y
3	5
5	7
7	9

C.

x	y
−1	2
1	2
3	2

D.

x	y
5	0
5	2
5	4

E.

x	y
1	16
2	8
4	4

5. In the equation $xy = c$, c is a constant. If $x = 4$ when $y = 12$, what is the value of x when $y = 6$?

6. In a printing company, if one machine can print 600 copies in 12 hours, how long would it take to print 1,200 copies with three identical machines working together?

Answers

1. B Since *inversely proportional* means that the product is always the same, solve $(12)(m) = (4)(6)$ to find that $24 = 12m$ and $m = 2$.

2. D Since y is directly proportional to x, you know that $y = kx$ for some constant k, and k is the slope of the line. In Choice D, the line crosses the origin, which implies that the y-intercept is 0. Using slope-intercept form $y = mx + b$ for the graph in Choice D, you have $b = 0$ and $y = mx$, which implies that y is directly proportional to x. Thus, the graph in Choice D could be the graph of $f(x)$.

3. C Since p is directly proportional to q, the ratio of p to q is a constant. You have $\frac{4}{6} = \frac{6}{k}$ or $\frac{6}{k} = \frac{10}{15}$. In either case, solve for k and you have $k = 9$.

4. E Since y is inversely proportional to x, $xy =$ constant. Of the given choices, the only table of values where the product of x and y is a constant is Choice E. Note that $(1)(16) = (2)(8) = (4)(4) = 16$. Therefore, of the given choices, Choice E is the only possible table of values for $f(x)$.

5. 8 Since $xy = c$, you know that x and y are inversely proportional. Therefore $(6)(x) = (4)(12)$ or $x = 8$.

6. 8 hours Since it takes 12 hours for one machine to print 600 copies, it would take 24 hours for one machine to print 1,200 copies. If three machines worked together to print 1,200 copies, it would take $\frac{24}{3} = 8$ hours.

You could also use an inverse proportion. The more machines you use, the less time it would require to print 1,200 copies.

Number of Machines	Hours	Number of Copies
1	24	1,200
3	x	1,200

Since the number of copies is the same, you have $(1)(24) = (3)(x)$ or $x = 8$ hours.

H. Functions

On the SAT, you're expected to answer questions involving functions and their graphs. Here are some important rules to keep in mind:

- If $y = f(g(x))$, then y is a composition of f and g. Evaluating $y = f(g(x))$ for a given value of x requires first substituting x in $g(x)$ and then substituting the answer for $g(x)$ in f. The order of substitution may not be reversed, since composition may not be commutative.
- Since the graph of a function is a picture of the ordered pairs that satisfy the equation, you can find values of the function by reading the graph. The accompanying figure is a typical graph that you may encounter.

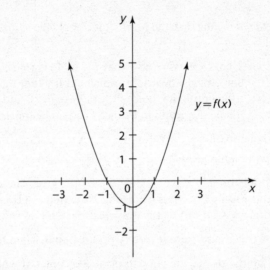

- If you need to find a function value, such as $f(2)$, from the graph, find the y-coordinate of the point on the graph where $x = 2$. In the accompanying figure, this is the point $(2,3)$. Since $y = 3$ when $x = 2$, using function notation, you would say $f(2) = 3$.
- If $f(b) = 3$ and you need to find the value of b, find the point(s) with y-coordinate 3. Remember that b is the x-coordinate when the y-coordinate is 3. Since there are two points, $(2,3)$ and $(-2,3)$, $b = \pm 2$.
- Many of the problems involving functions can be solved by using a graphing calculator (see the appendix).

Practice

1. If the function f is defined by $f(x) = 2x - 6$, which of the following is equivalent to $5f(x) + 10$?

   A. $10x - 40$
   B. $10x - 20$
   C. $10x + 4$
   D. $10x + 20$
   E. $7x + 4$

2. The life expectancy of a certain virus is given by the function $L(t) = \dfrac{12t + 36}{t + 1}$, $t \leq 120$, where t is the temperature, in Celsius, of the environment in which the virus is placed and L is the number of minutes that the virus will survive in that environment. What is the change in life expectancy, in minutes, if the temperature is raised from 7°C to 23°C?

   A. -16
   B. -2
   C. 15
   D. 16
   E. 30

3. Some of the values of the function f are shown in the accompanying table. If a function h is defined by $h(x) = 2f(x - 1)$, what is the value of $h(2)$?

x	f(x)
−3	−1
−2	0
−1	4
0	2
1	−3
2	4
3	5

   A. -6
   B. -3
   C. 4
   D. 5
   E. 7

4.

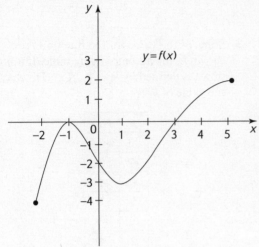

The graph of $y = f(x)$ for $-2 \le x \le 5$ is shown in the accompanying diagram. If $k < 0$ and $f(k) = 0$, what is the value of k?

A. -4

B. -2

C. -1

D. 0

E. 3

5.

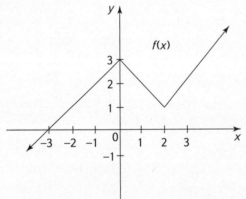

The graph of the function f is shown in the accompanying diagram. If the function h is defined by $h(x) = 3f(x - 1) + 1$, what is the value of $h(3)$?

6.

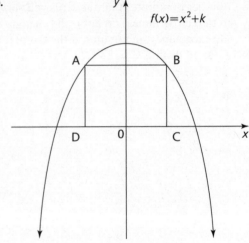

Not drawn to scale.

In the accompanying diagram, $ABCD$ is a rectangle with vertices A and B on the parabola, $f(x) = x^2 + k$, $k > 0$. If $AB = 4$ and the area of rectangle $ABCD$ is 32, what is the value of k?

Answers

1. **B** Since $f(x) = 2x - 6$, you have $5f(x) + 10 = 5(2x - 6) + 10$, which is equivalent to $10x - 20$.

2. **B** At 7°C, the life expectancy of the virus is $L(7) = \dfrac{12(7) + 36}{7 + 1} = \dfrac{120}{8} = 15$ minutes, and at 23°C is $L(23) = \dfrac{12(23) + 36}{23 + 1} = \dfrac{312}{24} = 13$ minutes. Therefore, the change in life expectancy is $13 - 15 = -2$ minutes.

3. **A** Since $h(x) = 2f(x - 1)$, $h(2) = 2f(2 - 1)$ or $h(2) = 2f(1)$. The table shows that $f(1) = -3$. Thus, $2f(1) = 2(-3)$ or -6.

4. **C** Since $f(k) = 0$ implies that k is a root of $f(x)$. The roots of $f(x)$ are the x-intercepts of the graph of $f(x)$. In this case, the x-intercepts are -1 and 3. Since $k < 0$, $k = -1$.

5. **4** Substituting $x = 3$, in $h(x) = 3f(x - 1) + 1$, you have $h(3) = 3f(2) + 1$. The graph of $f(x)$ shows that $f(2) = 1$. Therefore, $h(3) = 3(1) + 1 = 4$.

6. **4** You need to first find the coordinates of point B and then substitute to find k. Since $AB = 4$ and the graph of $f(x) = x^2 + k$ is symmetric with respect to the y-axis, the coordinates of B are $(2,y)$ and the coordinates A are $(-2,y)$. Because $AB = 4$ and the area of rectangle $ABCD = (AB)(BC) = 32$, you know that $4(BC) = 32$ or $BC = 8$ and the coordinates of point B are $(2,8)$. Since B is a point on the graph of $f(x) = x^2 + k$, substitute $(2,8)$ in $f(x) = x^2 + k$ to find that $8 = (2)^2 + k$ or $k = 4$.

XII. Geometry

A. Measurement of Angles and Line Segments

On the SAT, you'll be tested on angles and line segments. Here are the key rules to keep in mind:

- The sum of the measures of the three interior angles of a triangle is 180°.
- The measure of an exterior angle of a triangle is equal to the sum of the measures of the two nonadjacent interior angles.

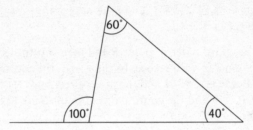

- The measure of an exterior angle of a regular polygon with n sides is $\frac{360}{n}$.

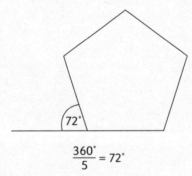

$$\frac{360°}{5} = 72°$$

- If two parallel lines are cut by a transversal, then the alternate interior angles are congruent.

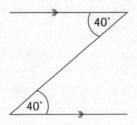

- If two parallel lines are cut by a transversal, then the corresponding angles are congruent.

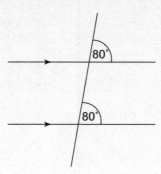

- If two lines intersect, then the vertical angles are congruent.

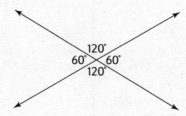

- The midpoint of a line segment divides the line segment into two congruent line segments.

Practice

1. The measure of the vertex angle of an isosceles triangle is 40°. What is the measure of a base angle of the triangle?

   A. 40°
   B. 60°
   C. 70°
   D. 80°
   E. 90°

2. Line *l* intersects $\overline{AB}$ and $\overline{BC}$ at D and E, respectively. What is the value of x?

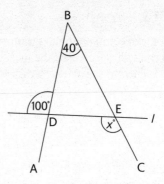

   A. 60
   B. 80
   C. 100
   D. 120
   E. 140

3. In the accompanying diagram, *ABCD* is a parallelogram. What is the value of *x*?

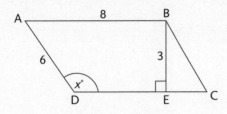

Not drawn to scale

   A.   60

   B.   80

   C.   100

   D.   120

   E.   150

4. Points *A*, *B*, *C*, and *D* lie on a line in that order. If *C* is the midpoint of $\overline{BD}$, $CD = 2AB$ and $AD = 60$, what is the length of $\overline{AC}$?

   A.   12

   B.   24

   C.   36

   D.   40

   E.   48

5. Points *A*, *B*, *C*, *D*, and *E* lie in that order on line *l*. *B* is the midpoint of $\overline{AC}$ and *D* is the midpoint of $\overline{CE}$. If $AB = 3DE$ and $BD = 60$, what is the length of $\overline{BE}$?

6. In the accompanying diagram, line *l* is parallel to line *m*. If $m\angle y = 100°$, what is the value of $m\angle x + m\angle y$?

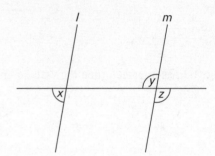

Answers

1. **C**   In the accompanying diagram, *x* represents the measure of one of the base angles. Because the given triangle is isosceles, the measures of base angles are equal. The sum of the measures of a triangle is 180°. Therefore, we have $x + x + 40 = 180$ or $2x = 140$. Thus $x = 70°$.

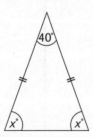

2. **D**   Since $m\angle BDE + 100° = 180°$, $m\angle BDE = 80°$. We know that the sum of the measures of the three angles of a triangle is 180°. Therefore, $80 + 40 + m\angle BED = 180$ or $m\angle BED = 60°$. Since $m\angle BED + x = 180$, we have $60 + x = 180$, or $x = 120°$.

3. E Opposite sides of a parallelogram are congruent; therefore $BC = 6$. In the right triangle $\triangle BEC$, BE = 3 and $BC = 6$. Note that $\overline{BC}$ is the hypotenuse and $\overline{BE}$ is a leg. Because the length of the hypotenuse is twice the length of a leg, $\triangle BEC$ is a 30°-60° right triangle. (This information is provided in the reference information at the beginning of every math section in the SAT.) Thus the $m\angle C = 30$. Also, in parallelogram $ABCD$, $\angle D$, and $\angle C$ are supplementary. Therefore, $m\angle D = 150$.

4. C Let $AB = x$. Since $CD + 2AB$, you have $CD = 2x$. Also, C is the midpoint of $\overline{BD}$; therefore, $BC = CD = 2x$. Since $AD = 60$, you have $x + 2x + 2x = 60$ or $5x = 60$, which leads to $x = 12$. The length of $\overline{AC}$ is $3x$ or $3(12) = 36$.

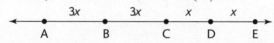

5. 75 Let $DE = x$, then $AB = 3(DE) = 3x$. Since B is the midpoint of AC, $AB = BC = 3x$, and since D is the midpoint of $\overline{CE}$, $CD = DE = x$. Since $BD = 60$ and $BD = BC + CD$, $3x + x + 60$ or $4x = 60$ or $x = 15$. Since $BE = BC + CD + DE$, $BE = 3x + x + x = 5x = 5(15) = 75$.

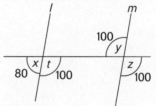

6. 180 Since $m\angle y = 100$ and also $\angle y$ and $\angle z$ are vertical angles, $m\angle y = m\angle z = 100$. Since $\angle z$ and $\angle t$ are corresponding angles, $m\angle z = m\angle t = 100$. Because $\angle x$ and $\angle t$ are supplementary, $m\angle x = 180 - 100 = 80$. Thus, $m\angle x + m\angle z = 180°$.

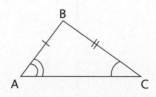

B. Properties of Triangles

Some of the questions on the SAT require you to apply the properties of triangles. Here are some of the important properties to remember:

- **The Triangle Inequality:** $a + b > c$

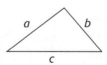

  The sum of the lengths of any two sides of a triangle is always greater than the length of the third side.
- **If the lengths of two sides of a triangle are unequal, the measures of the angles opposite these sides are unequal and the greater angle lies opposite the greater side.** Example: $BC > BA \Leftrightarrow m\angle A > m\angle C$.

- The shortest distance between a vertex of a triangle to the opposite side is the length of the altitude from the same vertex to the opposite side (perpendicular to the opposite side).

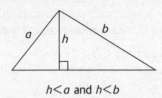

$$h < a \text{ and } h < b$$

The following information is given in the reference information box at the beginning of every math section in the SAT:

- **The Pythagorean theorem:** $a^2 + b^2 = c^2$

- **Special right triangle:** 30°-60° right triangle.

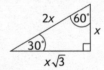

- **Special right triangle:** 45°-45° right triangle.

Practice

1. Starting from home, Mary drove 5 miles due east to Bill's house. She then drove 6 miles due south to Karen's house. Mary then drove 3 miles due east to Janet's house. What is the distance, in miles, between Mary's house and Janet's house?

   A. 4
   B. 8
   C. 10
   D. 14
   E. 16

2. In $\triangle DEF$, $DE = 6$ and $DF = 10$. What is the smallest possible integer length of side $\overline{EF}$?

   A. 4
   B. 5
   C. 6
   D. 15
   E. 16

3. In the accompanying diagram, *DEFG* is a parallelogram. What is the length of $\overline{GH}$?

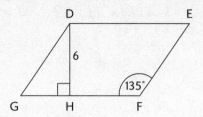

Not drawn to scale

A. 4
B. 6
C. 8
D. 10
E. 12

4. In the accompanying diagram, *a*, *b*, and *c* are the lengths of the three sides of the triangle. Which of the following must be true?

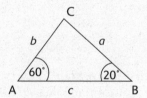

Not drawn to scale

A. $a > b > c$
B. $b > a > c$
C. $c > b > a$
D. $a > c > b$
E. $c > a > b$

5. Given three points *A*, *B*, and *C*, if the distance between *A* and *B* is 5, and the distance between *B* and *C* is 12, what is the shortest possible distance between *A* and *C*?

6. In the accompanying diagram, $\overline{BDC}$, $AD = 6$, and $DC = 8$. What is the smallest possible integer length of $\overline{AB}$?

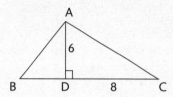

Answers

1. **C** In the accompanying diagram of Mary's trip, if you extend $\overline{MB}$ to A and draw $\overline{AJ}$, $\triangle MAJ$ is a right triangle and quadrilateral $BAJK$ is a rectangle with $BA = KJ = 3$ and $KJ = BA = 3$. $BK = AJ = 6$. Because $AM = 8$, $(AM)^2 + (AJ)^2 = (MJ)^2$ or $8^2 + 6^2 = (MJ)^2$ and $MJ = 10$.

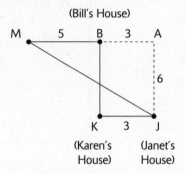

(Bill's House)

M   5   B   3   A

6

K   3   J

(Karen's   (Janet's
House)   House)

2. **B** Because you're looking for the smallest possible length of $\overline{EF}$, assume that $\overline{EF}$ is not the longest side of $\triangle DEF$. Applying the triangle inequality, you have $DE + EF > DF$ or $6 + \overline{EF} > 10$, which is equivalent to $EF > 4$. Because EF is an integer, the smallest possible value for EF is 5.

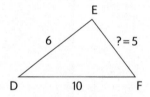

E

6   ? = 5

D   10   F

3. **B** Because $DEFG$ is a parallelogram, $m\angle G + m\angle F = 180$, which means $m\angle G + 135 = 180$ or $m\angle G = 45$. In the right triangle DGH, $m\angle G = 45$ implies that $m\angle GDH$ is also 45, and thus $\triangle DGH$ is isosceles. Therefore, $GH = DH$ or $GH = 6$.

4. **E** Because the sum of the measures of the three angles of a triangle is 180, $m\angle c = 180 - 60 - 20 = 100$. In a triangle, the longest side is always opposite the biggest angle. Thus, $c > a > b$.

5. **7** Points A, B, and C either form a triangle or they lie on the same line. If A, B, and C form a triangle, then $7 < AC < 17$ because the lengths of any two sides of the triangle must be greater than the third. If the points are collinear, then the shortest distance occurs when A is between B and C. Thus $AC = 12 - 5 = 7$.

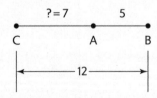

? = 7   5

C   A   B

12

6. **7** The shortest line segment connecting a point and a line is the perpendicular line. In this case, the shortest distance from A to $\overline{BC}$ is 6. Therefore, $AB > AD$ or $AB > 6$ and the smallest integer value for $\overline{AB}$ is 7. Note that $DC = 8$ is not relevant to the question.

C. Similarity

If two triangles are similar, then:

- Corresponding angles have the same measure.
- The lengths of any two corresponding line segments (including sides, altitudes, medians, and angle bisectors) have the same ratio.
- The ratio of the *perimeters* is equal to the ratio of the lengths of any pair of corresponding line segments.
- The ratio of the *areas* is equal to the square of the ratio of the lengths of any pair of corresponding line segments.

Practice

1. Kaela is 5 feet 6 inches tall and casts a shadow that is 11 feet long. If Dan is standing behind Kaela and he is 6 feet tall, how long is his shadow?

   A. 10 ft.
   B. 11 ft.
   C. 11 ft. 6 in.
   D. 12 ft.
   E. 12 ft. 6 in.

2. In the accompanying diagram, $\overline{DE} \parallel \overline{BC}$. If $AE = 2$, $EC = 4$, and $BC = 12$, find the length of DE.

   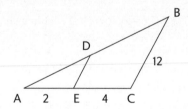

   Not drawn to scale

   A. 2
   B. 4
   C. 6
   D. 8
   E. 9

3. In the accompanying diagram, $\overline{AB} \parallel \overline{CD}$ and $\overline{AD}$ intersects $\overline{BC}$ at E. If $AB = 6$, $CD = 9$, and $BC = 30$, what is the length of $\overline{BE}$?

   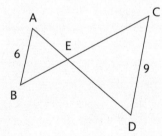

   A. 6
   B. 9
   C. 12
   D. 15
   E. 18

4. $\triangle LMN$ is similar to $\triangle PQT$. The area of $\triangle LMN$ is 16, and the length of its shortest side is 2. If the area of $\triangle PQT$ is 36, what is the length of its shortest side?

   A. 3
   B. 4.5
   C. 6
   D. 9
   E. 22

5. If $\triangle ABC$ is similar to $\triangle DEF$ and $\triangle ABC$ has a perimeter of 18cm and a longest side of 8cm, what is the perimeter of $\triangle DEF$ if $\triangle DEF$ has a the longest side of 6cm?

6. In the accompanying diagram, $\overline{DE}$ is perpendicular to $\overline{AC}$ and $\overline{BC}$ is perpendicular to $\overline{AC}$. If $AE = 3$, $EC = 3$, and $DE = 4$, what is the perimeter of $\triangle ABC$?

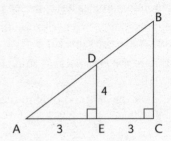

Answers

1. D

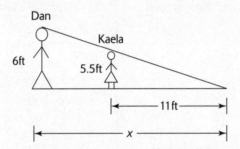

Since each triangle has a right angle and the triangles share an angle, they are similar. As long as all numbers are expressed in the same units with Kaela's height 5.5 feet instead of 5 feet 6 inches, Dan's height can be found using the equation

$$\frac{\text{Kaela's height}}{\text{length of Kaela's shadow}} = \frac{\text{Dan's height}}{\text{length of Dan's shadow}} \text{ or } \frac{5.5}{11} = \frac{6}{x} \text{ or } 5.5x = 66 \text{ or } x = 12.$$ Dan's shadow is 12 feet long.

2. B Because $DE \parallel BC$, congruent corresponding angles are formed with $\angle DEA \cong \angle BCA$ and $\triangle ADE \sim \triangle ABC$. Because the triangles are similar, their corresponding sides are in proportion and $\frac{DE}{BC} = \frac{AE}{AC}$. Notice that $EC = 4$ may not be used in this proportion because EC is not a side of either triangle. To find DE, solve $\frac{DE}{BC} = \frac{AE}{AC}$ or $\frac{DE}{12} = \frac{2}{6}$ or $DE = 4$.

3. C Because $AB \parallel CD$, pairs of congruent alternate interior angles are formed, $\angle B \cong \angle C$ and $\angle A \cong \angle D$, and so $\triangle ABE \sim \triangle DCE$. Because the triangles are similar, corresponding sides in proportion and $\frac{BE}{AB} = \frac{EC}{DC}$. To find BE, use x as the length BE and $(30 - x)$ as the length of $\overline{CE}$ and $\frac{x}{6} = \frac{30-x}{9}$ or $9x = 6(30 - x)$ or $9x = 180 - 6x$ or $x = 12$.

4. **A** Because $\triangle LMN \sim \triangle PQT$, the ratio of the areas is equal to the square of the ratio of any corresponding sides. Because the two shortest sides are a pair of corresponding sides, $\frac{16}{36} = \left(\frac{2}{x}\right)^2$ or $\frac{4}{9} = \frac{4}{x^2}$ or $4x^2 = 36$ or $x = \pm 3$. Because x must be positive, $x = 3$. The length of the shortest side of $\triangle PQT$ is 3.

5. **13.5** Because $ABC \sim DEF$ the ratio of their perimeters is equal to the ratio of a pair of corresponding sides. Since the two longest sides are a pair of corresponding sides, $\frac{18}{8} = \frac{p}{6}$ or $8p = 6(18)$ or $p = 13.5$.

6. **24** Because perpendicular lines form right angles, $\triangle ABC$ and $\triangle ADE$ are right triangles. Also, because both triangles contain $\angle A$, $\triangle ABC \sim \triangle ADE$. The ratio of their perimeters is the same as the ratio of their corresponding sides. Thus, $\frac{\text{perimeter } ABC}{\text{perimeter } ADE} = \frac{AC}{AE}$. Because $\triangle ADE$ is a right triangle with $AE = 3$ and $DE = 4$, using the Pythagorean theorem, $3^2 + 4^2 = (AD)^2$, you have $AD = 5$. The perimeter of $\triangle ADE = 3 + 4 + 5 = 12$ and $\frac{\text{perimeter } ABC}{\text{perimeter } ADE} = \frac{AC}{AE}$ becomes $\frac{\text{perimeter } ABC}{12} = \frac{6}{3}$ or perimeter $ABC = \frac{72}{3} = 24$.

D. Areas and Perimeters

On the SAT, perimeter and area problems are common questions. Here are the important formulas to keep in mind. Some of these formulas also appear in the reference information section at the beginning of each math section.

		Perimeter	Area
Triangle		$a + b + c$	$\frac{1}{2}bh$
Equilateral triangle		$3s$	$\frac{s^2\sqrt{3}}{4}$
Rectangle		$2(l + w)$	lw
Square		$4s$	s^2 or $\frac{d^2}{2}$

continued

		Perimeter	Area
Parallelogram		$2(a + b)$	bh
Trapezoid		$a + b + c + d$	$\frac{1}{2}h(a+b)$

Practice

1. If the area of a rectangle is 32 and the length and width of the rectangle are integers, what is the smallest possible perimeter of the rectangle?

    A. 12
    B. 24
    C. 36
    D. 64
    E. 66

2. In the accompanying diagram $ABCD$, is an isosceles trapezoid with $\overline{AB} \parallel \overline{DC}$. If $AB = 8$, $DC = 16$, and altitude $\overline{AE}$ has length 3, what is the perimeter of trapezoid $ABCD$?

    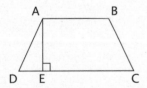

    Not drawn to scale

    A. 29
    B. 34
    C. 40
    D. 42
    E. 44

3. The area of an equilateral triangle is $9\sqrt{3}$. What is its perimeter?

    A. 6
    B. 12
    C. 18
    D. 24
    E. 36

4. If two sides of a triangle measure 6 and 8, what is the largest possible area for the triangle?

    A. 7
    B. 24
    C. 32
    D. 48
    E. 64

5. In the accompanying diagram, *ABCD* is a rectangle with side *AB* containing points *E* and *F* and *AE* = *EF* = *FB*. If the area of △*ADF* is 12, what is the area of quadrilateral *FBCD*?

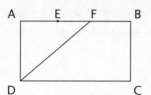

6. In the accompanying diagram, *ABCD* and *CEFG* are squares. If *DE* = 2 and *DC* = 4, what is the area of the entire figure?

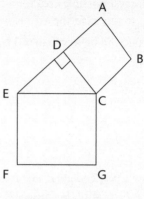

Not drawn to scale.

Answers

1. B To find the smallest perimeter, find the possible values for the length and width and calculate the perimeter. The possibilities are listed in the following table:

Area	Length	Width	Perimeter
32	1	32	66
32	2	16	36
32	4	8	24
32	8	4	24
32	16	2	36
32	32	1	66

Thus, the smallest possible perimeter of the rectangle is 24.

2. B To find the perimeter of trapezoid *ABCD* you need to know the length of *AD*. Because *AD* is also a side in right △*ADE*, $AD^2 = AE^2 + DE^2$. To find *DE*, draw an altitude from *B* intersecting $\overline{DC}$ at *F*. Because the trapezoid is isosceles, *DE* = *FC*, and because *EF* = 8 and *DE* + *EF* + *FC* = 16, the length of $\overline{DE}$ is 4, and $(AD)^2 = 3^2 + 4^2$ and *AD* = 5. Since the legs of an isosceles trapezoid are congruent, the perimeter of *ABCD* = 5 + 8 + 5 + 16 = 34.

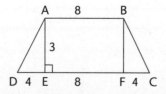

3. **C** The area of the equilateral triangle is $9\sqrt{3}$ and $A = \dfrac{s^2\sqrt{3}}{4}$, so $\dfrac{s^2\sqrt{3}}{4} = 9$. or $s^2 = 4(9)$ or $s = \pm 6$. Because s is the length of a side, $s = 6$, and the perimeter is $3(6) = 18$.

4. **B** The largest possible area for a triangle with two sides measuring 6 and 8 is the area of a right triangle. In this case, the area is $\dfrac{1}{2}(6)(8) = 24$. Notice that if the two sides 6 and 8 are not perpendicular, the altitude will be less than 6. Therefore, the area of the triangle would be less than 24.

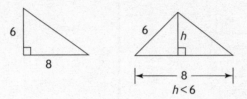

5. **24** Draw a perpendicular line from F to $\overline{DC}$ at point G. Note that the area of $\triangle AFD$ equals the area of $\triangle FDG = 12$. Because $AE = EF = FB$, we have $FB = \dfrac{1}{2}AF$. The area of rectangle $FBCG = \dfrac{1}{2}(\text{area of rectangle } AFGD)$, and the area of rectangle $AFGD$ is $12 + 12 = 24$. Therefore, the area of quadrilateral $FBCD$ is $12 + \dfrac{1}{2}(24) = 24$.

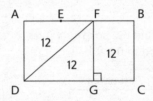

6. **40** To find the total area of the figure, you must find the area of each square, the area of the triangle, and the sum of these areas. The area of square $ABCD = s2 = 4^2 = 16$. The area of the right $DEC = \dfrac{1}{2}(DE)(DC) = \dfrac{1}{2}(2)(4) = 4$. Because CE is a side in square $CEFG$ and also the hypotenuse in $\triangle DEC$, the length of CE can be found using $(CE)^2 = (DE)2 + (DC)^2$ or $(CE)^2 = (2)^2 + (4)^2$ or $CE = \pm\sqrt{20}$ or $CE = \sqrt{20}$, and the area of square $CEFG = s2 = \left(\sqrt{20}\right)^2 = 20$. The area of the entire figure is $16 + 4 + 20 = 40$.

E. Solids, Volumes, and Surface Areas

On the SAT, some questions require you to find the volume and surface areas of solids. Here are the important formulas to keep in mind. Some of these formulas also appear in the reference information section at the beginning of each math section.

		Volume	Surface Area
Cube		s^3	$6s^2$

		Volume	Surface Area
Rectangular box		lwh	$2(lh + hw + lw)$
Right Circular Cylinder		$\pi r^2 h$	Total surface area $2\pi r^2 + 2\pi rh$ Lateral surface area $2\pi rh$
Sphere		$\frac{4}{3}\pi r^3$	$4\pi r^2$
Pyramids		$\frac{1}{3}(\text{base area})(\text{height})$	Base area + lateral surface areas
Right Circular Cone		$\frac{1}{3}\pi r^2 h$	Lateral: $\pi r\sqrt{r^2 + h^2}$ Total: $\pi r\sqrt{r^2 + h^2} + \pi r^2$ Usually not tested on the SAT.

Practice

1. If the length, width, and height of a rectangular box measure 1, 3, and 8, respectively, what is the total surface area of the box?

   A. 24
   B. 35
   C. 70
   D. 72
   E. 144

2. A red rectangular box has a volume of 12 cubic inches. If a blue rectangular box is made with each edge twice as large as the corresponding edge of the red box, what is the volume, in cubic inches, of the blue box?

   A. 24
   B. 36
   C. 48
   D. 72
   E. 96

3. If all faces of a pyramid (including the base) are equilateral triangles, and an edge of the pyramid measures 2cm, what is the total surface area, in cm², of the pyramid?

   A. 4
   B. $3\sqrt{3}$
   C. $4\sqrt{3}$
   D. 8
   E. 16

4. A sphere with a diameter measuring 3cm is inscribed in a cube. What is the length of a diagonal, in cm, of the cube?

   A. 3
   B. $3\sqrt{2}$
   C. $3\sqrt{3}$
   D. 6
   E. 27

5. A container in the shape of a cube is completely filled with water. An edge of the cube measures 12cm. A second container is in the shape of a rectangular box with length 8cm, width 12cm, and height 20cm. If all the water from the cubic container is emptied into the rectangular container, what is the height, in cm, of the water level in the rectangular container?

6. If the total surface area of a cube is 96, what is its volume?

Answers

1. **C** A rectangular box has six faces. The top and bottom faces both have surface areas (8)(3) = 24 for a total of 2(24) = 48. The front and back faces both have surface area (8)(1) = 8, for a total of 2(8) = 16. The left and right faces both have surface area (3)(1) = 3 for a total of 2(3) = 6. The surface area of the box is 48 + 16 + 6 = 70.

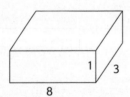

Not drawn to scale.

2. **E** Because the volume of the red box is *lwh* and the edges of the blue box are twice as large, the volume of the blue box is $(2l)(2w)(2h) = 8(lwh)$. The volume of the blue box is eight times the volume of the red box, so $8(12) = 96$.

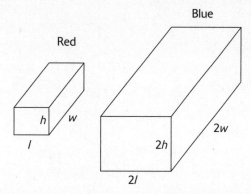

3. **C** Since *all* faces of the pyramid are congruent equilateral triangles, the total surface area of the pyramid is four times the area of one of the triangles. Each edge of the pyramid is also a side a triangle, and so the triangles are equilateral triangles with sides of length 2cm and the area of each triangle is $A = \dfrac{s^2\sqrt{3}}{4} = \dfrac{(2)^2\sqrt{3}}{4}$. The total surface area of the pyramid is $4\sqrt{3}\text{cm}^2$.

4. **C** Because the diameter of the sphere is 3cm, the length of each edge of the cube, including edges $\overline{AE}$, $\overline{EH}$, and $\overline{HG}$, is 3cm. To find a diagonal of the cube you must use the Pythagorean theorem twice— first to find EG and then to find AG. Because $\overline{EG}$ is a side in right $\triangle EHG$, $(EG)^2 = 3^2 + 3^2 = \sqrt{18}$. Since $\overline{AG}$ is a side in right $\triangle AEG$, $(AG)^2 = 3^2 + \left(\sqrt{18}\right)^2 = 9 + 18 = 27$ and $AG = \pm\sqrt{27} = \pm3\sqrt{3}$. The length of a diagonal is $3\sqrt{3}$ cm.

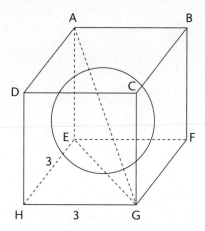

Not drawn to scale.

5. **18** Because the original container is completely filled, the volume of the water is $V = (12)^3$ cm^3 = 1,728 cm^3. When the water is poured into the second container, the volume of the water is the unchanged. Let x be the height of the water level in the rectangular box. Then $(8)(12)(x) = 1,728$ or $96x = 1,728$ or $x = 18$. The height of the water level is 18cm.

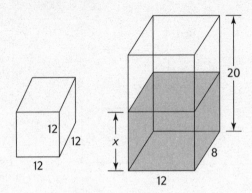

6. **64** To find the volume of the cube, you need to know the length of an edge. Because an edge of the cube is also a side, s, of the face of the cube and because the surface area is 96, s can be found using $6s^2 = 96$, $s^2 = 16$, and $s = \pm 4$. Because s is an edge, $s = 4$, the volume, $V = s^3 = 4^3 = 64$.

F. Properties of Circles

Given a circle O with radius r and diameter d:

- Circumference: $C = 2\pi r$ or $C = \pi d$
- Area: $A = \pi r^2$
- The length of an arc: $\dfrac{m\,\widehat{AB}}{2\pi r} = \dfrac{m\angle AOB}{360}$

- The area of a sector: $\dfrac{\text{area of sector } AOB}{\pi r^2} = \dfrac{m\angle AOB}{360}$

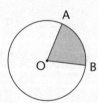

Practice

1. In the accompanying diagram, O is the center of the circle. If the area of sector AOB is 25π, what is the length of $\overset{\frown}{AB}$?

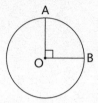

   A. 5
   B. 10
   C. $\dfrac{5\pi}{2}$
   D. 5π
   E. 10π

2. In the accompanying diagram, $\overline{AOB}$ and $\overline{COD}$ are diameters of the circle. If the length of $\overset{\frown}{AD}$ is 4π, what is the total area of the shaded regions?

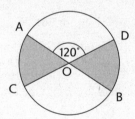

   A. 3π
   B. 6π
   C. 12π
   D. 24π
   E. 48π

3. In the accompanying diagram, a regular hexagon is inscribed in a circle. If $AB = 6$, what is the length of $\overset{\frown}{AB}$?

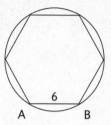

   A. 2
   B. π
   C. 2π
   D. 4π
   E. 6π

4. In the accompanying diagram, O is the center of the larger circle and $\overline{OA}$ and $\overline{OB}$ are diameters of the smaller circles. If the length of $\overline{AOB}$ is 12. What is the total area of the shaded regions?

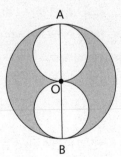

   A. 9π
   B. 18π
   C. 24π
   D. 27π
   E. 36π

5. In the accompanying diagram, O is the center of the circle and $\overline{AOB}$ is a diameter. If $\overline{BC} = 6$ and $m\angle B = 60$, what is the length of $\overparen{BC}$?

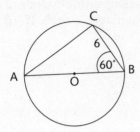

6. In the accompanying diagram, there are two concentric circles with center O. If $m\angle AOB = 60°$, $OD = 6$, $DB = 6$, and $\overline{ACO}$ and $\overline{BDO}$ are radii of the large circle, what is the area of the shaded region?

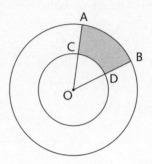

Answers

1. **D** First, find the radius of the circle. Use the proportion, $\dfrac{\text{area of sector } AOB}{\text{area of a circle}} = \dfrac{90}{360}$, which is equivalent to $\dfrac{25\pi}{\pi r^2} = \dfrac{1}{4}$ or $r^2 = 4(25)$. Thus, $r = 10$. Now use another proportion to find the length of $\overparen{AB}$, $\dfrac{\text{length of } \overparen{AB}}{\text{circumference of a circle}} = \dfrac{90}{360}$ or $\dfrac{\text{length of } \overparen{AB}}{2\pi(10)} = \dfrac{1}{4}$. Thus the length of $AB = 5\pi$.

2. **C** Begin by finding the area of the circle. To do that, you need to find the radius. Using the proportion, $\dfrac{\text{length of } \overparen{AD}}{2\pi r} = \dfrac{120}{360}$, you have $\dfrac{4\pi}{2\pi r} = \dfrac{1}{3}$ or $r = 6$. The area of the circle is πr^2 or 36π. Since $\overline{AOB}$ is a diameter, $m\angle DOB + 120 = 180$, and thus $m\angle DOB = 60$. Also, $\angle AOC$ and $\angle DOB$ are vertical angles, so $m\angle AOC = 60$. Now use a proportion to find the area of sector DOB: $\dfrac{\text{area of sector } DOB}{\text{area of a circle}} = \dfrac{60}{360}$. The proportion is equivalent to $\dfrac{\text{area of sector } DOB}{36\pi} = \dfrac{1}{6}$ or area of sector $DOB = 6\pi$, and the total area of the shaded regions is $2(6\pi)$ or 12π.

3. **C** A regular hexagon is both equilateral and equiangular. Therefore, $m\angle AOB = 60$. Also, $\overline{AO}$ and $\overline{BO}$ are radii and thus $m\angle OAB = m\angle OBA = 60$, and $\triangle AOB$ is an equilateral triangle. To find the length of $\overparen{AB}$, we use the proportion $\dfrac{\text{length of } \overparen{AB}}{\text{circumference of circle}} = \dfrac{60}{360}$, which is equivalent to $\dfrac{\text{length of } \overparen{AB}}{2\pi6} = \dfrac{1}{6}$ or length of $AB = 2\pi$.

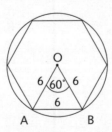

4. **B** Because $\overline{OA}$ and $\overline{OB}$ are radii of the larger circle and $\overline{AOB}$ is 12, we have $OA = OB = 6$. The area of the larger circle is $\pi(6)^2 = 36\pi$. The two smaller circles are congruent and the length of the radius, for both small circles is 3. The area of each small circle is $\pi(3)^2 = 9\pi$, and the total area of both small circles is 18π. Therefore, the area of the shaded regions is $36\pi - 18\pi = 18\pi$.

5. **2π** Diameter $\overline{AOB}$ divides the circle into two semicircles. Therefore, $\angle ACB$ is inscribed in a semicircle, which means $m\angle ACB = 90$. In $\triangle ABC$, $m\angle A = 30°$ and $\triangle ABC$ is a 30°-60° right triangle. In 30°-60° right triangle, the length of the hypotenuse is twice the length of the leg opposite the 30° angle. Thus, $AB = 2(6)$ or 12. (The relationship among the sides of a 30°-60° right triangle is given in the reference information at the beginning of each math section on the SAT.) The circumference of the circle is 12π. Because $\overset{\frown}{ACB}$ is a semicircle, its length is 6π. $\angle B$ and $\angle C$ are inscribed angles and $m\angle B = 2m\angle C$, so the length of $\overset{\frown}{AC} = $ twice the length of $\overset{\frown}{BC}$, and you have $2x + x = 6\pi$ or $x = 2\pi$. Thus, the length of BC is 2π.

6. **18π** The area of shaded region = the area of sector AOB – the area of sector COD. The radius of the small circle is 6, and its area is $\pi(6)^2 = 36\pi$. Using a proportion, $\dfrac{\text{area of sector } COD}{\text{area of small circle}} = \dfrac{60}{360}$, you have $\dfrac{\text{area of sector } COD}{36\pi} = \dfrac{1}{6}$ or the area of sector $COD = 6\pi$. The radius of the large circle is 12, and its area is $\pi(12)^2 = 144\pi$. Using a proportion, $\dfrac{\text{area of sector } AOB}{\text{area of small circle}} = \dfrac{60}{600}$, you have $\dfrac{\text{area of sector } AOB}{144\pi} = \dfrac{1}{6}$ or area of sector $AOB = 24\pi$. Therefore, the area of the shaded region is $24\pi - 6\pi = 18\pi$.

G. Coordinate Geometry

Given $A(x_1, y_1)$ and $B(x_2, y_2)$:

- The midpoint of $\overline{AB}$: $\left(\dfrac{x_1 + x_2}{2}, \dfrac{y_1 + y_2}{2}\right)$. Think of a midpoint as the "average."
- The distance between A and B (the length of $\overline{AB}$): $d_{\overline{AB}} = \sqrt{(x_2 - x_1)^2 + (y_2 - y_1)^2}$.
- The slope of $\overline{AB}$: $m_{\overline{AB}} = \dfrac{y_2 - y_1}{x_2 - x_1}$. (Practice problems for slope are given in the next section.)

Practice

1. In the coordinate plane, if $M(2,-1)$ is the midpoint of the line segment joining points $A(4, a)$ and $B(0,b)$, what is the value of $a + b$?

A. -2
B. -1
C. 0
D. 3
E. 6

2. Which of the following is a relation that contains the ordered pairs (x,y) listed in the table below?

x	0	1	2
y	0	3	8

A. $y = 3x$
B. $y = 3x^2$
C. $y = x^3$
D. $y = x^2 + 2x$
E. $y = x^3 + 2x$

3. In a *xy*-coordinate plane, point C with coordinates (2,1) is the center of a circle and point A with coordinate (7,1) is on the circle, which of the following could be the coordinates of point B, if B is also a point on the circle?

   A. (−7,1)
   B. (1,7)
   C. (4,6)
   D. (6,4)
   E. (7,6)

4. Which of the following points on the accompanying graph has coordinates that satisfy the equation, $-|3x| + |y| = 2$?

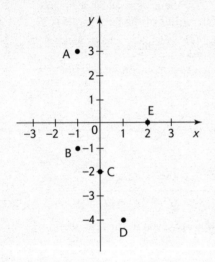

   A. *A*
   B. *B*
   C. *C*
   D. *D*
   E. *E*

5. In a coordinate plane, the distance between point $A(10,5)$ and point $B(-2,b)$ is 13. If $b > 0$, what is the value of b?

6. In a *xy*-coordinate plane, a circle in the second quadrant is tangent to the *x*-axis, the *y*-axis, and the line $x = -8$. If point $C(h,k)$ is the center of the circle, what is the value of $h + k$?

Answers

1. **A** Applying the midpoint formula, you have the coordinates of M as $\left(\frac{4+0}{2}, \frac{a+b}{2}\right)$. Because the coordinates of M are given as $(2,-1)$, you have $\frac{a+b}{2} = -1$ or $a+b = -2$. Notice that you do not need to find the individual values of a and b. They are not relevant to the question.

x	0	1	2
y	0	3	8

2. **D** A relation contains the given ordered pair if substituting the given value of x produces the given value of y. To determine which of the equations contains all three pairs, choose an equation and substitute $x = 0$. If the answer is $y = 0$, test the next value of x by substituting $x = 2$. If that answer is $y = 3$, test the third value of x and see if when you substitute 2 for x, the answer is $y = 8$. Only $y = x^2 + 2x$ contains all three pairs.

Note: If you use a graphing calculator you can solve this problem without substitution. Just use the $[y_1 =]$ function to enter each equation and check for the three ordered pairs using TABLE.

3. **D** Because $\overline{CA}$ is a radius of the circle, the length of the radius of the circle is $\sqrt{(7-2)^2 + (1-1)^2} = 5$. Because B is a point on the circle, $\overline{CB}$ must also be a radius with length 5. Using the distance formula with each choice, only when the coordinates of B are (6,4) does the length equal to $\sqrt{(6-2)^2 + (4-1)^2} = 5$.

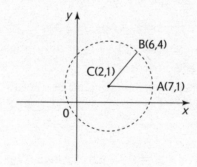

Another approach is to note that the equation of the circle is $(x - 2)^2 + (y - 1)^2 = 5^2$ because the center is (2,1) and the length of the radius is 5. Substitute the coordinates of the point in each choice in the equation and see if the equation is true.

Note: You can save time if you graph the points. Because $\overline{CA}$ is horizontal, you can find the length of the radius using $7 - 2 = 5$, and you can see that choices A, B, and E appear to be too far from C to be on the circle. Now only two points require checking with the distance formula.

4. **C** A point satisfies an equation if substituting produces an equation that is true. Substitute the coordinates of each point into the equation $-|3x| + |y| = 2$. Only when the coordinates of $C(0,-2)$ are substituted is the resulting equation true: $-|3(0)| + |2| = 0 + 2 = 2$.

5. 10 Using the distance formula, you have $d_{\overline{AB}} = \sqrt{(10-(-2))^2 + (5-b)^2} = 13$, or $\sqrt{144 + (5-b)^2} = 13$. Square both sides of the equation and you have $144 + (5-b)^2 = 169$ or $(5-b)^2 = 25$. Take the square root of both sides and you get $5 - b = 5$ or $5 - b = -5$, which implies $b = 0$ or $b = 10$. Because $b > 0$, $b = 10$.

6. 0 Draw a sketch of the coordinate plane and the line $x = -8$. The circle is tangent to both axes and the line $x = -8$, so its diameter must be 8, which means the radius is 4. Therefore, the center must be 4 units from all three lines, making its coordinates $(-4,4)$. Thus, the value of $h + k = (-4) + (4) = 0$.

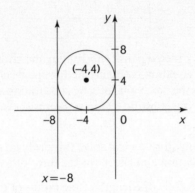

H. Slopes and Lines

On the SAT, you'll be asked to find the slope of a line. Here are some important facts you should know:

- The slope of the line through the points (x_1,y_1) and (x_2,y_2) is $\frac{y_2 - y_1}{x_2 - x_1}$.
- The graph of $y = mx + b$ is a straight line with slope m and y-intercept b.
- If two lines are parallel, their slopes are equal.
- If two lines are perpendicular, their slopes are negative reciprocals and the product of their slopes is -1.

Practice

1. In the xy-plane, $y = 4x + 1$ and $cx + 2y = d$ are parallel lines. What is the value of c?

   A. -8
   B. -4
   C. $-\frac{1}{4}$
   D. 4
   E. 8

2. In the xy-plane, the point $(-4,-2)$ is on the line $-3x + y = k$. What is the value of k?

   A. -14
   B. -10
   C. 10
   D. 12
   E. 18

3. In the accompanying diagram, what is the slope of line *l*?

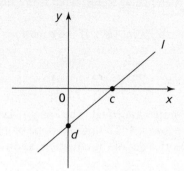

A. $\dfrac{-d}{c}$

B. $\dfrac{-c}{d}$

C. $\dfrac{d}{c}$

D. $\dfrac{c}{d}$

E. $\dfrac{1}{d}$

4. In the accompanying diagram, if a line is drawn through any two of the given points, which of the following is the smallest possible value for the slope of the line?

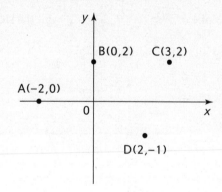

A. -4

B. $-\dfrac{3}{2}$

C. $-\dfrac{1}{4}$

D. 0

E. $\dfrac{2}{5}$

5. In the xy-plane, the coordinates of three given points are $A(2,4)$, $B(1,1)$, and $C(4,2)$. If line l is drawn passing through point A and perpendicular to $\overrightarrow{BC}$, what is the slope of line l?

6. In the xy-plane, two lines intersect at point (l,k). If the equations of the two lines are $y = -x$ and $y = 2x + h$. What is the value of h?

Answers

1. **A** If two lines are parallel, their slopes are equal. The line $y = 4x + 1$ is written in slope-intercept form $y = mx + b$. The slope of this line is $m = 4$. To find the slope of $cx + 2y = d$, rewrite the equation in $y = mx + b$ form. Subtract cx from both sides of the equation, and you have $2y = -cx + d$ and dividing both sides by 2, you have $y = \frac{-cx}{2} + \frac{d}{2}$. Therefore, the slope of this line is $m = -\frac{c}{2}$. Since the two lines are parallel, the slopes are equal. Set $-\frac{c}{2} = 4$ and you have $c = -8$.

2. **C** The coordinates of a point on a line satisfy the equation of the line. Therefore, substitute -4 for x and -2 for y in the equation $-3x + y = k$ and you have $-3(-4) + (-2) = k$ or $k = 10$.

3. **A** The coordinates of the two points are $(c,0)$ and $(0,d)$. The slope of a line passing through two given points is defined as $m = \frac{y}{x}$ or $\frac{y_2 - y_1}{x_2 - x_1}$. In this case, the slope of line l is $m = \frac{0 - d}{c - 0}$ or $\frac{-d}{c}$. Remember that you must use the same order when subtracting the x and y coordinates.

4. **B** Six lines can be drawn. Lines $\overrightarrow{AB}$, $\overrightarrow{DC}$, and $\overrightarrow{AC}$ have slopes that are positive, lines $\overrightarrow{AD}$ and $\overrightarrow{BD}$ have slopes that are negative, and $\overrightarrow{BC}$ has a slope of zero. The smallest value for slope will be the smaller of the two negative slopes. The slope of $\overrightarrow{AD} = \frac{-1 - 0}{2 - (-2)} = \frac{-1}{4}$ and the slope of $\overrightarrow{BD} = \frac{-1 - 2}{2 - 0} = \frac{-3}{2}$. Because $\frac{-3}{2} < \frac{-1}{4}$, the smallest value for the slope is $\frac{-3}{2}$.

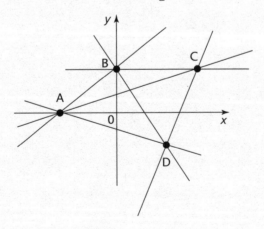

5. (–3) Draw a sketch of the xy-plane including the points A, B, and C. If two lines are perpendicular, their slopes are negative reciprocals. The slope of $\overleftrightarrow{BC}$ is $m_{\overline{BC}} = \frac{2-1}{4-1} = \frac{1}{3}$. Therefore, the slope of a line perpendicular to $\overleftrightarrow{BC}$ is –3.

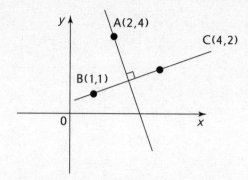

Note: The fact that the line passes through point A is not relevant. There are infinitely many lines perpendicular to $\overleftrightarrow{BC}$, and the slopes of all of these lines is 3.

6. (–3) If two lines intersect, the coordinates of the intersection point satisfy the equations of both lines. Substitute $(1,k)$ into both equations, and you have $k = -1$ and $k = 2(1) + h$. Therefore $-1 = 2 + h$ or $h = -3$.

I. Transformations and Symmetry

Given the graph of $y = f(x)$:

- Shifting vertically

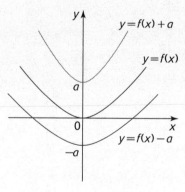

- Shifting horizontally

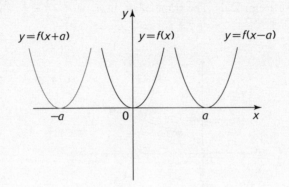

- Reflecting about an axis

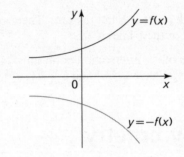
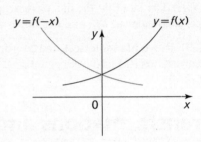

- Rotating a figure

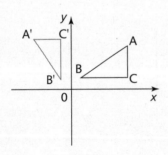
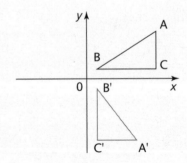

- Symmetry

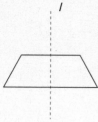

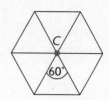

Line symmetry in
line *l*

Point symmetry
in point *A*

Rotation symmetry of 60°
about *C*

Practice

1. Line *l* is shown in the accompanying diagram. The graph of which of the following equations is the reflection of line *l* in the *y*-axis?

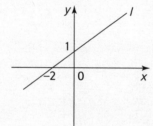

A. $y = -2x + 1$

B. $y = -2x - 1$

C. $y = \frac{1}{2}x + 2$

D. $y = -\frac{1}{2}x + 1$

E. $y = -\frac{1}{2}x - 1$

2. In the accompanying diagram, the graph of $y = f(x)$ is shown. Which of the following could be the graph of $f(x + 2)$?

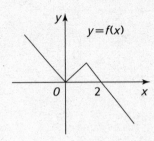

A.

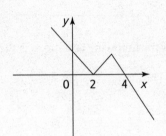

B.

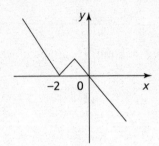

C.

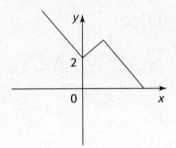

D.

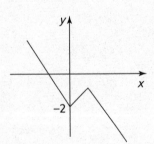

E.

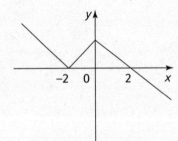

3. In the accompanying diagram, a triangle and the line $y = x$ are shown. Which of the following would be the image of the triangle reflected in the line $y = x$?

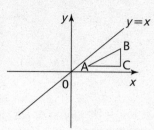

A.

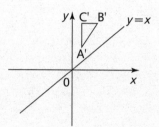

B.

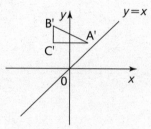

C.

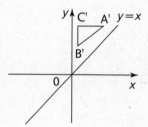

D.

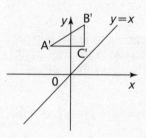

E.

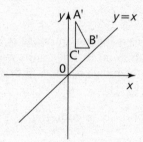

4. In the accompanying diagram, the figure is a regular hexagon. How many lines of symmetry does the hexagon have?

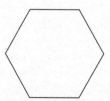

A. 1
B. 2
C. 3
D. 4
E. 6

5. In the accompanying diagram, how many lines of symmetry does the figure have?

6. In the accompanying diagram, a portion of the graph of $h(x)$ is shown. If $h(x) = h(x + 4)$ for all values of x, how many distinct values of x are there such that $h(x) = 0$ and $0 \le x \le 40$?

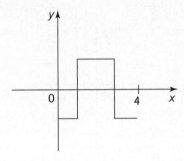

Answers

1. **D** The reflection of line l in the y-axis is the mirror image of line l with the y-axis as the mirror. The image of the point $(-2,0)$ is $(2,0)$. This point $(0,1)$ is on the y-axis, and therefore the image of $(0,1)$ is itself. Now you have two points on the image of line l: $(2,0)$ and $(0,1)$. The slope of the image is $\frac{1-0}{0-2} = -\frac{1}{2}$, and the equation is $y - 1 = -\frac{1}{2}(x - 0)$ or $y = -\frac{1}{2} + 1$.

   Note: You could also enter the equations into your graphing calculator and see which one is the reflection of line l.

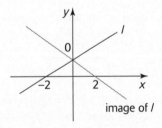

   image of l

2. **B** The graph of $f(x + 2)$ is the same as the graph of $f(x)$ shifted two units to the left. Therefore, $(0,0)$ is shifted to $(-2,0)$ and $(2,0)$ becomes $(0,0)$. Thus, Choice A is the graph of $f(x + 2)$.

3. **A** The triangle and its image match perfectly along the line of reflection. Imagine folding the graph on the line $y = x$. The base of the triangle $\overline{AC}$ (a horizontal line segment) will be reflected to become a vertical line. The height of the triangle $\overline{BC}$ (a vertical line segment) will become a horizontal line segment. Also, the image of $\triangle ABC$ should have vertex A below side $\overline{BC}$ Thus the graph in Choice A is the image.

4. **E** A line of symmetry divides a figure into two parts, each the mirror image of the other. As illustrated in the following diagram, six such lines are possible.

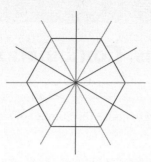

5. **0** A line of symmetry divides a figure into two parts, each the mirror image of the other. In this case, it is not possible to divide the figure into mirror images. Thus, there is no line of symmetry.

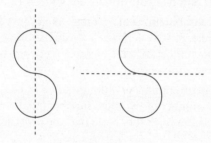

No mirror images

6. **20** The fact that $h(x) = h(x + 4)$ implies that $h(x)$ is periodic—the graph repeats itself every four units. In this case, the portion of the graph will appear ten times on the interval [0,40]. Also, the *x-value* satisfying $h(x) = 0$ are the *x*-intercepts. Because the graph crosses the *x*-axis twice for $0 \leq x \leq 4$, it will cross the *x*-axis 2(10) or 20 times for $0 \leq x \leq 40$.

XIII. Probability, Statistics, and Data Analysis

A. Counting Problems, Combinations, and Permutations

On the SAT, some questions require you to count the number of ways an event can happen. Here are some of the rules to remember:

- **Fundamental Counting Principle:** If one activity can occur in m ways, and then following that a second activity can occur in n ways, then the number of ways both activities can occur in that order is mn. For example, if you own three different jackets and four different pairs of slacks, then the number of outfits consisting of one jacket and one pair of slacks is $4 \times 3 = 12$.

- **Combinations:** The number of combinations of n things taken r at a time is $_nC_r = \frac{_nP_r}{r!}$, where $n! = n(n-1)(n-2)\ldots 1$. For example, $5! = 5 \cdot 4 \cdot 3 \cdot 2 \cdot 1 = 120$. Another example: If there are three players on the school's tennis team, the number of ways of selecting two players to play doubles is $_3C_2 = 3$. Note that the order in which the players are selected does *not* matter.

- **Permutations:** The number of permutations of n things taken r at a time is $_nP_r = \frac{n!}{(n-r)!}$. For example, given the digits 3, 4, and 5, the number of two-digit numbers that we can get by selecting two of the three given digits without repetition is $_3P_2 = 6$. Note that the order in which the digits appear (34 versus 43) *does* matter.

When you're solving these problems on the SAT, keep the following tips in mind:

- Use combination if order does *not* matter. Use permutation if order *does* matter.
- $_nP_1 = n$ and $_nP_n = n!$
- $_nC_1 = n$ and $_nC_n = 1$
- You'll save a lot of time if you use your calculator to evaluate $_nC_r$ and $_nP_r$.

Practice

1. At a restaurant, the menu consists of 2 varieties of salad, 5 different entrees, and 3 desserts, of which one is apple pie. If the Tuesday night dinner special consists of 1 salad, 1 entree, and apple pie for desert, how many different Tuesday night dinner specials are there?

   A. 5
   B. 7
   C. 10
   D. 15
   E. 30

2. The junior class is holding an election for president, vice president, and secretary, and six students are candidates. If any of the candidates could be elected president, vice president, or secretary but no one can hold more than one position, how many different outcomes are possible?

   A. 6
   B. 20
   C. 36
   D. 72
   E. 120

3. If the local post office only has three denominations of stamps available, $0.01 stamps, $0.10 stamps, and $0.20 stamps, how many different sets of stamps can be used to form $0.41?

   A. 4
   B. 5
   C. 8
   D. 9
   E. 10

4. What is the total number of distinct diagonals that can be drawn in an octagon? (An octagon has eight sides.)

   A. 7
   B. 20
   C. 28
   D. 40
   E. 56

5. Katie, Cristen, Johnny, and Juliet have all been promoted to senior management positions in a company. They are to be assigned to four new offices, of which only one is a corner office with a panoramic view. How many different ways can the four of them be assigned to their new offices with either Cristen or Johnny having a corner office?

6. Four table-tennis players—Bill, Mary, Janet, and Karen—put their paddles on a table during a break. After the break, Bill picked up his own paddle. However, Mary, Janet, and Karen picked up each other's paddles but not their own. In how many ways can this happen?

Answers

1. **C** Use the Fundamental Counting Principle to determine the number of different dinner specials. Since there are 2 choices for salad, 5 choices for the entree, and 1 choice for dessert (because dessert must be apple pie), there are $(5)(2)(1) = 10$ different dinner specials.

2. **E** This is a permutation problem because order matters. You could have the same three students elected to different positions. Thus, the number of different outcomes is $_6P_3$, which is $6(5)(4) = 120$.

3. **D** This problem involves not only selecting from three subgroups of stamps, but also factoring in the values of these stamps. This is not a permutation or combination problem. One way to do this problem is to list all the possible outcomes. Summarizing the outcomes, you have the following table:

$0.01	$0.10	$0.20
1	0	2
1	2	1
11	1	1
21	0	1
1	4	0
11	3	0
21	2	0
31	1	0
41	0	0

There are 9 possible sets of stamps to make $0.41.

4. **B** There eight vertices in an octagon. From each vertex, five diagonals can be drawn. So, you have (8)(5) = 40 diagonals. However, each diagonal was counted twice. For example, a diagonal drawn from vertex *A* to vertex *C* is the same as the diagonal drawn from vertex *C* to vertex *A*. Therefore, the total number of distinct diagonals in an octagon is $\frac{40}{2} = 20$.

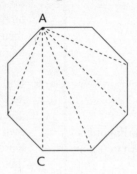

5. 12

Corner office	Office A	Office B	Office C
2	3	2	1

Let's call the 4 offices: corner office and offices A, B, and C. You have two choices (Cristen and Johnny) for the corner office. After that, you have two choices for office A, two for office B, and one for office C. Therefore, you have (2)(3)(2)(1) = 12 ways of assigning the four offices with Cristen or Johnny occupying the corner office.

6. 2

Janet	Karen	Mary
K	M	J
M	J	K

There are three decisions to investigate: (1) Which paddle did Janet pick up, (2) Which paddle did Mary pick up, and (3) Which paddle did Karen pick up? Janet picked up either Mary's paddle or Karen's paddle. If Janet picked up Mary's paddle, then Mary had Karen's paddle, and Karen had Janet's paddle. This is one possible outcome. If Janet picked up Karen's paddle then Mary had Janet's paddle and Karen had Mary's paddle. This is the only other possible outcome. Thus, there are two possible ways that Janet, Karen, and Mary could have picked up the wrong paddles.

B. Probability

On the SAT, you'll be tested on simple probability. Here are some of the rules to keep in mind:

- Probability that an event A will occur is $P(A) = \dfrac{\text{number of ways event A can occur}}{\text{total number of possible outcomes}}$.
- Probability that event A will occur is $0 \le P(A) \le 1$.
- Probability that event A will not occur is $P(\text{not } A) = 1 - P(A)$.
- The probability that event A or event B will occur is: $P(A \text{ or } B) = P(A) + P(B) - P(A \text{ and } B)$.

Practice

1. If a number is randomly selected from the set $\{1,2,3,4,5,6,7,8,9\}$, what is the probability that it will be a prime number?

   A. $\dfrac{2}{9}$

   B. $\dfrac{3}{9}$

   C. $\dfrac{4}{9}$

   D. $\dfrac{5}{9}$

   E. 3

2. In Janet's classroom, she labeled all her books as either fiction or nonfiction. She has 30 non-fiction books. If a book is picked at random, the probability that it is fiction is $\dfrac{3}{5}$. What is the total number of books in her classroom?

   A. 50
   B. 60
   C. 75
   D. 90
   E. 150

3. Victoria has 3 quarters and 2 dimes in her piggybank. If 2 coins are taken out of the piggybank at random, what is the probability that both coins are dimes?

   A. $\dfrac{1}{20}$

   B. $\dfrac{1}{10}$

   C. $\dfrac{2}{5}$

   D. $\dfrac{2}{3}$

   E. $\dfrac{4}{5}$

4. In a box, there are 10 red balls and 8 blue balls. What is the minimum number of balls that have to be removed in order for the probability of picking a red ball at random from the box to be $\dfrac{2}{3}$?

   A. 0
   B. 2
   C. 3
   D. 4
   E. 6

5. In the accompanying diagram, O is the center of both circles with $OB = 6$ and $AB = 2$. If a point is picked at random from the larger circle, what is the probability of getting a point that lies in the shaded region.

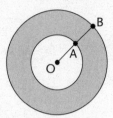

Not drawn to scale

6. There are 24 students in Mr. Faseoli's music class, each of whom is a member of either the orchestra or the band or both. If 16 of these students are in the orchestra and 14 are in the band, and if a student is randomly chosen, what is the probability that the student picked is in both the orchestra and the band?

Answers

1. **C** $P(\text{a prime number}) = \dfrac{\text{number of prime numbers in the set}}{\text{total number of elements in the set}}$. There are 4 prime numbers in the set: 2, 3, 5, and 7. There are 9 numbers in total. Therefore the probability of getting a prime number is $\dfrac{4}{9}$.

2. **C** Since $P(\text{fiction}) = \dfrac{3}{5}$, $P(\text{nonfiction}) = 1 - \dfrac{3}{5} = \dfrac{2}{5}$, use x to represent the total number of books. There are 30 nonfiction books. Therefore, $\dfrac{\text{the number of nonfiction books}}{\text{total number of books}} = \dfrac{2}{5}$ or $\dfrac{30}{x} = \dfrac{2}{5}$, which is equivalent to $2x = 30(5)$ or $x = 75$. There are 75 books in total in Janet's classroom.

3. **B** $P(\text{2 dimes}) = \dfrac{\text{number of ways of picking 2 dimes}}{\text{total number of picking 2 coins from 5 coins}}$. The number of ways of picking 2 dimes is $_2C_2 = 1$. The number of ways of picking 2 coins from 5 coins is $_5C_2 = 10$. Therefore, $P(\text{2 dimes}) = \dfrac{1}{10}$. Another approach is as follows: $P(\text{2 dimes}) = P(\text{first coin is a dime}) \times P(\text{second coin is a dime}) = \dfrac{2}{5}\left(\dfrac{1}{4}\right) = \dfrac{1}{10}$.

4. **C** The probability of picking a red ball equaling $\dfrac{2}{3}$ implies that the total number of balls in the box has to be divisible by 3. Initially, there are 10 red and 8 blue balls in the box totaling 18, which is divisible by 3. However, the probability of picking a red ball is $\dfrac{10}{18}$, which is $\dfrac{5}{9}$, not $\dfrac{2}{3}$. The next number divisible by 3 is 15. If there are 15 balls in the box and the probability of picking a red is $\dfrac{2}{3}$, then you have $\dfrac{x}{15} = \dfrac{2}{3}$, x being the number of red balls. Solve the proportion and note that $x = 10$. So you need 10 red balls and 5 blue balls. Since there are 10 red and 8 blue balls initially, you must remove 3 blue balls from the box.

5. $\left(\dfrac{5}{9}\right)$ Note that $P(\textit{getting a point in the shaded region}) = \dfrac{\text{the area of the shaded region}}{\text{the area of the larger circle}}$. The area of the shaded region = (area of the larger circle) – (area of the smaller circle). The length of the radius of the larger circle is 6. The area of the larger circle is $\pi(6)^2 = 36\pi$. The radius of the smaller circle is $6 - 2 = 4$. The area of the smaller circle is $\pi(4)^2 = 16\pi$. Thus, the area of the shaded region is $36\pi - 16\pi = 20\pi$. The probability of getting a point from the shaded region is $\dfrac{20\pi}{36\pi}$ or $\dfrac{5}{9}$.

6. $\frac{1}{4}$ $P\left(\text{picking a student in both orchestra and band}\right)=\dfrac{\text{the number of students in both orchestra and band}}{\text{total number of students in class}}$.

The number of students in either orchestra or band is $16 + 14 = 30$. Since there are only 24 students in the class, there must be $30 - 24 = 6$ students in both orchestra and band. Thus,

$P\left(\text{picking a student in both orchestra and band}\right)=\dfrac{6}{24}$ or $\dfrac{1}{4}$.

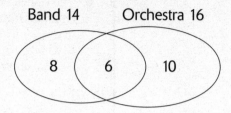

Band 14   Orchestra 16

8   6   10

C. Mean, Median, and Mode

On the SAT, you'll be asked to find the mean, median, and mode of a given set of numbers or algebraic expressions. Here are the key definitions:

- The **mean** of a set of numbers or algebraic expressions is the average of the set. For example:
  - The average of 5, 6, and 10 is $\dfrac{5+6+10}{3} = 7$.
  - The average of $x + 8$ and $5x - 4$ is $\dfrac{x+8+5x-4}{2} = 3x + 2$.
- The **median** of a list of numbers is the middle value, when arranged in numerical order. For example:
  - The median of 2, 6, 10, 11, and 14 is 10.
  - The median of 2, 6, 8, and 20 is $\dfrac{6+8}{2}$ or 7. (When there are an even number of values, you take the average of the two middle numbers.)
- The **mode** of a list of numbers is the number that appears most often. For example:
  - The mode of 2, 3, 5, 5, 5, 6, 6, and 8 is 5.
  - The mode of 2, 3, 6, 6, 8, 8, 12, and 15 is 6 and 8.
- If you know the average of a set of numbers, then you know the sum. For example: The average of x and y is 10, then the sum of $x + y$ is $2(10) = 20$.

Practice

1. If the average (arithmetic mean) of 6, m, and n is 10, what is the average of m and n?

    A.   4
    B.   12
    C.   18
    D.   24
    E.   36

2. If the average (arithmetic mean) of x and $3x - 4$ is p and the average of $6 - 2x$ and $14 - 2x$ is q, what is the average of p and q?

    A.   4
    B.   16
    C. $4 - 2x$
    D. $2x + 4$
    E. $8x+16$

3. Rebecca's test grades in her math class for the first quarter are 90, 84, 80, 92, 84, and 98. Of the 6 grades in the first quarter, if p is the mean, q is the median, and r is the mode, which of the following inequalities is true?

A. $r < q < p$
B. $r < p < q$
C. $p < r < q$
D. $q < p < r$
E. $p < q < r$

4. Given $3x - 2$, $-\dfrac{1}{x}$ and x^2, if x^2 is the median, which of the following could be the value of x?

A. -3
B. -2
C. $-\dfrac{1}{2}$
D. $\dfrac{1}{2}$
E. 3

5. $16, 6, 4, 21, k, 3$

If 8 is the median of the 6 numbers shown, what is the value of k?

6. The Cohen family consists of 2 parents and 3 children. If the average height of the 5 people in the family is 5 feet 8 inches, and the average height of the 2 parents is 5 feet 5 inches, what is the average height of the 3 children?

Answers

1. **B** Knowing the average implies knowing the sum. Because $\dfrac{6+m+n}{3} = 10$, you know that $6 + m + n = 30$ by multiplying both sides of the equation by 3. Then $m + n = 24$, and the average of m and n is $\dfrac{m+n}{2}$, which is $\dfrac{24}{2} = 12$.

2. **A** Because the average of x and $3x - 4$ is p, you have $p = \dfrac{(x)+(3x-4)}{2} = \dfrac{4x-4}{2} = 2x - 2$. Similarly, $q = \dfrac{(6-2x)+(14-2x)}{2} = \dfrac{20-4x}{2} = 10 - 2x$. The average of p and q can be obtained by $\dfrac{(2x-2)+(10-2x)}{2} = \dfrac{8}{2} = 4$.

3. **A** The mean is the average; $p = \dfrac{90+84+80+92+84+98}{6} = 88$. The median is q, which is the middle value of 80, 84, 84, 90, 92, and 98 or $\dfrac{84+90}{2} = 87$. The mode is r, which is the value that appears the most often: 84. Thus, $r < q < p$.

4. C Substitute the given numbers into the three expressions:

x	$3x-2$	x^2	$-\dfrac{1}{x}$
-3	-11	9	$\dfrac{1}{3}$
-2	-8	4	$\dfrac{1}{2}$
$-\dfrac{1}{2}$	$-3\dfrac{1}{2}$	$\dfrac{1}{4}$	2
$\dfrac{1}{2}$	$-\dfrac{1}{2}$	$\dfrac{1}{4}$	-2
3	7	9	$-\dfrac{1}{3}$

Notice that when $x=-\frac{1}{2}$, you have $-3\frac{1}{2}$, $\frac{1}{4}$, and 2, making x^2 the median.

5. 10 Arrange the numbers, not including k, in ascending order: 3, 4, 6, 16, and 21. If k is not one of the two numbers in the middle, such as in the sequence 3, 4, 6, 16, k, 21, then the median is $\frac{6+16}{2}=11$ or, as in the sequence k, 3, 4, 6, 16, 21, then the median is $\frac{4+6}{2}=5$. These two cases are not possible since the median is 8. Therefore, k must be one of the two numbers in the middle, such as in the sequence 3, 4, 6, k, 16, 21 or as in the sequence 3, 4, k, 6, 16, 21. The median is $\frac{6+k}{2}=8$ or $k=10$.

6. (5 feet 10 inches) The average height of the 5 persons is :

$$\frac{\left(\text{sum of heights of 2 parents}\right)+\left(\text{sum of heights of 3 children}\right)}{5}=5 \text{ feet 8 inches.}$$

Multiply both sides of the equation by 5, and you have: (sum of heights of 2 parents) + (sum of heights of 3 children) = 25 feet 40 inches. The average height of the 2 parents is: $\frac{\text{sum of heights of 2 parents}}{2}=5$ feet 5 inches, or the sum of heights of 2 parents is 10 feet 10 inches. Therefore, the sum of heights of the 3 children is (25 feet 40 inches) – (10 feet 10 inches) = 15 feet 30 inches. Thus, the average height of the 3 children is $\frac{15\,\text{feet 30 inches}}{3}$ or 5 feet 10 inches.

D. Data Interpretation

Data analysis questions involve using information that is presented in a graph, chart, or table. Always take the time to carefully read the labels. The unit of measure used in the graph, chart, or table may not be the same as the unit of measure in the question. In that case, you should use the unit of measure from the graph and extract the needed information; work out the problem and express your final answer in the unit of measure in which the question is asked.

Practice

1. In the accompanying diagram, the line graph shows the number of books sold by Whitman Bookstore in each month from January through May. What percent of the number of books sold in February is equal to the number of books sold in May?

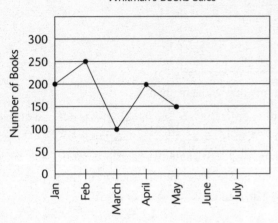

Whitman's Books Sales

A. 25
B. 40
C. 60
D. 75
E. 80

2. In 2008, students who attended Washington High School and Adams High School were allowed to participate in only one sport for the year: tennis, soccer, swimming, or basketball. Based on the information provided in the accompanying bar graph, how many more students at Washington High School than Adams High School participated in a sport in 2008?

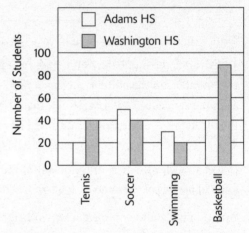

Number of Students in Four Sports at Washington HS and Adams HS

A. 40
B. 50
C. 70
D. 140
E. 190

3. In the accompanying diagram, the double line graph shows the revenues and expenses of Concord Electronics for the past five years. Which year had the greatest profit?

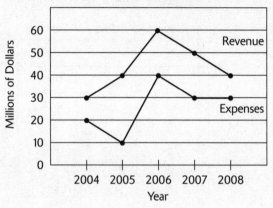

A. 2004
B. 2005
C. 2006
D. 2007
E. 2008

4. Janet and Karen are meeting at a library to work on their math project. Because there are five libraries in town, they have decided to choose the library that would result in their traveling the smallest total distance. The accompanying scatter plot graph shows the distances that Karen would have to travel to go to each of the five libraries and the distances that Janet would have to travel to go to each of the five libraries. Which library should they choose?

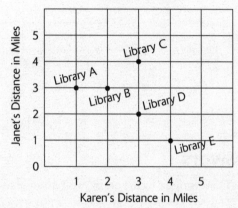

A. A
B. B
C. C
D. D
E. E

5. Janet was saving a part of her salary every month so she could buy a house. In four months she saved a total of $2,000. If the accompanying table shows the total amount of money that Janet had saved by the end of each month, how much did she save in March?

Janet's Savings

Month	Total Amount in Dollars
January	500
February	800
March	1,400
April	2,000

6. Karen gets a fixed allowance for lunch and entertainment every week. The accompanying bar graph shows the amount that she spent on lunch for the past five weeks. If she spent 60% of her allowance on lunch during the second week, what percent of her allowance did she spend on her lunch during the fourth week?

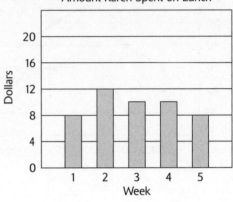

Amount Karen Spent on Lunch

Answers

1. **C** According to the graph, you know that the number of books sold in February is 250 and the number of books sold in May is 150. Use the proportion $\frac{150}{250} = \frac{x}{100\%}$, which is equivalent to $x = \frac{100(150)}{250}\% = 60\%$.

2. **B** At Washington High School, 40 students played tennis, 40 played soccer, 20 were swimmers, and 90 played basketball totaling 40 + 40 + 20 + 90 = 190 students who participated in a sport. At Adams High School, 20 students played tennis, 50 played soccer, 30 were swimmers, and 40 played basketball, totaling 20 + 50 + 30 + 40 = 140 students who participated in a sport. The number of additional students who participated in sports at Washington High School than at Adams High School is 190 − 140 = 50.

3. **B** Profit = Revenue − Expenses. According to the line graph, in 2005, revenue was $40 million and expenses were $10 million. Profit for that year was $30 million, the largest for the five years.

	2004	2005	2006	2007	2008
Revenue	30	40	60	50	40
Cost	20	10	40	30	30
Profit	10	30	20	20	10

4. **A** According to the scatter plot, the distance from library A to Karen's house is 1 mile and to Janet's house is 3 miles. Thus, the total distance from library A, to their houses is 4 miles, the smallest.

	A	B	C	D	E
Distance to Karen's house	1	2	3	3	4
Distance to Janet's house	3	3	4	2	1
Total Distance	4	5	7	5	5

5. **$600** The amount shown in the savings account is cumulative. In other words, the amount shown in March reflects what was saved in January, February, and March. Since Janet saved a total of $800 for January and February and a total of $1,400 for January, February, and March, she must have saved $1,400 – $800 = $600 for the month of March.

6. **50%** According to the bar graph, Karen spent $12 out of her allowance for lunch. Since $12 is 60% of her allowance, use the proportion $\frac{12}{\text{allowance}} = \frac{60}{100}$, which is equivalent to allowance $= \frac{100(12)}{60} = 20$. In the fourth week, Karen spent $10 on lunch. Therefore, $\frac{\$10}{\$20}$, which is $\frac{1}{2}$ or 50%.

XIV. Logic and Problem Solving

A. Ω, * , ∇, and Other Unusual Symbols

On the SAT, you may encounter problems in which an unusual symbol is used to define a series of operations. In these cases, you have to substitute and then do some arithmetic to find your answer. For example:

- **Given $a* = 3a + 5$, what is the value of $a*$ if $a = 2$?** Use 2 for a and then do the arithmetic: $2* = 3(2) + 5 = 11$.

- **If $m \, \Omega \, n = m^2 - n^2$, find the value of $3 \, \Omega \, 2$.** Use 3 for m and 2 for n, and then do the arithmetic: $3 \, \Omega \, 2 = 3^2 - 2^2 = 5$.

- **If 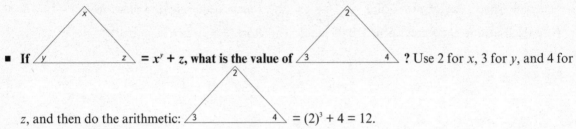 $= x^y + z$, what is the value of** 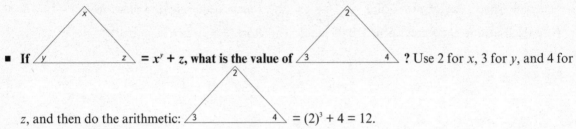 **? Use 2 for x, 3 for y, and 4 for

z, and then do the arithmetic: 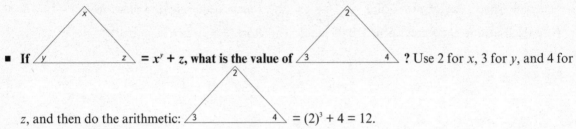 $= (2)^3 + 4 = 12$.

Remember: The symbol itself doesn't matter. What matters is what the problem is telling you the symbol means.

When you're solving these problem, keep in mind that order matters! Be sure to substitute in the correct order as you follow the given pattern.

Most of the questions involving an unusual symbol can be solved using a TI-89 graphing calculator. (See the appendix for more on working with the TI-89 graphing calculator.)

Practice

1. Let $n*$ be defined as $n = n^2 - 3n$ for all integers n. What is the value of $n*$ if $n = -4$?

   A. −28
   B. −4
   C. 4
   D. 16
   E. 28

2. For all real numbers m and n. If $m \, \nabla \, n$ is defined as $m \, \nabla \, n = m^2 - 2n$, what is the value of $4 \, \nabla \, (3 \, \nabla \, 2)$?

   A. 5
   B. 6
   C. 21
   D. 23
   E. 123

3. For all integers n, let $n \blacklozenge$ be defined as $n \blacklozenge = 2n + 8$. Which of the following has the same value as $\dfrac{80\blacklozenge}{2\blacklozenge}$?

A. $2\blacklozenge$
B. $3\blacklozenge$
C. $406\blacklozenge$
D. $40\blacklozenge$
E. 40

4. For all positive numbers of x, x^* is defined as $x^* = x - 2\sqrt{x}$. If $x^* = k$, and k is a positive integer, which of the following is a possible value of x?

A. -4
B. 1
C. 2
D. 4
E. 9

5. Let $@p$ be defined as $2^p - 1$ for all integers p. What is the value of $@(@3)$?

6. Let the following be defined as $bc - ad$ for all real numbers a, b, c, and d.

a	c
b	d

What is the value of the following?

-3	-4
0	2

Answers

1. **E** Use -4 for n and do the arithmetic: $(-4)^2 - 3(-4) = 16 + 12 = 28$.

2. **B** Because the symbol ∇ is used twice in the equation, you have to substitute and follow the pattern twice. First, work inside the parentheses: Use 3 for m, 2 for n, and $m \nabla n = m^2 - 2n$ to find that $3 \nabla 2 = (3)^2 - 2(2) = 5$. Next, use 5 in place of $(3 \nabla 2)$ in the original problem. Then $4 \nabla (3 \nabla 2) = 4 \nabla 5$. Use 4 for m, 5 for n, and $m \nabla n = m^2 - 2n$ to find that $4 \nabla 5 = (4)^2 - 2(5) = 6$.

3. **B** Because $n \blacklozenge = 2n + 8$, $80 \blacklozenge = 2(80) + 8 = 168$, and $2 \blacklozenge = 2(2) + 8 = 12$. Therefore, $\dfrac{80\blacklozenge}{2\blacklozenge} = \dfrac{168}{12}$ $= 14$. Evaluating the five choices, you have $3 \blacklozenge = 2(3) + 8 = 6 + 8 = 14$. Thus, Choice B, $3\blacklozenge = \dfrac{80\blacklozenge}{2\blacklozenge}$.

4. **E** Try to eliminate choices and then evaluate the remaining choices. You can eliminate Choice A, because $\sqrt{-4}$ is not a real number. You can eliminate Choice C, because $\sqrt{2}$ is irrational. Now find the value of the remaining choices. Choice B $= 1^* = 1 - 2\sqrt{1} = -1$, which is not a positive integer and Choice D $= 4^* = 4 - 2\sqrt{4} = 0$, which also is not a positive integer. Choice E $= 9^* = 9 - 2\sqrt{9} = 3$, which is a positive integer. Thus, Choice E, $x = 9$.

5. **127** Because $@$ is used twice, you have to substitute twice. First, work inside the parenthesis using 3 for p. You have $@3 = (2)^3 - 1 = 7$. Next, use 7 for p. You have $@7 = (2)^7 - 1 = 127$.

6. **6** Determine the values of a, b, c, d and substitute in $bc - ad$. Based on location, $a = -3$, $c = -4$, $b = 0$, and $d = 2$ and $(0)(-4) - (-3)(2) = 0 - (-6) = 6$.

B. Word Problems

The key to solving word problems is to read the problem closely. Start by identifying what you need to find. Then find it by setting up and solving an equation or by guessing and checking.

Be sure to answer the question that is asked. The solution to your equation may not be the final answer to the question. For example: If the sum of two consecutive integers is 15, then $x + (x + 1) = 15$ and $x = 7$. However, if the question asks for the value of the larger integer, the larger integer is 8.

Be aware that sometimes a question may contain information not relevant to the solution.

Practice

1. Three times a number is the same as the number added to 60. What is the number?

   A.   15
   B.   20
   C.   30
   D.   45
   E.   180

2. Rebecca has twice as much money as Rachel. If Rebecca gives Rachel $60, then the two of them will have the same amount of money. How much money does Rebecca have?

   A. $60
   B. $90
   C. $120
   D. $180
   E. $240

3. There are 200 marbles in a box. All the marbles are either red or blue. If there are 40 more red marbles than blue, how many red marbles are there in the box?

   A.   40
   B.   80
   C.   120
   D.   160
   E.   180

4. Erica used a car service that charges $5 per mile plus an additional initial fee of $20. If the total cost for the car service was $110, what was the distance traveled, in miles?

   A.   16
   B.   18
   C.   20
   D.   22
   E.   26

5. The cube root of a positive number is the same as the number divided by four. What is the number?

6. Tom can paint a house in 12 hours, and Hunter can paint the same house in 6 hours. Working together, how long will Tom and Hunter take to paint the house?

Answers

1. **C** Let x be the number. Then, you have $3x = x + 60$, which is equivalent to $2x = 60$, or $x = 30$. The number is 30.

2. **E** Let x be the amount of money that Rachel has. Then $2x$ represents the amount of money that Rebecca has. Since Rebecca gave Rachel $60 and they have the same amount of money, we can write the equation $2x - 60 = x + 60$. Subtracting x from both sides of the equation, we have $x - 60 = 60$, or $x = 120$. Thus, Rachel has $120, and Rebecca has $240.

3. **C** Let x be the number of blue marbles, and $x + 40$ be the number of red marbles. There are 200 marbles in the box, so you have $x + x + 40 = 200$, which is equivalent to $2x + 40 = 200$, or $x = 80$. Thus, the number of red marbles is $x + 40 = 120$.

4. **B** Let x be the number of miles of Erica's trip. Then $5x + 20 = 110$, which is equivalent to $5x = 90$ or $x = 18$. Thus the distance of Erica's trip is 18 miles.

5. **8** Let x be the number. Then $\sqrt[3]{x} = \frac{x}{4}$ or $x^{\frac{1}{3}} = \frac{x}{4}$. Raising both sides to the third power, you have $\left(x^{\frac{1}{3}}\right)^3 = \left(\frac{x}{4}\right)^3$, which is equivalent to $x = \frac{x^3}{64}$. Multiplying both sides by 64, you have $64x = x^3$ or $0 = x^3 - 64x$. Factor $x^3 - 64x$ and you have $0 = x(x^2 - 64)$ or $0 = x(x - 8)(x + 8)$. Thus $x = -8, 0,$ or 8. Because x is a positive number, you know that $x = 8$.

6. **4 hours** Tom can paint a house in 12 hours, so he can paint $\frac{1}{12}$ of the house in one hour. Similarly, Hunter can paint $\frac{1}{6}$ of the house in one hour. If they work together, in one hour they can paint $\frac{1}{12} + \frac{1}{6} = \frac{1}{12} + \frac{2}{12} = \frac{3}{12}$ or $\frac{1}{4}$ of the house. Tom and Hunter can paint $\frac{1}{4}$ of the house in an hour, it will take them $1 \div \left(\frac{1}{4}\right)$ or 4 hours to paint the whole house.

C. Logical Reasoning

Logical reasoning questions require the reasoning skills that you strengthen as you study mathematics. They may be more complicated and take extra time to solve, but they're not worth any extra points on the test.

Use your time wisely. Look at the choices provided before trying to solve the problem. Often, you can eliminate some choices quickly and tip the odds in your favor if you decide to guess the answer. Look at the following example.

EXAMPLE:

If three painters working together can paint a house in 2 hours, how long will it take for nine painters working together at the same rate to paint the same house?

- **A.** 8 hours
- **B.** 6 hours
- **C.** 3 hours
- **D.** 48 minutes
- **E.** 40 minutes

Because there are more painters painting the house, it should take less time than 2 hours. Thus, you can eliminate choices A, B, and C. This is an inverse proportion because the more painters you have, the less time it will take. The formula for an inverse proportion is $(x_1)(y_1) = (x_2)(y_2)$, and in this case, $(3)(2) = (9)(y)$ or $y = \frac{2}{3}$ hour which is 40 minutes.

Practice

1. In the following diagram, there are 25 squares numbered from 1 to 25. Each square is to be painted either red or blue, and no two squares sharing a common side can have the same color. If square number 15 is painted red, how many squares are painted blue?

1	2	3	4	5
6	7	8	9	10
11	12	13	14	15
16	17	18	19	20
21	22	23	24	25

   A. 5
   B. 12
   C. 13
   D. 14
   E. 15

2. Multiply: $xy \times 8x = 3,154$. xy represents a two-digit number with x being the tens digit and y the units digit, and $8x$ represents another two-digit number with 8 being the tens digit and x being the units digit. If the product of xy and $8x$ is 3,154, what is the value of y?

   A. 2
   B. 3
   C. 4
   D. 6
   E. 8

3. If no member of Mary's family plays football, which of the following statements must be true?

   A. If Phillip does not play football, then Phillip is a member of Mary's family.
   B. If Jonathan is not a member of Mary's family, then he plays football.
   C. If Richard is not a member of Mary's family, then he does not play football.
   D. If Bill plays table tennis, then he is a member of Mary's family.
   E. If David plays football, then he is not a member of Mary's family.

4. In the accompanying diagram of Lyons County, five highway routes and their ten points of intersection are drawn. The county wants to have two restaurants and two gas stations located along each route. The restaurants and gas stations must be located at points of intersection. Three gas stations and two restaurants have already been placed at the locations indicated in the diagram. Of the remaining intersections labeled A, B, C, D and E, which intersection must have a restaurant?

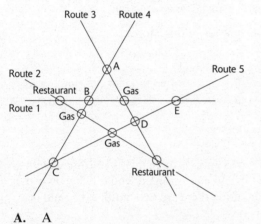

A. A
B. B
C. C
D. D
E. E

5. *ABCD* is a square that has been divided into 16 smaller congruent squares. How many squares are in *ABCD*?

6. The following table shows three columns of numbers. If the numbers in each column are interrelated and the same relationship exists for all three columns, what is the value of x?

2	4	6
6	12	18
10	18	x

Answers

1. **B** Because no two squares sharing a common side can be painted the same color, the squares must be painted every other red and every other blue. Begin with red on square number 15, and continue with every other red. After completing all 25 squares, count the number of blue squares and there are 12.

   An alternative approach is that, because 15 is red, that means all the odd numbers will be colored red, and all the even numbers will be colored blue. There are 13 odd numbers and 12 even numbers. Thus, 12 will be blue.

2. **E** Solve this problem by narrowing down the possibilities for x and y. Begin with x. Because x is the tens digit in xy, and the product of xy and $8x$ is about 3,000, x must be less than 4. If $x = 4$, the product of 40 and 84 is 33,366, which is greater than 3,154. Try $x = 3$ because the product is close to 3,000. The problem becomes $3y \times 83 = 3,154$. The units digits are y and 3, and the units digit in the product 3,154 is 4. Therefore, three times y must lead to a number whose units digit is 4. Thus, $y = 8$. Check the product of 38 and 83 and you have 3,154. So, the value of y is 8.

3. **E** Use reasoning skills. Because no one in Mary's family plays football, if you play football you are not in Mary's family. Another approach is to use formal logic. Here are some of the rules of logic:

- Statement: If A, then B.
- Converse: If B, then A.
- Inverse: If not A, then not B.
- Contrapositive: If not B, then not A.

Note: A statement and the contrapositive always have the same truth value.

In this problem, "No member of Mary's family plays football" can be written as "If you are a member of Mary's family, then you do not play football." The contrapositive of this statement is "If you play football, then you are not a member of Mary's family." Thus, Choice E is true.

4. **C** Use trial and error. Begin by listing all the possible new restaurant stops:

- Route 1: B, E
- Route 2: None
- Route 3: A, D
- Route 4: A, B, C
- Route 5: C, D, E

Start with Route 1 or Route 3, because there are only two options there instead of three. Let's say you begin with Route 1. There are already a restaurant stop and a gas stop on Route 1, so you can have one more restaurant stop and one more gas stop. Therefore, there are two options: B could be a restaurant stop and E could be a gas stop or vice versa:

- Option 1: If B is a restaurant stop and E is a gas stop, then in Route 5, C and D are both restaurant stops and in Route 3, A must be a gas stop.

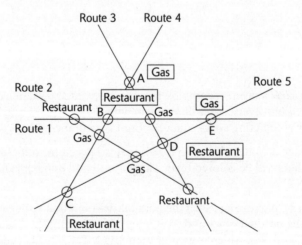

■ Option 2: If B is a gas stop and E is a restaurant stop. In Route 4, A and C must be restaurant stops. In Route 3, D must be a gas stop.

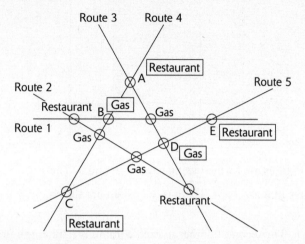

In both cases, C is a restaurant stop.

5. **30** Categorize the squares by size and then count within each category. The smallest squares are 1×1. There are 16 squares that are 1×1.

Next count the 2×2 squares. Start by counting the 2×2 squares formed using row 1 and row 2. Three 2×2 squares are formed.

Similarly, three 2×2 squares are formed using rows 2 and 3 and then again using rows 3 and 4. There are 9 squares that are 2×2.

Next count the squares that are 3×3. Start by counting the 3×3 squares formed using row 1, row 2, and row 3. Two squares are formed.

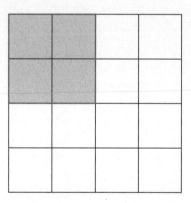

Similarly, two 3×3 squares are formed using rows 2, 3, and 4. There are 4 squares that are 3 x 3.

Next count the squares that are 4×4. There is only 1 square that is 4×4. There are $16 + 9 + 4 + 1 = 30$ squares.

6. **26** Look for a pattern. The second number in each column is 3 times the first. The third number is the sum of the first and second number plus 2 — for example, $10 = (2 + 6) + 2$ and $18 = (4 + 12) + 2$. Therefore $x = (6 + 18) + 2$ or $x = 26$. Another approach is to note that the third number is 4 times the first plus 2 — for example, $10 = 4(2) + 2$ and $18 = 4(4) + 2$. Thus, $x = 4(6) + 2 = 26$.

XV. Full-Length Practice Test with Answer Explanations

The total time for the entire exam is 3 hours and 20 minutes.

Note: Because this practice test does not have the experimental section, it is shorter than the SAT exam you'll take on test day. When you take the SAT, you'll spend 3 hours and 45 minutes, because of the added experimental section. (See the Introduction for more information.)

Answer Sheet

Section 1

CUT HERE

CUT HERE

Section 2

1 (A) (B) (C) (D) (E)	21 (A) (B) (C) (D) (E)
2 (A) (B) (C) (D) (E)	22 (A) (B) (C) (D) (E)
3 (A) (B) (C) (D) (E)	23 (A) (B) (C) (D) (E)
4 (A) (B) (C) (D) (E)	24 (A) (B) (C) (D) (E)
5 (A) (B) (C) (D) (E)	
6 (A) (B) (C) (D) (E)	
7 (A) (B) (C) (D) (E)	
8 (A) (B) (C) (D) (E)	
9 (A) (B) (C) (D) (E)	
10 (A) (B) (C) (D) (E)	
11 (A) (B) (C) (D) (E)	
12 (A) (B) (C) (D) (E)	
13 (A) (B) (C) (D) (E)	
14 (A) (B) (C) (D) (E)	
15 (A) (B) (C) (D) (E)	
16 (A) (B) (C) (D) (E)	
17 (A) (B) (C) (D) (E)	
18 (A) (B) (C) (D) (E)	
19 (A) (B) (C) (D) (E)	
20 (A) (B) (C) (D) (E)	

Section 3

1 (A) (B) (C) (D) (E)
2 (A) (B) (C) (D) (E)
3 (A) (B) (C) (D) (E)
4 (A) (B) (C) (D) (E)
5 (A) (B) (C) (D) (E)
6 (A) (B) (C) (D) (E)
7 (A) (B) (C) (D) (E)
8 (A) (B) (C) (D) (E)
9 (A) (B) (C) (D) (E)
10 (A) (B) (C) (D) (E)
11 (A) (B) (C) (D) (E)
12 (A) (B) (C) (D) (E)
13 (A) (B) (C) (D) (E)
14 (A) (B) (C) (D) (E)
15 (A) (B) (C) (D) (E)
16 (A) (B) (C) (D) (E)
17 (A) (B) (C) (D) (E)
18 (A) (B) (C) (D) (E)
19 (A) (B) (C) (D) (E)
20 (A) (B) (C) (D) (E)

Section 4

1 (A) (B) (C) (D) (E)	21 (A) (B) (C) (D) (E)
2 (A) (B) (C) (D) (E)	22 (A) (B) (C) (D) (E)
3 (A) (B) (C) (D) (E)	23 (A) (B) (C) (D) (E)
4 (A) (B) (C) (D) (E)	24 (A) (B) (C) (D) (E)
5 (A) (B) (C) (D) (E)	25 (A) (B) (C) (D) (E)
6 (A) (B) (C) (D) (E)	26 (A) (B) (C) (D) (E)
7 (A) (B) (C) (D) (E)	27 (A) (B) (C) (D) (E)
8 (A) (B) (C) (D) (E)	28 (A) (B) (C) (D) (E)
9 (A) (B) (C) (D) (E)	29 (A) (B) (C) (D) (E)
10 (A) (B) (C) (D) (E)	30 (A) (B) (C) (D) (E)
11 (A) (B) (C) (D) (E)	31 (A) (B) (C) (D) (E)
12 (A) (B) (C) (D) (E)	32 (A) (B) (C) (D) (E)
13 (A) (B) (C) (D) (E)	33 (A) (B) (C) (D) (E)
14 (A) (B) (C) (D) (E)	34 (A) (B) (C) (D) (E)
15 (A) (B) (C) (D) (E)	35 (A) (B) (C) (D) (E)
16 (A) (B) (C) (D) (E)	
17 (A) (B) (C) (D) (E)	
18 (A) (B) (C) (D) (E)	
19 (A) (B) (C) (D) (E)	
20 (A) (B) (C) (D) (E)	

Section 5

1 (A) (B) (C) (D) (E)	21 (A) (B) (C) (D) (E)
2 (A) (B) (C) (D) (E)	22 (A) (B) (C) (D) (E)
3 (A) (B) (C) (D) (E)	23 (A) (B) (C) (D) (E)
4 (A) (B) (C) (D) (E)	24 (A) (B) (C) (D) (E)
5 (A) (B) (C) (D) (E)	
6 (A) (B) (C) (D) (E)	
7 (A) (B) (C) (D) (E)	
8 (A) (B) (C) (D) (E)	
9 (A) (B) (C) (D) (E)	
10 (A) (B) (C) (D) (E)	
11 (A) (B) (C) (D) (E)	
12 (A) (B) (C) (D) (E)	
13 (A) (B) (C) (D) (E)	
14 (A) (B) (C) (D) (E)	
15 (A) (B) (C) (D) (E)	
16 (A) (B) (C) (D) (E)	
17 (A) (B) (C) (D) (E)	
18 (A) (B) (C) (D) (E)	
19 (A) (B) (C) (D) (E)	
20 (A) (B) (C) (D) (E)	

CUT HERE

Section 6

1	Ⓐ Ⓑ Ⓒ Ⓓ Ⓔ
2	Ⓐ Ⓑ Ⓒ Ⓓ Ⓔ
3	Ⓐ Ⓑ Ⓒ Ⓓ Ⓔ
4	Ⓐ Ⓑ Ⓒ Ⓓ Ⓔ
5	Ⓐ Ⓑ Ⓒ Ⓓ Ⓔ
6	Ⓐ Ⓑ Ⓒ Ⓓ Ⓔ
7	Ⓐ Ⓑ Ⓒ Ⓓ Ⓔ
8	Ⓐ Ⓑ Ⓒ Ⓓ Ⓔ

9. 10. 11.

12. 13. 14. 15.

16. 17. 18.

Section 7

1. Ⓐ Ⓑ Ⓒ Ⓓ Ⓔ
2. Ⓐ Ⓑ Ⓒ Ⓓ Ⓔ
3. Ⓐ Ⓑ Ⓒ Ⓓ Ⓔ
4. Ⓐ Ⓑ Ⓒ Ⓓ Ⓔ
5. Ⓐ Ⓑ Ⓒ Ⓓ Ⓔ
6. Ⓐ Ⓑ Ⓒ Ⓓ Ⓔ
7. Ⓐ Ⓑ Ⓒ Ⓓ Ⓔ
8. Ⓐ Ⓑ Ⓒ Ⓓ Ⓔ
9. Ⓐ Ⓑ Ⓒ Ⓓ Ⓔ
10. Ⓐ Ⓑ Ⓒ Ⓓ Ⓔ
11. Ⓐ Ⓑ Ⓒ Ⓓ Ⓔ
12. Ⓐ Ⓑ Ⓒ Ⓓ Ⓔ
13. Ⓐ Ⓑ Ⓒ Ⓓ Ⓔ
14. Ⓐ Ⓑ Ⓒ Ⓓ Ⓔ
15. Ⓐ Ⓑ Ⓒ Ⓓ Ⓔ
16. Ⓐ Ⓑ Ⓒ Ⓓ Ⓔ
17. Ⓐ Ⓑ Ⓒ Ⓓ Ⓔ
18. Ⓐ Ⓑ Ⓒ Ⓓ Ⓔ
19. Ⓐ Ⓑ Ⓒ Ⓓ Ⓔ

Section 8

1. Ⓐ Ⓑ Ⓒ Ⓓ Ⓔ
2. Ⓐ Ⓑ Ⓒ Ⓓ Ⓔ
3. Ⓐ Ⓑ Ⓒ Ⓓ Ⓔ
4. Ⓐ Ⓑ Ⓒ Ⓓ Ⓔ
5. Ⓐ Ⓑ Ⓒ Ⓓ Ⓔ
6. Ⓐ Ⓑ Ⓒ Ⓓ Ⓔ
7. Ⓐ Ⓑ Ⓒ Ⓓ Ⓔ
8. Ⓐ Ⓑ Ⓒ Ⓓ Ⓔ
9. Ⓐ Ⓑ Ⓒ Ⓓ Ⓔ
10. Ⓐ Ⓑ Ⓒ Ⓓ Ⓔ
11. Ⓐ Ⓑ Ⓒ Ⓓ Ⓔ
12. Ⓐ Ⓑ Ⓒ Ⓓ Ⓔ
13. Ⓐ Ⓑ Ⓒ Ⓓ Ⓔ
14. Ⓐ Ⓑ Ⓒ Ⓓ Ⓔ
15. Ⓐ Ⓑ Ⓒ Ⓓ Ⓔ
16. Ⓐ Ⓑ Ⓒ Ⓓ Ⓔ

Section 9

1. Ⓐ Ⓑ Ⓒ Ⓓ Ⓔ
2. Ⓐ Ⓑ Ⓒ Ⓓ Ⓔ
3. Ⓐ Ⓑ Ⓒ Ⓓ Ⓔ
4. Ⓐ Ⓑ Ⓒ Ⓓ Ⓔ
5. Ⓐ Ⓑ Ⓒ Ⓓ Ⓔ
6. Ⓐ Ⓑ Ⓒ Ⓓ Ⓔ
7. Ⓐ Ⓑ Ⓒ Ⓓ Ⓔ
8. Ⓐ Ⓑ Ⓒ Ⓓ Ⓔ
9. Ⓐ Ⓑ Ⓒ Ⓓ Ⓔ
10. Ⓐ Ⓑ Ⓒ Ⓓ Ⓔ
11. Ⓐ Ⓑ Ⓒ Ⓓ Ⓔ
12. Ⓐ Ⓑ Ⓒ Ⓓ Ⓔ
13. Ⓐ Ⓑ Ⓒ Ⓓ Ⓔ
14. Ⓐ Ⓑ Ⓒ Ⓓ Ⓔ

CUT HERE

Section 1: Essay

Time: 25 minutes

Directions: This essay gives you a chance to develop your own ideas and express them in essay form. Read the question carefully, think about your point of view, present your ideas clearly in logical fashion, and be sure to use standard written English.

You must write your essay in the space provided; you must use only the lines within the margin. You should write on every line (do not skip lines), avoid wide margins, and keep your handwriting to a reasonable size. You may write or print, but try to write as legibly as you can.

You will have 25 minutes for this section. Be sure to write on the topic. An off-topic essay, no matter how well written, will receive a score of zero.

Think about the issue presented below:

> We are living in a world in which teamwork and cooperation are essential tools for survival. As John Donne said, "No man is an island." Yet, there are times when a person must separate himself or herself from a group and speak or act as an individual, even if to do so means rejecting the will of the group and breaking the bonds.

> **Assignment:** Is it sometimes more important to stand as an individual rather than as a member of a group? Plan and write an essay in which you develop your point of view on this question. Be sure to support your position with reasons and examples taken from personal experience, observation, reading, or studies.

Be sure to write only in the space provided on your answer sheet.

IF YOU FINISH BEFORE TIME IS CALLED, CHECK YOUR WORK ON THIS SECTION ONLY. DO NOT WORK ON ANY OTHER SECTION IN THE TEST.

Section 2: Critical Reading

Time: 25 minutes

24 questions

Directions: Each sentence below has either one or two blanks. Each blank indicates that a word or words have been left out. Beneath the sentence are five words or sets of words labeled A through E. Choose the word or set of words that, when inserted in the sentence, *best* fits the meaning of the sentence as a whole.

EXAMPLE:

The regeneration of the Pine Barrens after the devastating wildfire did not take place overnight; on the contrary, the regrowth was _____.

    A.   expected
    B.   encouraged
    C.   gradual
    D.   infinite
    E.   rapid

The correct answer is C.

1. Although there have been sporadic reports of sightings and even blurry photographs of the Abominable Snowman, most scientists remain skeptical; consequently, the existence of the Yeti has been _____ the realm of legend.

    A.   compounded with
    B.   relegated to
    C.   interested in
    D.   ignored by
    E.   disrupted by

2. Some health professionals believe that the excessive use of disinfectants is _____ to a person's health because these products _____ the microbes that may help fight infection.

    A.   useful . . . defuse
    B.   peripheral . . . reject
    C.   detrimental . . . destroy
    D.   acceptable . . . justify
    E.   vital . . . deactivate

3. School officials were surprised by the _____ of plagiarism in the school: a survey indicated that 70% of students had included undocumented material in their research papers.

    A.   brevity
    B.   scrupulousness
    C.   pervasiveness
    D.   reliability
    E.   inflexibility

4. The first-time author was surprised by the pejorative reviews of the critics who found her novel _____ and insipid.

    A.   concise
    B.   trite
    C.   inspiring
    D.   profound
    E.   articulate

5. We would have thought the commentator's remarks regarding the _____ in the recent campaign hyperbolic had we not seen proof of political trickery.

   A. chicanery
   B. effrontery
   C. subtlety
   D. solidarity
   E. meticulousness

6. The prosecuting attorney was concerned by the lack of _____ proof in the case; he feared the _____ nature of the evidence would lead the jury to acquit the defendant.

   A. irrefutable . . . valid
   B. sentimental . . . hybrid
   C. personal . . . illusory
   D. solid . . . incisive
   E. factual . . . circumstantial

7. The chief executives of the company, all characterized by ruthless _____, embezzled thousands of dollars from the employees' pension fund.

   A. indolence
   B. avarice
   C. wrath
   D. irresolution
   E. altruism

8. Fearing the _____ of the incumbent mayor, the nominating committee decided to replace her with a more _____ candidate.

   A. abrasiveness . . . conciliatory
   B. rebelliousness . . . heretical
   C. passivity . . . nondescript
   D. stupidity . . . inane
   E. gentility . . . respectable

Directions: Read the following passage and answer the questions that follow on the basis of what is directly stated and what is implied in the passage and in the introductory information provided.

Questions 9–10 are based on the passage that follows.

Of no English poet, except Shakespeare, can we say with approximate truth that he is the poet of all times. The subjective breath of their own epoch dims the mirror which they hold up to
(5) nature. Missing by their limitation the highest universality, they can only be understood in their setting. It adds but little to our knowledge of Shakespeare's work to regard him as the great Elizabethan; there is nothing temporary in his dra-
(10) mas, except petty incidents and external trappings—so truly did he dwell amidst the elements constituting man in every age and clime. But this cannot be said of any other poet, not even of Chaucer or Spenser, far less of Milton or Pope or
(15) Wordsworth. In their case, the artistic form and the material, the idea and its expression, the beauty and the truth, are to some extent separable. We can distinguish in Milton between the Puritanic theology, which is perishable, and the art whose
(20) beauty can never pass away. The former fixes his kinship with his own age, gives him a definite place in the evolution of English life; the latter is independent of time, a thing which has supreme worth in itself.

9. In the passage, the assertion that "there is nothing temporary in his dramas" (line 9–10) is best understood to mean

   A. Shakespeare's great tragedies focus on leaders whose downfall was brought about through their own tragic flaws.
   B. The themes of Shakespeare's works are universal and require no understanding of the Elizabethan setting to be meaningful.
   C. The Elizabeth Period, often called the Golden Age of Drama, lasted but a few years.
   D. The great poets of the Elizabethan Age, although popular in their time, are no longer read with the same intensity as when they were alive.
   E. Poets who reflect the specific conception of beauty and truth in their lifetimes will stand the test of time.

10. The author mentions Chaucer, Spenser, Milton, Pope, and Wordsworth as examples of poets

   A. who are notable for the their Puritanic philosophy
   B. whose work has transcended the time period in which they lived
   C. whose artistic form is completely inseparable from their content
   D. who are linked inextricably with the epoch in which they lived
   E. whose talents are diminished by comparison to those of Shakespeare

Questions 11–12 are based on the passage that follows.

Since scientists now have evidence to prove that the moon is not made of "green cheese" as the old myth suggests, attention has turned from the composition of the lunar body to theories of its
(5) origin. One of the early theories proposes that the moon formed at the same time as the earth from the same elements. However, samples collected from the moon's surface by lunar probes show that moon rocks do not contain iron, an element
(10) common in Earth samples. The model currently in favor postulates that the moon was formed when a large planetary body struck Earth's surface and broke off a chunk, which spun into orbit. This theory explains the missing iron by theorizing that
(15) the iron in the Earth had drifted into its core, leaving an iron-free outer layer from which the moon was formed.

11. The primary purpose of this passage is to

   A. criticize a method
   B. present a single position
   C. offer alternative explanations
   D. correct a long-standing factual error
   E. refute statistical evidence

12. The author refers to "green cheese" (line 2) to

   A. provide a transition
   B. discredit a silly theory
   C. show how science can explain natural phenomena
   D. provoke a controversy
   E. recognize the role of myth in the natural world

Questions 13–24 are based on the passages that follow.

The first passage was written by a 19th-century American essayist. The second passage is from the State of the Union Address by John Quincy Adams.

Passage 1

I heartily accept the motto,—"That government is best which governs least"; and I should like to see it acted up to more rapidly and systematically. Carried out, it finally amounts to
(5) this, which also I believe,—" That government is best which governs not at all"; and when men are prepared for it, that will be the kind of government which they will have. Government is at best but an expedient; but most governments
(10) are usually, and all governments are sometimes, inexpedient. The objections which have been brought against a standing army, and they are many and weighty, and deserve to prevail, may also at last be brought against a standing gov-
(15) ernment. The standing army is only an arm of the standing government. The government

the standing government. The government itself, which is only the mode which the people have chosen to execute their will, is equally lia-
(20) ble to be abused and perverted before the people can act through it. Witness the present Mexican war, the work of comparatively a few individuals using the standing government as their tool; for, in the outset, the people would
(25) not have consented to this measure.

This American government—what is it but a tradition, though a recent one, endeavoring to transmit itself unimpaired to posterity, but each instant losing some of its integrity? It has not the
(30) vitality and force of a single living man; for a single man can bend it to his will. It is a sort of wooden gun to the people themselves. But it is not the less necessary for this; for the people must have some complicated machinery or other, and
(35) hear its din, to satisfy that idea of government which they have. Governments show thus how successfully men can be imposed on, even impose on themselves, for their own advantage. It is excellent, we must all allow. Yet this government
(40) never of itself furthered any enterprise, but by the alacrity with which it got out of its way. *It* does not keep the country free. *It* does not settle the West. *It* does not educate. The character inherent in the American people has done all that has been
(45) accomplished; and it would have done somewhat more, if the government had not sometimes got in its way. For government is an expedient by which men would fain succeed in letting one another alone; and, as has been said, when it is most expe-
(50) dient, the governed are most let alone by it. Trade and commerce, if they were not made of India rubber, would never manage to bounce over the obstacles which legislators are continually putting in their way; and, if one were to judge these men
(55) wholly by the effects of their actions, and not partly by their intentions, they would deserve to be classed and punished with those mischievous persons who put obstructions on the railroads.

Passage 2

The organization of the militia is yet more indispensable to the liberties of the country. It is only by an effective militia that we can at once enjoy the repose of peace and bid defiance
(5) to foreign aggression; it is by the militia that we are constituted an armed nation, standing in perpetual panoply of defense in the presence of all the other nations of the earth. To this end it would be necessary, if possible, so to shape its
(10) organization as to give it a more united and active energy. There are laws establishing an uniform militia throughout the United States and for arming and equipping its whole body. But it is a body of dislocated members, without
(15) the vigor of unity and having little of uniformity but the name. To infuse into this most important institution the power of which it is susceptible and to make it available for the defense of the Union at the shortest notice and
(20) at the smallest expense possible of time, of life, and of treasure are among the benefits to be expected from the persevering deliberations of Congress.

The condition of the various branches of the
(25) public service resorting from the Department of War, and their administration during the current year, will be exhibited in the report of the Secretary of War and the accompanying documents herewith communicated. The organization and disci-
(30) pline of the Army are effective and satisfactory. To counteract the prevalence of desertion among the troops it has been suggested to withhold from the men a small portion of their monthly pay until the period of their discharge; and some expedient
(35) appears to be necessary to preserve and maintain among the officers so much of the art of horsemanship as could scarcely fail to be found wanting on the possible sudden eruption of a war, which should take us unprovided with a single corps of
(40) cavalry.

225

13. The author's main argument in passage 1 is that

    A. A government must reflect the will of the majority.
    B. The democratic form of government is the most expedient in that it is both effective and inclusive.
    C. The best form of government is one that least interferes in the lives of its citizens.
    D. Power in the hands of the state government is more suitable to the American character than a powerful federal government.
    E. Laws imposed by legislatures on individuals violate the due process amendment of the Constitution.

14. The phrase *many and weighty* (passage 1, line 13) refers to

    A. the reasons to support the establishment of a state militia
    B. arguments against the formation of a permanent army
    C. objections to a government that interferes little in the every day lives of its citizens
    D. heated discussions of the U.S. involvement in the Mexican War
    E. refutation of the refusal of the government to simplify its bureaucracy

15. By using the word *expedient* (line 9) to refer to the government, the author of passage 1 indicates his belief that the U.S. government is

    A. an effective and desirable institution
    B. a brutal regime used to oppress
    C. a traditionally successful organization
    D. a quick fix for all the ills of society
    E. an unfortunate but necessary tool

16. The word *mode* (passage 1, line 17) most nearly means

    A. style
    B. method
    C. world
    D. mannerism
    E. approach

17. The repetition of the word *It* (passage 1, lines 28–30) serves to

    A. distinguish between the governing body and the character of the populace
    B. indicate the inadvisability of a military arm that does not reflect the will of the people
    C. defend the use of force to protect the nation from foreign invasion
    D. reinforce the constitutional insistence on a system of checks and balances
    E. disparage the need for a legislature that employs complicated machinery to accomplish simple tasks

18. The author refers to "India rubber" (passage 1, lines 50–51) to make the point that

    A. the U.S. should engage in profitable trade with India
    B. a comparison of the actions of the government and the action of men reveals they are both inherently flexible
    C. a comparison of the actions of the government and the action of men reveals their inherent flexibility
    D. without its innate resilience, commercial trade would be thwarted by government regulations
    E. the free enterprise system, if unrestricted, will allow trade to flourish

19. The word *vigor* (passage 2, line 15) most nearly means

   A. life
   B. difficulty
   C. drive
   D. enthusiasm
   E. strength

20. The author of passage 2 believes that the benefits of the "persevering deliberations of Congress" (lines 22–23) are

   I.   to energize and strengthen the militia
   II. to save money
   III. to protect the lives of soldiers
   IV. to work efficiently

   A. I and II
   B. I, II, and III
   C. I, III, and IV
   D. II and IV
   E. I, II, III, and IV

21. The author of passage 2 acknowledges all of the following as problems of the militia EXCEPT

   A. preserving the art of horsemanship
   B. an absence of organization and discipline
   C. a disunity in the militia
   D. desertion among the ranks
   E. a lack of dynamism

22. The authors of the two passages most strongly disagree on

   A. the effectiveness of discipline in the armed forces
   B. the indispensability of a permanent military force in the U.S.
   C. the organizational plan of the three branches of the government
   D. the role of the cavalry in case of a sudden attack
   E. the need for an educated populace to protect the liberties granted by the Constitution

23. The attitude of the author of passage 2 toward the assertion of the author of passage 1 that "*It* does not keep the country free" (lines 40–41) would most likely be

   A. whole-hearted agreement
   B. qualified approval
   C. complete disagreement
   D. guarded ambivalence
   E. sympathetic tolerance

24. The author of passage 1 would most likely argue that the justification for a "perpetual panoply of defense" (passage 2, line 7) is

   A. substantiated by the threat of foreign aggression
   B. not meant to be taken literally
   C. of dubious validity
   D. driven by political expedience
   E. solid as witnessed by the example of the Mexican War

IF YOU FINISH BEFORE TIME IS CALLED, CHECK YOUR WORK ON THIS SECTION ONLY. DO NOT WORK ON ANY OTHER SECTION IN THE TEST.

Section 3: Mathematics

Time: 25 minutes
20 questions
Calculator allowed

Reference Information

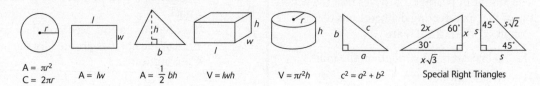

$A = \pi r^2$
$C = 2\pi r$

$A = lw$

$A = \frac{1}{2}bh$

$V = lwh$

$V = \pi r^2 h$

$c^2 = a^2 + b^2$

Special Right Triangles

The complete arc of a circle measures 360°.

The sum of the measures of the angles of a triangle is 180°.

---

1. If 75% of n is $\frac{3}{4}$, what is the value of n?

   A. $\frac{1}{4}$
   B. $\frac{3}{4}$
   C. 1
   D. $\frac{4}{3}$
   E. 75

2. If x and y are positive integers, and $x^2 + y^2 = 25$, which of the following could be a value of y?

   A. −3
   B. −1
   C. 0
   D. 3
   E. 5

3. If $\frac{1}{2}\left(\frac{x}{y}\right) = 4$, then $\frac{y}{x} =$

   A. $\frac{1}{8}$
   B. $\frac{1}{2}$
   C. 1
   D. 8
   E. Cannot be determined

4. If $2x + y > 18$ and $x < 5$, which of the following must be true?

   A. $y = 8$
   B. $x = 5$
   C. $y < 18$
   D. $y > 8$
   E. $y > 10$

5. If x and y are integers, which of the following must be an odd integer?

   A. $x + y$
   B. $2x + y$
   C. $x + 2y$
   D. $3(x + y)$
   E. $2(x + y) + 1$

6. If $4k + 5$ is divided by 7, the remainder is 3. Which of the following could be the value of k?

   A. 0
   B. 1
   C. 2
   D. 3
   E. 4

7. In the accompanying diagram, $\triangle ABC$ is isosceles with $AB = AC$, and points D, C, and B are on a line. If the measure of $\angle A$ is 80°, what is the measure of $\angle ACD$?

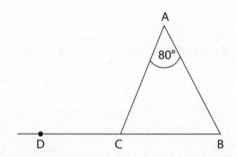

   A. 80°
   B. 100°
   C. 120°
   D. 130°
   E. 150°

8. Points A, B, C, and D are on line l. How many line segments are there, each having 2 of these four points as its endpoints?

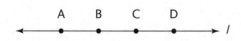

   A. 3
   B. 4
   C. 6
   D. 11
   E. 12

9. In the accompanying diagram, 2 lines intersect. If $a > 90°$, which of the following must be true?

   I. $b < 90°$
   II. $c < 90°$
   III. $a + d > 180°$

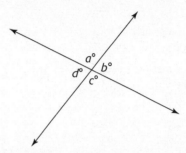

   A. I only
   B. II only
   C. III only
   D. II and III only
   E. I, II, and III

10. Let $a \# b$ be defined as $a \# b = ab - 2b$ for all real numbers. What is the value of $(4 \# 0) \# 3$?

   A. −12
   B. −6
   C. 0
   D. 6
   E. Undefined

11. If $x^4 + y^4 = 10$ and $x^2 + y^2 = 5$, what is the value of $2x^2y^2$?

   A. 5
   B. 10
   C. 15
   D. 20
   E. 25

12. Set A = {–4, –2, 0, 2, 4, 6, 8}. If Set B contains only members obtained by multiplying every member of set A by 7, what is the average of set B?

A. 0
B. 7
C. 14
D. 28
E. 42

13. If a function g is defined as $g(x) = 3x - 3$, what is the value of $3g(3) + 3$?

A. 0
B. 6
C. 21
D. 27
E. 45

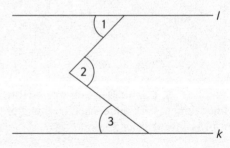

14. If $4^3 + 8^2 = 2(2^n)$, what is the value of n?

A. 4
B. 5
C. 6
D. 7
E. 8

15. In the accompanying diagram, which of the following points could represent the coordinates of $B + 2D$?

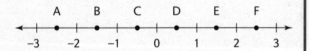

A. A
B. B
C. C
D. F
E. E

16. In the accompanying figure, $\triangle ABC$ is equilateral. If $A(0, 6\sqrt{3})$ and $B(h,k)$, what is the value of h?

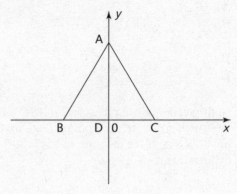

A. $-6\sqrt{3}$
B. -6
C. -3
D. 6
E. 12

17. In the accompanying figure, line l is parallel to line k. If $m\angle 2 = 4x$ and $m\angle 1 = 2x + 4$, which of the following is the measure of $\angle 3$?

A. $2x - 4$
B. $2x$
C. $2x + 4$
D. $3x + 2$
E. $4x$

18. There are 2 roads connecting Smithtown and Jones Village, and there are 3 roads connecting Jones Village and Glen Cove. How many different ways can a person travel from Smithtown to Glen Cove and back, each way passing through Jones Village without using any of the roads more than once?

A. 5
B. 6
C. 12
D. 24
E. 36

19. A video store charges $4 for a monthly membership and $2 for each video rental. In December, Amanda rented 10 videos. What is the average cost per rental for that month?

A. $2
B. $2.20
C. $2.40
D. $3.00
E. $3.20

20. In the accompanying circle, the length of diameter $\overline{EOF}$ is 12, and the $m\angle DFE$ is twice the $m\angle DEF$. What is the length of DF?

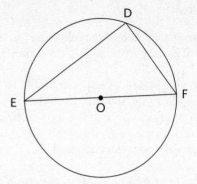

A. 3
B. $3\sqrt{3}$
C. 6
D. $6\sqrt{3}$
E. 8

IF YOU FINISH BEFORE TIME IS CALLED, CHECK YOUR WORK ON THIS SECTION ONLY. DO NOT WORK ON ANY OTHER SECTION IN THE TEST.

STOP

Section 4: Writing

Time: 25 minutes

35 questions

Directions: Read each of the following questions carefully. Then select the best answer from the choices provided. Fill in the corresponding circle on your answer sheet.

The following sentences test your ability to recognize correctness and effectiveness of expression. In each sentence, part of the sentence or the entire sentence is underlined. Underneath each sentence you will find five ways of phrasing the underlined material. Choice A is the same as the original sentence in the question; the other four choices are different. If you think the original sentence is correct as written, select Choice A; if not, carefully consider choices B, C, D, and E, and select the one you think is the best.

In making your selection, follow the requirements of standard written English. Carefully consider the grammar, diction (word choice), sentence construction, and punctuation of each sentence. When you make your choice, select the most effective sentence, the one that is clear and precise, without any awkwardness or ambiguity.

EXAMPLE:

The high fuel efficiency and low emissions of a newly released hybrid car <u>account for its popularity</u> with those who are environmentally aware.

A. account for its popularity
B. accounts for its popularity
C. account for their popularity
D. are the reason why it has popularity
E. accounts for their popularity

The correct answer is A.

---

1. Statistics indicate that avalanches can be <u>equally as dangerous to expert skiers as</u> to novices.

   A. equally as dangerous to expert skiers as
   B. equal in danger to expert skiers as
   C. equally dangerous to expert skiers as
   D. as dangerous to expert skiers as
   E. as equally dangerous to expert skiers as

2. <u>When one buys products online,</u> you should be sure you know the return policy of the company.

   A. When one buys products online,
   B. When you buy products online,
   C. When one is buying products online,
   D. If one buys products online,
   E. If one wants to buy products online,

3. Usually busy transporting needed supplies, <u>as the demand for fuel has declined the huge supertankers filled with oil are currently floating offshore</u>.

   A. as the demand for fuel has declined the huge supertankers filled with oil are currently floating offshore.

   B. and floating offshore, the huge supertankers are filled with oil as the demand for fuel has declined.

   C. huge supertankers filled with oil are currently floating offshore as the demand for fuel has declined.

   D. huge supertankers, as the demand for fuel has declined, filled with oil are currently floating offshore.

   E. the decline in the demand for fuel has left huge supertankers filled with oil currently floating offshore.

4. In 1992 the Korean group Seo Taiji and Boys became a wildly popular sensation, <u>playing innovative dance music that had a tremendous impact on Korean youth culture</u>.

   A. playing innovative dance music that had a tremendous impact on Korean youth culture.

   B. and playing innovative dance music that had a tremendous impact on Korean youth culture.

   C. they played innovative dance music that had a tremendous impact on Korean youth culture.

   D. playing innovative dance music and while they were having a tremendous impact on Korean youth culture.

   E. they played innovative dance music and had a tremendous impact on Korean youth culture.

5. Green technology companies <u>are to help create innovative ways in which industry can meet the needs of society</u> without damaging or depleting natural resources.

   A. are to help create innovative ways in which industry can meet the needs of society

   B. are helping creating innovative ways in which industry can meet the needs of society

   C. being created innovative ways in which industry can meet the needs of society

   D. have been formed to help create innovative ways in which industry can meet the needs of society

   E. are forming in order to help create innovative ways for which industry can meet the needs of society

6. <u>The birds of New Zealand had no natural predators, wings became unnecessary, and many varieties, including the kiwi and the kakapo parrot, became flightless</u>.

   A. The birds of New Zealand had no natural predators, wings became unnecessary, and many varieties, including the kiwi and the kakapo parrot, became flightless.

   B. The birds of New Zealand had no natural predators; wings becoming unnecessary and many varieties, including the kiwi and the kakapo parrot, becoming flightless.

   C. Because the birds of New Zealand had no natural predators, wings are becoming unnecessary, and many varieties, including the kiwi and the kakapo parrot, are becoming flightless.

   D. Since the birds of New Zealand had no natural predators; wings became unnecessary and many varieties, including the kiwi and the kakapo parrot, became flightless.

   E. Because the birds of New Zealand had no natural predators, wings became unnecessary, and many varieties, including the kiwi and the kakapo parrot, became flightless.

7. The Heisman Trophy, <u>is named for football coach John Heisman, and it is awarded to the most outstanding college football player, and it is a very prestigious award</u>.

   A. is named for football coach John Heisman, and it is awarded to the most outstanding college football player, and it is a very prestigious award.

   B. named for football coach John Heisman, is a very prestigious award presented to the most outstanding college football player.

   C. which is named for football coach John Heisman, and is awarded to the most outstanding college football player, is a very prestigious award.

   D. named for football coach John Heisman, it is a very prestigious award presented to the most outstanding college football player.

   E. is named for football coach John Heisman, which is awarded to the most outstanding college football player, and it is a very prestigious award.

8. A trip to Greenland is an arctic <u>adventure: visitors can dog-sled on the tundra, traverse icy glaciers, and they can go explore magnificent fjords</u>.

   A. adventure: visitors can dog-sled on the tundra, traverse icy glaciers, and they can go explore magnificent fjords.

   B. adventure, visitors dog-sledding on the tundra, traversing icy glaciers, and they can go exploring magnificent fjords.

   C. adventure with visitors dog-sledding on the tundra, traversing icy glaciers, and going on explorations of magnificent fjords.

   D. adventure: visitors can dog-sled on the tundra, traverse icy glaciers, and explore magnificent fjords.

   E. adventure being that visitors can go dog-sledding on the tundra, traversing icy glaciers, and they can go explore magnificent fjords.

9. The young deer <u>were gathered in the clearing, and each of them ate their</u> fill of leaves in the quiet pre-dawn hours.

   A. were gathered in the clearing, and each of them ate their

   B. was gathered in the clearing, and each of them ate their

   C. were gathered in the clearing, and each of them ate its

   D. were gathering in the clearing, and each of them were eating their

   E. was gathered in the clearing, and they ate their

10. Scientists studying geological formations of volcanic <u>origin have been surprised when they studied and found that the depth of many volcanoes exceed 1,000 feet</u>.

    A. origin have been surprised when they studied and found that the depth of many volcanoes exceed 1,000 feet.

    B. origin have been surprised when they found that the depth of many volcanoes exceed 1,000 feet.

    C. origin have been surprised when they studied and found that the depth of many volcanoes exceeds 1,000 feet.

    D. origin has been surprised when they studied and found that the depth of many volcanoes exceeds 1,000 feet.

    E. origin have been surprised when they found that the depth of many volcanoes exceeds 1,000 feet.

11. <u>Neither the weather reports or the almanac predict a snowfall large enough to close school</u>.

   A.   Neither the weather reports or the almanac predict a snowfall large enough to close school.
   B.   Neither of the weather reports or the almanac predicts the snowfall will be sufficient to close school.
   C.   Neither the weather reports nor the almanac predicts a snowfall large enough to close school.
   D.   Neither the weather reports nor the almanac predict a snowfall sufficient enough to close school.
   E.   Neither of the weather reports nor of the almanac are predicting the snowfall will be sufficient to close school.

Directions: In the following questions, you will be tested on your ability to recognize errors in grammar and usage. Every sentence below contains either one error or no error. None of the sentences contains more than one error. If the sentence contains an error, it will be in one of the underlined parts of the sentence. You should find the part of the sentence that needs to be changed to make the sentence correct. If you think the sentence is correct as written, select Choice E, no error. Keep the requirements of standard written English in mind as you carefully read the sentences.

EXAMPLE:

As the doors to Carnegie Hall <u>slowly opened</u> and the audience <u>began to</u> flow in, each of the musi-
                                   A   B

cians <u>in the orchestra</u> tuned <u>their</u> instrument before striking the opening chords of the symphony.
            C   D

<u>No error</u>.
   E
The correct answer is D.

12. <u>Through an</u> intensive exercise program at
         A
   <u>home</u> and proper diet, many people have
      B
   <u>become</u> physically fit without <u>doing it at</u> a
      C   D
   gym. <u>No error</u>.
            E

13. Just when the school's <u>administrators</u>
                                  A
   <u>thought</u> the transition to the new building
   had <u>gone smooth</u>, they discovered that all the
            B
   <u>plumbing in</u> the bathrooms <u>was faulty</u>.
         C   D
   <u>No error</u>.
      E

14. <u>Although</u> the essay was fascinating and well
    A
    written, the <u>editor felt</u> compelled to
    B
    <u>comment about</u> the obvious <u>use of</u> uncited
    C D
    sources. <u>No error</u>.
    E

15. Marlee and Ava were shocked that
    <u>they had won</u> the scene contest; <u>indeed</u>, they
    A B
    considered <u>their</u> competitor's performance
    C
    <u>superior to theirs</u>. <u>No error</u>.
    D E

16. <u>All of the basketball players</u> except Olivia
    A
    and <u>I</u> <u>have agreed</u> to meet at the school for
    B C
    practice <u>before the play-off game</u>. <u>No error</u>.
    D E

17. <u>While</u> the plays of Christopher Marlowe
    A
    <u>were enormously</u> successful <u>during his life-</u>
    B C
    time, most contemporary critics find them
    inferior to <u>William Shakespeare</u>. <u>No error</u>.
    D E

18. <u>Of the two paintings</u> by Renoir hanging
    A
    <u>in the lobby</u> of the museum, the <u>one of</u> the
    B C
    dancer is the <u>most admired</u>. <u>No error</u>.
    D E

19. <u>Within the courtyard</u> of the palace <u>grows</u> the
    A B
    cherry trees <u>that produce</u> the luscious fruit
    C
    <u>for which</u> the region is known. <u>No error</u>.
    D E

20. <u>When entertaining</u> guests <u>for dinner</u> in my
    A B
    home, I often prefer <u>serving</u> my own dessert
    C
    <u>more than</u> serving a ready made cake from
    D
    the bakery. <u>No error</u>.
    E

21. The Alvin Ailey American Dance Theater,
    <u>led by</u> Artistic Director Judith Jamison,
    A
    <u>is a troupe</u> that has earned <u>its</u> reputation
    B C
    <u>by celebrating</u> the grace and beauty of
    D
    African American culture. <u>No error</u>.
    E

22. <u>After</u> the torrential rainstorm, it was
    A
    <u>clear that</u> neither of the football teams <u>were</u>
    B C
    able <u>to play well</u> on the muddy expanse that
    D
    had once been a grassy field. <u>No error</u>.
    E

23. <u>By the end</u> of this year, Olympic champion
    A
    Michael Phelps will have <u>swum</u> the equiva-
    B
    lent <u>of twice</u> the <u>width of</u> the Atlantic Ocean.
    C D
    <u>No error</u>.
    E

24. Ricardo was <u>preparing for</u> his chemistry
    A
    project <u>at home</u> all morning, <u>but</u> he
    B C
    <u>was studying</u> in the library the night before.
    D
    <u>No error</u>.
    E

25. <u>During last week's</u> lecture on the environ-
    A
    ment, Mr. Simon made several <u>illusions</u> to
    B
    the <u>swamp reclamation</u> plan <u>created by</u> his
    C D
    team of graduate students. <u>No error</u>.
    E

26. That there had been a recent infestation of
     A   B

termites in the house became evident

as soon as the contractors removed the old
 C   D

paneling. No error.
          E

27. Opposite to what most people think, the
    A

lavender herb is not always lavender; in fact,
         B   C

it appears in almost every shade of the rain-
               D

bow. No error.
     E

28. Although the Boston Marathon is a grueling
    A   B

route that covers 26 miles of hilly terrain,
     C

thousands of runners stagger across the fin-
                   D

ish line each year since 1897. No error.
                        E

29. Owners of ski resorts all over the United

States have been concerned about the
       A

frequency of avalanches, noting that it has
    B   C

become a severe hazard in the past few
                   D

seasons. No error.
     E

Questions 30–35 are based on the following passage.

The following passage is an early draft of an essay that needs some editing and revision. First, read the passage; then, consider the questions that follow. Some questions will ask you to revise a particular sentence or will ask you to find the best version of the sentence. Other questions will ask you about the structure or organization of the essay. Always consider your revisions in the context of the whole essay. In choosing your answers, follow the requirements of standard written English.

(1) Can you imagine digging in a field and making a discovery that some consider the newest wonder of the world? (2) This is what happened in 1974 to a group of Chinese farmers in a field outside the city of Xi'an in central China. (3) These were men which were digging a well when they unearthed some terra cotta figures of soldiers. (4) This accidental find led to one of the most amazing archeological events of the century.

(5) Chinese experts arrived to supervise the digging, they uncovered the terra cotta army that had been raised to protect the tomb of Emperor Qin, he lived in 221 B.C. (6) To protect himself in the afterlife, Qin ordered slaves to create an army of baked clay. (7) It is estimated that slaves constructed 7,000 lifelike and life-size warriors along with 520 horses and 130 chariots. (8) What is most incredible is that each soldier is distinct. (9) Each of the warriors varies in facial characteristics, clothing, footwear, and weapons. (10) There are four main categories of figures: chariot warriors, infantrymen, cavalrymen, and horses. (11) Nevertheless, there are generals, middle-ranking officers, lower-ranking officers, ordinary soldiers, and armored soldiers. (12) They are all made of baked clay called terra cotta. (13) When the army was completed to the Emperor's satisfaction, the terra cotta figures were placed in the pits in precise military formation.

(14) The Chinese have built a huge hall to enclose all the warriors and to protect them from the weather. (15) They are constantly working to repair those clay figures that have been damaged by time and weather so that the whole army will be restored. (16) You should see this sight some time.

30. In the first paragraph (sentences 1–4), the author is primarily

    A. relating a personal anecdote
    B. explaining a misconception
    C. setting up a contrast
    D. introducing the topic
    E. arguing a position

31. In context, which of the following is the best revision of sentence 3 (reproduced below)?

These were men which were digging a well when they unearthed some terra cotta figures of soldiers.

A. As it is now.
B. These men, who were digging a well, unearthing some terra cotta figures of soldiers.
C. They were digging a well when they unearthed some terra cotta figures of soldiers.
D. They were digging a well and unearthing some terra cotta figures of soldiers.
E. They have been digging a well and unearthing some terra cotta figures of soldiers.

32. What is the best revision of sentence 5 (reproduced below) ?

Chinese experts arrived to supervise the digging, they uncovered the terra cotta army that had been built to protect the tomb of Emperor Qin, he lived in 221 B.C.

A. Chinese experts who arrived to supervise the digging, uncovered the terra cotta army that had been raised to protect the tomb of Emperor Qin, he lived in 221 B.C.
B. When Chinese experts arrived to supervise the digging, they uncovered the terra cotta army that had been raised in 221 B.C. to protect the tomb of Emperor Qin.
C. Arriving to supervise the digging, they uncovered the terra cotta army that had been raised in 221 B.C. to protect the tomb of Emperor Qin.
D. Chinese experts arrived to supervise the digging and uncovered the terra cotta army that had been raised to protect the tomb of Emperor Qin, he lived in 221 B.C.
E. Supervising the digging, the Chinese experts uncovered the terra cotta army that had been raised to protect the tomb of Emperor Qin and he lived in 221 B.C.

33. What is the best way to revise and improve sentence 11 (reproduced below)?

Nevertheless, there are generals, middle-ranking officers, lower-ranking officers, ordinary soldiers, and armored soldiers.

A. As it is now.
B. There are, however, generals, middle-ranking officers, lower-ranking officers, ordinary soldiers, and armored soldiers.
C. Among the warriors are generals, middle-ranking officers, lower-ranking officers, ordinary soldiers, and armored soldiers.
D. Thus, there are generals, middle-ranking officers, lower-ranking officers, ordinary soldiers, and armored soldiers.
E. Furthermore generals, middle-ranking officers, lower-ranking officers, ordinary soldiers, and armored soldiers are there.

34. Which of the following should be done with sentence 12 (reproduced below)?

They are all made of baked clay called terra cotta.

A. Leave it as it is for it adds an important detail.
B. Move it before sentence 8.
C. Move it to the end of the first paragraph.
D. Delete it; the point has already been made.
E. Insert the words *In fact* at the beginning.

35. Which would be the best sentence to replace sentence 16 (reproduced below)?

You should see this sight some time.

A. A visit to Xi'an to see the Terra Cotta warriors has become a must for all tourists to China.

B. Visiting China, especially Xi'an don't miss the amazing warriors.

C. For every tourist, a visit to see the warriors are a required sight.

D. If you go to China, a tourist should not miss going to see the amazing warriors of Xi'an.

E. In conclusion, visiting Xi'an to see the terra cotta warriors have become a must for all tourists to China.

IF YOU FINISH BEFORE TIME IS CALLED, CHECK YOUR WORK ON THIS SECTION ONLY. DO NOT WORK ON ANY OTHER SECTION IN THE TEST.

Section 5: Critical Reading

Time: 25 minutes

24 questions

Directions: Each sentence below has either one or two blanks. Each blank indicates that a word has been left out. Beneath the sentence are five words or sets of words labeled A through E. Choose the word or set of words that, when inserted in the sentence, *best* fits the meaning of the sentence as a whole.

EXAMPLE:

The regeneration of the Pine Barrens after the devastating wildfire did not take place overnight; on the contrary, the regrowth was _____.

A. expected
B. encouraged
C. gradual
D. infinite
E. rapid

The correct answer is C.

---

1. Hoping to _____ the black mark from his record, Bart conducted himself with proper decorum during the remainder of his tenure.

A. exacerbate
B. extol
C. exchange
D. explicate
E. expunge

2. Beth professed an interest in diverse styles of art: her _____ collection consisted of Native American sand paintings, Renaissance oils, and Pop Art sculpture.

A. egregious
B. educational
C. effervescent
D. elusive
E. eclectic

3. Aromas of the holiday season evoke childhood memories of family visits to my grandmother's apartment, her kitchen _____ of traditional dishes lovingly prepared.

A. solicitous
B. redolent
C. conscious
D. defiant
E. contemptuous

4. Unable to determine the authenticity of the purportedly ancient document, the Egyptologist was forced to declare it _____.

A. apocryphal
B. primordial
C. ritualistic
D. illegible
E. inevitable

5. The inclusion of Jeff Koons's whimsical sculptures in a recent exhibition at the Chateau de Versailles has excited some fierce protests from a right-wing group of French critics who object to the _____ of his _____ pieces with the serious grandeur of the 17th-century palace.

A. contradiction . . . serious
B. individualism . . . archaic
C. enormity . . . palatial
D. provincialism . . . aesthetic
E. juxtaposition . . . playful

Directions: Read the following passages and answer the questions that follow on the basis of what is directly stated and what is implied in the passages and in the introductory information provided.

Questions 6–9 are based on the passages that follow.

Passage 1

Many people have an impression that the more ornate an article is, the more work has been lavished upon it. There never was a more erroneous idea. The diligent polish in order to secure nice (5) plain surfaces, or the neat fitting of parts together, is infinitely more difficult than adding a florid casting to conceal clumsy workmanship. Of course certain forms of elaboration involve great pains and labor; but the mere fact that a piece of (10) work is decorated does not show that it has cost any more in time and execution than if it were plain—frequently many hours have been saved by the device of covering up defects with cheap ornament. How often one finds that a simple chair with (15) a plain back costs more than one which is apparently elaborately carved! The reason is that the plain one had to be made out of a decent piece of wood, while the ornate one was turned out of a poor piece, and then stamped with a pattern in (20) order to attract the attention from the inferior material of which it was composed.

Passage 2

Although we decline to give specific directions about what varieties of furniture should constitute the furnishings of a house, or to illustrate its style or fashion by drawings, and content ourselves (5) with the single remark, that it should, in all cases, be strong, plain, and durable—no sham, nor ostentation about it—and such as is made for use: mere trinkets stuck about the room, on center tables, in corners, or on the mantelpiece, are the foolishest (10) things imaginable. They are costly; they require a world of care, to keep them in condition; and then, with all this care, they are good for nothing, in any sensible use. We have frequently been into a country house, where we anticipated better things, and, (15) on being introduced into the "parlor," actually found everything in the furniture line so dainty and "prinked up," that we were afraid to sit down on the frail things stuck around by way of seats, for fear of breaking them; and everything about it (20) looked so gingerly and inhospitable, that we felt an absolute relief when we could fairly get out of it, and take a place by the wide old fireplace, in the common living room, comfortably ensconced in a good old easy, high-backed, split-bottomed (25) chair—there was positive comfort in that, when in the "parlor" there was nothing but restraint and discomfort.

6. Both authors would most likely agree with which saying?

    A. Necessity is the mother of invention.

    B. Simplicity is indeed often the sign of truth and a criterion of beauty.

    C. An Englishman's home is his castle.

    D. Time is a great healer, but a poor beautician.

    E. Beauty is no quality in things themselves: it exists merely in the mind which contemplates them.

7. The assertion in passage 1, lines 1–4 ("Many . . . idea") corresponds to which idea in passage 2?

    A. "we anticipated better things" (line 14)

    B. "nothing but restraint and discomfort" (lines 26–27)

    C. "everything about it looked so gingerly and inhospitable" (lines 19–20)

    D. "trinkets stuck about the room" (line 8)

    E. "no sham, nor ostentation about it" (lines 6–7)

8. Unlike passage 1, passage 2 relies on

    A. literary allusion

    B. historical data

    C. direct citation

    D. anecdote

    E. scholarly research

9. Both passages support the point that

    A. highly elaborate furnishings are a sign of excellent workmanship

    B. a comfortable, soft easy chair is essential in every home

    C. the most desirable furniture is plain and simple

    D. decorative details personalize a home and stamp it with the owner's personality

    E. the more work that goes into a piece of furniture, the more beautiful it will be

Questions 10–19 are based on the passage that follows.

The following excerpt is from a British novel first published in 1871. Dorothea Brooke and her sister Celia are well-to-do young ladies living in an English village.

      Miss Brooke had that kind of beauty which seems to be thrown into relief by poor dress. Her hand and wrist were so finely formed that she could wear sleeves not less bare of style than those

(5) in which the Blessed Virgin appeared to Italian painters; and her profile as well as her stature and bearing seemed to gain the more dignity from her plain garments, which by the side of provincial fashion gave her the impressiveness of a fine quo-

(10) tation from the Bible,—or from one of our elder poets,—in a paragraph of today's newspaper. She was usually spoken of as being remarkably clever, but with the addition that her sister Celia had more common-sense. Nevertheless, Celia wore scarcely

(15) more trimmings; and it was only to close observers that her dress differed from her sister's, and had a shade of coquetry in its arrangements; for Miss Brooke's plain dressing was due to mixed conditions, in most of which her sister shared. . . .

(20)   The rural opinion about the new young ladies, even among the cottagers, was generally in favour of Celia as being so amiable and innocent-looking, while Miss Brooke's large eyes seemed, like her religion, too unusual and striking. Poor Dorothea!

(25) compared with her, the innocent-looking Celia was knowing and worldly-wise; so much subtler is a human mind than the outside tissues which make a sort of blazonry or clock-face for it. . . .

    Yet those who approached Dorothea, though

(30) prejudiced against her by this alarming hearsay, found that she had a charm unaccountably reconcilable with it. Most men thought her bewitching when she was on horseback. She loved the fresh air and the various aspects of the country, and

(35) when her eyes and cheeks glowed with mingled pleasure she looked very little like a devotee. Riding was an indulgence which she allowed herself in spite of conscientious qualms; she felt that she enjoyed it in a pagan sensuous way, and always

(40) looked forward to renouncing it. She was open,

ardent, and not in the least self-admiring; indeed, it was pretty to see how her imagination adorned her sister Celia with attractions altogether superior to her own, and if any gentleman appeared to come to (45) the Grange from some other motive than that of seeing Mr. Brooke, she concluded that he must be in love with Celia: Sir James Chettam, for example, whom she constantly considered from Celia's point of view, inwardly debating whether it would (50) be good for Celia to accept him. That he should be regarded as a suitor to herself would have seemed to her a ridiculous irrelevance. Dorothea, with all her eagerness to know the truths of life, retained very childlike ideas about marriage.

10. The author's primary purpose for writing this passage is

   A. to argue that the rural setting of the story is more appropriate than an urban setting
   B. to expose the rivalry between two sisters
   C. to create a character sketch
   D. to explain the artistic source from which the subject of the novel will be drawn
   E. to account for the somewhat prejudiced opinions of the villagers

11. The author refers to the Bible (line 10) and today's newspaper (line 11) to suggest

   A. the epic cadences of the Bible are far more expressive of Miss Brooke's beauty than ordinary journalistic prose
   B. the inappropriateness of the religious content of a paragraph in the local paper
   C. his displeasure with modern styles, which should reflect the modesty of more ancient garments
   D. the refined and enduring simplicity of Miss Brooke's dress
   E. his conviction that provincial journalists should refer to the Bible as a model for eloquent writing

12. The word *addition* (line 13) most nearly means

   A. qualification
   B. sum
   C. total
   D. completion
   E. accumulation

13. The author implies that close observers (lines 15–16)

   A. would be the only ones to notice the slightly flirtatious nature of Celia's garments
   B. would have the discernment to tell the two sisters apart for they were so similar in appearance
   C. were necessary to chaperone the two young women
   D. would note the poor quality of the arrangements made for the sisters
   E. were never able to overcome their prejudice against the bolder, more worldly-wise sister

14. The word *shade* (line 17) most nearly means

   A. color
   B. shadow
   C. dimness
   D. hint
   E. gloom

15. The author suggests that the cottagers (line 21) found Dorothea's religious views

   A. traditional and innocent
   B. passionate and pagan
   C. extraordinary and remarkable
   D. subtle and charming
   E. imaginative and childlike

16. Which of the following statements, if true, would most undermine the author's arguments about Dorothea's attitude towards riding?

    A. She unabashedly adored riding and had no qualms about indulging in this exercise every day.

    B. She was somewhat embarrassed by the sensual pleasure she received from riding.

    C. Horseback riding was considered too wild an activity for well-bred young women of the time.

    D. Men found Miss Brooke especially appealing when she rode with abandon.

    E. Riding gave Miss Brooke a sense of freedom from the restrictions of her religious life.

17. According to Dorothea, any man who came to the Grange not to see Mr. Brooke was motivated by

    A. the desire to ask her father for her hand in marriage

    B. religious zeal

    C. interest in purchasing horses

    D. love for Celia

    E. curiosity about her reputation as a witch

18. The word *adorned* (line 42) most nearly means

    A. decorated
    B. admired
    C. envied
    D. supported
    E. credited

19. The quality of Dorothea that the author seems to admire most is

    A. her religious piety
    B. her horseback riding skill
    C. her physical attractiveness
    D. her ingenuousness passion
    E. her love for rustic pleasures

Questions 20–24 are based on the passage that follows.

The following article was written by a recent graduate of the Columbia Business School.

If you interviewed a random sample of business school students in 1988, the concept of environmental markets would have been foreign to virtually everyone you spoke with. If you did the
(5) same in 1968, the concept of "environment" itself would have been foreign to most. As we look forward in 2008 at the opportunities for growth and investment both in the U.S. and globally in the two decades ahead, the specter of the effects of
(10) global warming and the pressure placed on natural resources from an expanding global population with ever-increasing rates of per-capita consumption will result in increased value placed on any activities, which lessen the impact of development
(15) on natural systems, including climate, air, water, biodiversity, etc.

So what exactly do we mean when we say "environmental markets" and how are these markets going to impact the business landscape? First,
(20) the basics: Anytime a unit of exchange arises from an underlying activity that is perceived to benefit the environment by either the buyer of that unit or the governing body that created the units of exchange, the main ingredients of an environmen-
(25) tal market are present. In a cap-and-trade system, the governing body places a cap on the total amount of air or water pollution that may be emitted by issuing an equivalent number of allowances, denominated in units of pollution. These
(30) allowances may be issued by the government to the business entities that are regulated by the program in amounts similar to their expected production, to lessen the economic impact, or those entities may have to purchase the allowances from
(35) the government in an auction. At the end of each specified period, usually a year, the business entities will have to surrender a number of allowances, or permits, equal to their generation of pollution during the period. As the governing
(40) entity reduces the supply of allowances available to the market in each subsequent year, the price will go up unless the regulated businesses invest

in technologies that will reduce their pollution per unit of output, thereby reducing their demand and
(45) the overall market demand for allowances. Environmental markets that are not set up as cap-and-trade markets in the U.S. include the state-level markets for renewable energy credits, which are granted to producers of renewable energy and
(50) given value because utilities must purchase an amount of these credits determined by the state, and the voluntary market for greenhouse gas emissions, in which credits arising from a unit of greenhouses gas emissions avoided are granted to
(55) owners of qualifying project activities by accredited third-party verifiers and sold to voluntary buyers, primarily to conform with the buyer's goals becoming "carbon neutral." Companies can claim to be carbon neutral if they purchase an
(60) amount of these credits for avoided greenhouse gas emissions equivalent to the total amount of emissions they produce. This is increasingly important from a public relations and corporate responsibility perspective in the United States,
(65) even in the absence of federal legislation governing greenhouse gas emissions.

Adapted and reprinted with permission of the author, Jonathan Rappe.

20. The purpose of the first two sentences of the passage ("If . . . most") is to

A. suggest that the environmental movement had its roots in the recent past

B. give examples of years in which foreign markets were environmentally savvier than U.S. markets

C. imply that astute business students need to recognize and capitalize on unanticipated trends

D. chastise those leaders in business education who reject the implications of global warming

E. contrast practices in the past with those needed to ensure a secure environmental future

21. According to the author's use of the term, all of the following would require a "cap" (line 26) EXCEPT

A. a coal-burning power plant

B. an automobile powered only by electricity

C. a waste incinerator

D. a farm in which fertilizer runs off into a stream

E. mining companies that dump mining waste directly into rivers

22. The word *allowances* (line 30) refers to

A. the amount of pollution an entity is permitted to emit

B. the funds a business must set aside to pay for pollution clean-up

C. the total government penalty issued to those companies who pollute the air and water

D. the economic impact of the reduction of emissions in a given year

E. a system by which allowable pollution units are increased as pollution increases

23. The author believes that it is important for a company to become "carbon neutral" (line 58) because

I. The company will benefit from a good public image.

II. The company will demonstrate its awareness of accountability.

III. The company will be complying with government regulations.

A. I only

B. I and III

C. I and II

D. II only

E. I, II, and III

24. The author of this passage most likely would agree that

    A. government regulations that control allowable greenhouse emissions are too stringent.

    B. the U.S. has a history of refusing to address environmental problems, a position that will adversely affect the growth of business in this country.

    C. renewable resources in the United States are so abundant as to make regulations that govern their use superfluous.

    D. in the future, more value will be placed on any activities that lessen the impact of development on natural systems.

    E. the realistic goal of the environmental movement should be to completely eliminate air and water pollution in the United States.

IF YOU FINISH BEFORE TIME IS CALLED, CHECK YOUR WORK ON THIS SECTION ONLY. DO NOT WORK ON ANY OTHER SECTION IN THE TEST.

Section 6: Mathematics

Time: 25 minutes
18 questions
Calculator allowed

Reference Information

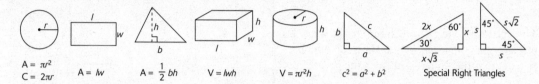

$A = \pi r^2$
$C = 2\pi r$ $A = lw$ $A = \frac{1}{2} bh$ $V = lwh$ $V = \pi r^2 h$ $c^2 = a^2 + b^2$ Special Right Triangles

The complete arc of a circle measures 360°.

The sum of the measures of the angles of a triangle is 180°.

1. If $2x + 1 = 3$, what is the value of $-2x + 1$?

   A. -2
   B. -1
   C. 1
   D. 2
   E. 4

2. In a math class there are 12 girls. If 25% of the students in the class are boys, what is the total number of students in the class?

   A. 15
   B. 16
   C. 24
   D. 36
   E. 48

3. Given the sequence 1, 2, 4, 8, . . . , what is the 10th term divided by the 5th term?

   A. 2
   B. 16
   C. 32
   D. 64
   E. 128

4. In the accompanying figure, line l is perpendicular to line m. What is the value of y, in degrees, in terms of x?

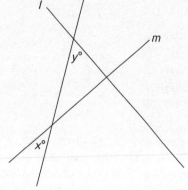

   A. x
   B. $90 - x$
   C. $90 + x$
   D. $2x$
   E. $180 - 2x$

5. Ten years from now, Janet will be *m* years old, and she will be exactly half her father's age. Which of the following represents the difference of their ages today?

A. *m* – 10
B. *m*
C. *m* + 10
D. 2*m* – 10
E. 2*m*

6. The accompanying graph summarizes the sales of a company over six years. Between which two years is the increase in sales the greatest?

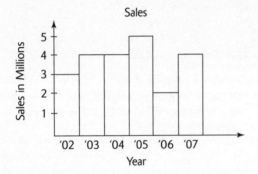

A. '02–'03
B. '03–'04
C. '04–'05
D. '05–'06
E. '06–'07

7. Let *S* be a set of all positive integers *k* such that k^2 is equal to the product of all integral divisors of *k*. (For example, 6 is a member of *S* because $6^2 = 1 \times 2 \times 3 \times 6$). Which of the following numbers is a member of *S*?

A. 4
B. 8
C. 9
D. 12
E. 16

8. In the accompanying diagram, the figure is a rectangular solid with *HG* = 6, *GF* = 4, and *CG* = 2, what is the total surface area?

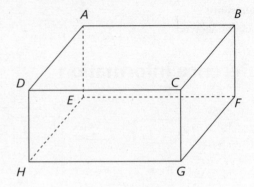

Not drawn to scale.

A. 22
B. 36
C. 44
D. 48
E. 88

Directions for Student-Produced Response Questions (Grid-ins): Questions 9–18 require you to solve the problem and enter your answer by carefully making the circles on the special grid. Examples of the appropriate way to mark the grid follow.

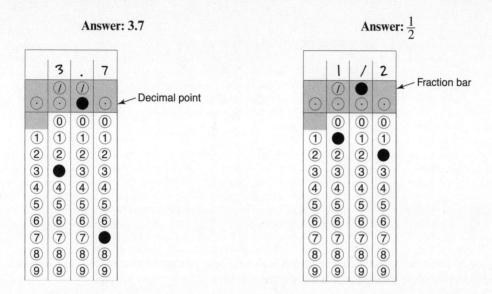

Answer: 3.7

Answer: $\frac{1}{2}$

Do not grid in mixed numbers in the form of mixed numbers. Always change mixed numbers to improper fractions or decimals.

Answer: $1\frac{1}{2}$

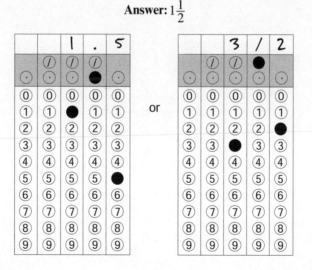

or

Answer: 123

Space permitting, answers may start in any column. Each grid-in answer below is correct.

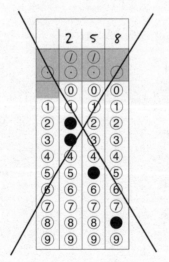

Note: Circles must be filled in correctly to receive credit. Mark only one circle in each column. No credit will be given if more than one circle in a column is marked. Example:

Answer: 258 (no credit)

Answer: $\frac{8}{9}$

Always enter the most accurate decimal value that the grid will accommodate. For example, an answer such as .8888 . . . can be gridded as .888 or .889. Gridding this value as .8, .88, or .89 is considered inaccurate and, therefore, not acceptable. The acceptable grid-ins of $\frac{8}{9}$ are:

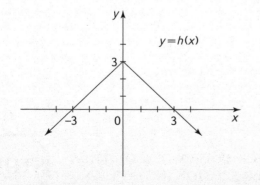

Be sure to write your answers in the boxes at the tops of the circles before doing your gridding. Although writing out the answers above the columns is not required, it is very important to ensure accuracy. Even though some problems may have more than one correct answers, grid only one answer. Grid-in questions contain no negative answers.

9. If 18 doughnuts cost $9.00, how much would 24 doughnuts cost (in dollars) at the same rate?

10. Given the accompanying diagram, $g(x) = h(x - 2)$. What is the value of $g(3)$?

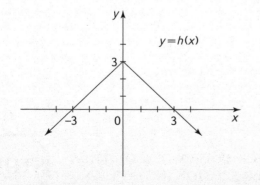

11. The vertices of a triangle are $A(-1,1)$, $B(3,1)$, and $C(3,4)$. What is the perimeter of $\triangle ABC$?

12. How many different three-digit numbers greater than 200 can be formed using the digits 1, 2, 3, and 4 if repetition of digits is allowed?

13. The average score of 4 math tests is 90. If the highest score is 98, and all scores are integers with no two scores the same, what is the lowest possible score?

14. The function $h(x)$ is defined as $h(x) = x - 1$. If n is a positive integer and $2h(n^2) = 70$, what is the value of n?

15. If $\dfrac{2k}{k^{\frac{2}{3}} - 1} = \dfrac{16}{m}$, k and m are positive integers, what is the value of m?

251

16. If k is a positive number, and the square of k is the same as k divided by 2, what is the value of k?

17. Given that h is a positive odd integer and that if h is increased by 100%, the result is between 40 and 50, what is one possible value of h?

18. A square is inscribed in a circle as shown in the accompanying diagram. The area of the circle is 16π. What is the area of the square?

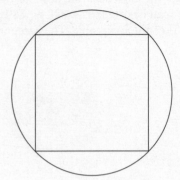

IF YOU FINISH BEFORE TIME IS CALLED, CHECK YOUR WORK ON THIS SECTION ONLY. DO NOT WORK ON ANY OTHER SECTION IN THE TEST.

Section 7: Critical Reading

Time: 20 minutes

19 questions

Directions: Each sentence below has either one or two blanks. Each blank indicates that a word has been left out. Beneath the sentence are five words or sets of words labeled A through E. Choose the word or set of words that, when inserted in the sentence, *best* fits the meaning of the sentence as a whole.

EXAMPLE:

The regeneration of the Pine Barrens after the devastating wildfire did not take place overnight; on the contrary, the regrowth was _____.

A. expected

B. encouraged

C. gradual

D. infinite

E. rapid

The correct answer is C.

---

1. Some visitors found the starkly modern geometric form of the new museum unwelcoming and preferred the _____ architecture of the original, older building.

   A. austere

   B. cold

   C. abstract

   D. melancholy

   E. traditional

2. Dr. Judith Burns shifted the focus of her experiments from a purely theoretical vein to a more _____ application when she discovered a way to improve the nutritional value of corn.

   A. cooperative

   B. influential

   C. coherent

   D. practical

   E. fundamental

3. Tombs have been erected in most New Orleans cemeteries because a swelling water table would thwart _____ burials.

   A. tropic

   B. subterranean

   C. arboreal

   D. spiritual

   E. secular

4. Author Toni Morrison's work is both _____ and _____ in that she infuses magic into very real and emotionally painful situations.

   A. mystical . . . poignant

   B. deceptive . . . unfulfilling

   C. gullible . . . tragic

   D. universal . . . definitive

   E. enigmatic . . . perceptive

5. Concerned that youthful inexperience had led some graduate students to conclusions based on unwarranted assumptions, Dr. Noah David admonished his research team that _____ data can result in _____ deductions.

   A. dubious . . . explicit
   B. fallacious . . . unjustified
   C. distinct . . . unclear
   D. obscure . . . perspicacious
   E. confidential . . . revelatory

6. Far from being a _____ lecturer, the professor had a _____ style that his students found soporific.

   A. scintillating . . . pedantic
   B. banal . . . tedious
   C. enlightening . . . dynamic
   D. scholarly . . . recondite
   E. brief . . . flamboyant

Directions: Read the following passage and answer the questions that follow on the basis of what is directly stated and what is implied in the passage and in the introductory information provided.

Questions 7–19 are based on the passage that follows.

The following excerpt is from a work of science writing about the role of human encroachment in the startling disappearance of the great predatory beasts. Two wildlife specialists set out to test their speculations that the australopithecine ape-men did not subsist on a diet of nuts and berries but were predatory hunters who lived by their red-blooded hunting skills.

(5) There had undoubtedly been protohumans walking the mean streets of prehistoric Africa. They had left behind hip bones and craniums whose attachments and orientations could only subscribe to an upright, vertical mode of existence. In the ancient ash bed of a Tanzanian volcano, they had left footprints more than three million years old, bipedaling across the plain of Laetoli. One way or another, the protohuman was out there

(10) competing in the open among big and dangerous beasts, and winning its share of the contests.

That fact left a world of speculation as to how on earth the little australopithecine ape-men had pulled it off. That they had lived large on the tree-

(15) less spaces suggested they had sustained themselves on something more than a simple gathering of nuts and fruits, tubers and roots. The richest concentrations of calories on the plains were those giant packages of meat wandering the grasslands

(20) in herds. As hard as it was to imagine the little near-humans tackling zebra, gazelle, and wildebeest, never mind elephants—all the while fending off the saber-tooths and leopards and roaming gangs of hyenas—it was harder to imagine getting

(25) by without them.

In 1968, wildlife biologist George Schaller and anthropologist Gordon Lowther decided to test their speculations. They set out into the predator-rich plains of East Africa's Serengeti in search of

(30) carrion and game like two australopithecine scavengers, on foot and unarmed. . . .

The australopithecine experiment had given visceral support for the possibilities of early man as the lone predatorial biped of the African plains.

(35) With the scavenging lifestyle came ready explanations for human hallmarks such as family groups and divisions of labor (more hands to quickly tackle, butcher, and cache meat; more eyes to note incoming enemies). With the preda-

(40) tory component came an answer for the rudiments of speech and the process of planning. ("Look out, leopard in the bush!" or "Meet me on the far side of the water hole. Limping zebra there.")

Along with the ecological emergence of meat-

(45) chasing man-apes in the African plains came physical revolutions. The jutting jaw gradually flattened, the cheek teeth began to shrink. And the volume of brain all but erupted. In the relative heartbeat of a million years, between the chim-

(50) plike *Australopithecines* and the human form of *Homo sapiens,* the size of the brain tripled. It had become the fastest-growing organ in the history of life.

(55) That brain, along with the stone and bone tools it produced, would indeed come in handy for the hunting life. But it turns out the most important vehicles blazing the hunter's path may have been his own legs. When, in the 1980s, anthropologists began questioning the human stereotype as a hopeless
(60) slowpoke plodding about the plains, they uncovered one of nature's purist talents for pursuit. Hunting cultures were to be found running down the fleetest quadrupeds on the planet. A deconstruction of ancient anatomy and physiology revealed one of the
(65) greatest long-distance runners of all time.

As the ancestral humans left the trees and hit the ground walking, their physiques and physiologies responded in kind. The bipeds grew tall and erect, their heads bobbing freely atop a long neck
(70) anchored to a stable platform of broadening shoulders. Leg bones lengthened, arms shortened, hips and waists narrowed. Midsoles of the feet began to arch; additional spring was added with the arrival of the Achilles tendon. They were the loco-
(75) motory antithesis of the pig-necked, bowlegged, knuckle-shuffling chimpanzee life-form.

In a race with the furred and four-legged, the naked ape also ran cooler and more consistently than the competition. The running hominid vented
(80) heat not only through the panting mouth but also through the evaporative cooling from the sweatiest skin on the savanna. Running erect heightened the thermal advantage, exposing a minimum of bodily surface area to the sun.
(85) These were just a few of the examined traits that padded the *Homo sapiens'* racing pedigree. The contests were, admittedly more of a tortoise-and-hare affair, with the slow and steady human ultimately gaining the advantage. But long-dis-
(90) tance endurance may well have meant the difference between a life tied to the trees and a career as a big-brained biped competing in the carnivores' kingdom. *Homo sapiens* was born to run.

The marathon-man hypothesis came replete
(95) with anecdotes of modern cultures still known to run for their supper: North American Navajos chasing pronghorn antelope to exhaustion, Australian Aborigines running down kangaroos, African Bushmen overtaking zebra and wildebeest.

Excerpt from Where the Wild Things Were *by William Stolzenburg: Permission to reprint granted by Bloomsbury USA.*

7. The primary purpose of the passage is to

A. offer physiological and speculative evidence to support a theory
B. advocate a solution to a seemingly insurmountable obstacle
C. demonstrate the unreliability of anecdotal evidence
D. provide incontrovertible empirical proof for a new model of prehistoric man
E. refute a long-standing belief held by anthropologists about the eating habits of large carnivorous beasts

8. The phrase "mean streets" (line 2) refers to

A. cities in Africa that have been historically plagued by crime
B. areas in prehistoric Africa in which wild animals roamed freely
C. nature preserves in which the most dangerous predators have been confined
D. volcanoes whose instability sporadically threatened human settlements
E. treeless spaces where the hazards were too perilous to allow human habitation

9. It can be inferred from the passage that George Schaller and Gordon Lowther

A. survived their experiment by subsisting on indigenous vegetation
B. successfully scavenged sufficient meat to support the competitive biped theory
C. discovered the existence of predators who hunted leopards and gazelle
D. brought packages of high-calorie freeze-dried meat with them into the wilderness
E. debunked the myth of the australopithecine scavenger

255

10. The purpose of the parenthetical comments on lines 37–39 is to

   A. argue against the wilderness survival theories of Schaller and Lowther
   B. imply that predatory instincts preclude the formation of family units
   C. connect the hunting propensities of early hominids to the development of social structural forces
   D. blur the line between the protohumans and the "hopeless slowpoke plodding about the plains"
   E. link physiological changes in hominids to merging lifestyle changes

11. The word *cache* (line 38) most nearly means

   A. prepare
   B. replenish
   C. store
   D. heat
   E. render

12. The author uses the parenthetical comments in lines 41–43 to explain

   A. physiological adaptations in eye structure
   B. the development of organized language
   C. the growth of the brain
   D. contradictions in animal behavior
   E. the importance of water sources to social groups

13. The word *revolutions* (line 46) suggests

   A. political upheaval
   B. rebellion against authority
   C. gradual transformation
   D. dramatic leaps
   E. societal reverses

14. The author uses the phrase *relative heartbeat* (lines 48–49) to

   A. note changes in the coronary arteries that allowed early bipeds to run faster
   B. emphasize the formation of family units based on emotional needs
   C. highlight anatomical structures that disprove a connection between australopithecines and *Homo sapiens*
   D. dramatize the briefness of the span of time between protohumans and the modern species man
   E. underscore the longevity of *Homo sapiens* compared to that of large predators

15. According to the passage, the physical attribute most critical to the hunting life was

   A. brain
   B. heart
   C. shoulders
   D. eyes
   E. legs

16. The phrase *padded the* Homo sapiens' *racing pedigree* (line 86) suggests the author's belief that

   A. running ability was a major contributing factor to humanity's predatorial heritage.
   B. human beings have a history of being able to outrun those predators who stalk them.
   C. the ability to run long distances has hindered the intellectual development of bipeds.
   D. marathons are often won by those who maintain a slow steady pace.
   E. those same traits that fostered endurance in early hominids also made them vulnerable to attack by carnivores.

17. All of the following support the author's contention that "*Homo sapiens* was born to run" (line 93) EXCEPT

    A. "the sweatiest skin on the savanna" (lines 81–82)

    B. "a stable platform of broadening shoulders" (lines 70–71)

    C. "the arrival of the Achilles tendon" (lines 73–74)

    D. "heads bobbing freely" (line 69)

    E. "pig-necked, bowlegged . . . life-form" (lines 75–76)

18. Which of the following, if true, would most undermine the author's main argument?

    A. Studies of teeth and bones of proto-humans reveal that they did not have the capacity to chew and digest meat.

    B. Running erect exposed the least bodily surface area to the sun.

    C. The rapid physical growth of the brain was not accompanied by parallel intellectual growth.

    D. The hunting culture led to disintegration of the family unit.

    E. Rather than the stereotype of the long-armed apelike protohumans, the ancestors of *Homo sapiens* were upright and vertical.

19. The tone of the passage is best described as

    A. wistfully nostalgic

    B. stridently polemical

    C. solemnly didactic

    D. amusingly informative

    E. respectfully ambivalent

IF YOU FINISH BEFORE TIME IS CALLED, CHECK YOUR WORK ON THIS SECTION ONLY. DO NOT WORK ON ANY OTHER SECTION IN THE TEST.

Section 8: Mathematics

Time: 20 minutes

16 questions

Calculator allowed

Reference Information

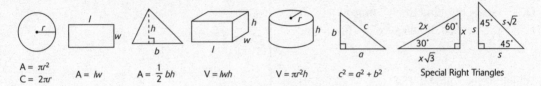

$A = \pi r^2$
$C = 2\pi r$

$A = lw$

$A = \frac{1}{2}bh$

$V = lwh$

$V = \pi r^2 h$

$c^2 = a^2 + b^2$

Special Right Triangles

The complete arc of a circle measures 360°.

The sum of the measures of the angles of a triangle is 180°.

1. If a fair die is tossed, what is the probability that it will show an even number?

   A. 3

   B. $\frac{1}{6}$

   C. $\frac{1}{4}$

   D. $\frac{1}{3}$

   E. $\frac{1}{2}$

2. If x is an integer and $2\,|\,x\,| < 2$, then what is the value of x?

   A. -1

   B. $-\frac{1}{2}$

   C. 0

   D. $\frac{1}{2}$

   E. 1

3. If $2^3 + 2^3 = 2^n$, what is the value of n?

   A. 2

   B. 4

   C. 6

   D. 8

   E. 9

4. If the average of x and y is 10 and the average of x, y, and z is 8, what is the value of z?

   A. 4

   B. 8

   C. 9

   D. 14

   E. 24

5. If *a* is directly proportional to *b*, which of the following tables could be the values of *a* and *b*?

A.

a	b
4	7
6	9
8	11

B.

a	b
3	0
5	2
7	4

C.

a	b
0	5
1	6
2	11

D.

a	b
−4	−8
0	2
4	12

E.

a	b
−3	−12
1	4
3	12

6. If *m* and *n* are nonzero integers and $m = -n$, what is the value of $m^2 - n^2$?

A. −2
B. −1
C. 0
D. 1
E. 2

7. If $\overline{HK} \parallel \overline{NP}$, what is the length of $\overline{MH}$?

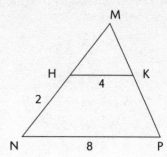

A. 1
B. 2
C. 3
D. 4
E. 6

8. If the slope of the line passing through $A(-4,0)$ and $B(2,k)$ is 2, what is the value of *k*?

A. −12
B. −6
C. 4
D. 63
E. 12

9. In the accompanying diagram, the radius of circle O is 6. $\triangle AOB$ is equilateral. What is the area of the shaded region?

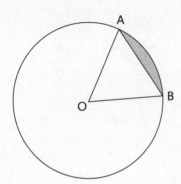

   A. $6\pi - 18\sqrt{3}$
   B. $6\pi - 9\sqrt{3}$
   C. $6\pi + 9\sqrt{3}$
   D. $12\pi - 9\sqrt{3}$
   E. $12\pi + 9\sqrt{3}$

10. How many different two-digit numbers that are formed by using the digits 1, 3, 5, 7, and 9 are divisible by 5 if repetition of digits is allowed?

   A.   4
   B.   5
   C.   10
   D.   25
   E.   120

11. Two concentric circles have center O, and $AB = 2$, and $\overline{OA}$ is a radius of the larger circle. If the area of the larger circle is 36π, what is the area of the smaller circle?

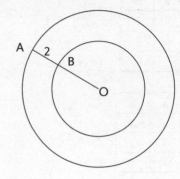

   A. 4π
   B. 8π
   C. 16π
   D. 32π
   E. 34π

12. If b is a positive integer and $a + b = 1$ and $ab = -6$, what is the value of a?

   A. -3
   B. -2
   C. 0
   D. 2
   E. 3

13. Which of the following could be an equation of the accompanying figure?

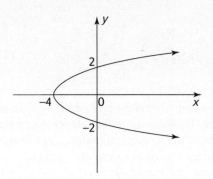

A. $x = y^2 + 2$
B. $x = y^2 - 4$
C. $x = -y^2 - 4$
D. $x = -y^2 + 4$
E. $y = x^2 - 4$

14. In the accompanying circle O, $ABCO$ is a square and the area of sector AOC is 4π. Which is the perimeter of the shaded region?

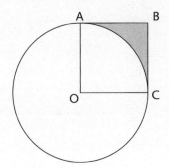

A. $4 + 8\pi$
B. $8 + 2\pi$
C. $8 + 4\pi$
D. $16 + 2\pi$
E. $16 + 8\pi$

15. If $h(t) = nt^2 + t - 2$ such that n is a constant and $h(2) = -4$, what is the value of $h(-2)$?

A. -8
B. -4
C. 0
D. 4
E. 8

16. If $4x^2 - 4x + 1$ is equivalent to $\left(mx + \dfrac{h}{2}\right)^2$, what is the value of $m + h$?

A. -4
B. -1
C. 0
D. 1
E. 4

IF YOU FINISH BEFORE TIME IS CALLED, CHECK YOUR WORK ON THIS SECTION ONLY. DO NOT WORK ON ANY OTHER SECTION IN THE TEST.

Section 9: Writing

Time: 10 minutes

14 questions

Directions: Read each of the following questions carefully. Then select the best answer from the choices provided. Fill in the corresponding circle on your answer sheet.

The following sentences test your ability to recognize correctness and effectiveness of expression. In each sentence, part of the sentence or the entire sentence is underlined. Underneath each sentence you will find five ways of phrasing the underlined material. Choice A is the same as the original sentence in the question; the other four choices are different. If you think the original sentence is correct as written, select Choice A; if not, carefully consider choices B, C, D, and E, and select the one you think is the best.

In making your selection, follow the requirements of standard written English. Carefully consider the grammar, diction (word choice), sentence construction, and punctuation of each sentence. When you make your choice, select the most effective sentence, the one that is clear and precise, without any awkwardness or ambiguity.

EXAMPLE:

The high fuel efficiency and low emissions of a newly released hybrid car <u>account for its popularity</u> with those who are environmentally aware.

    A. account for its popularity
    B. accounts for its popularity
    C. account for their popularity
    D. are the reason why it has popularity
    E. accounts for their popularity

The correct answer is A.

---

1. Dr. Burns, the team podiatrist, diagnosed the football player's painful foot as turf toe, a potentially career-ending injury <u>caused by running on hard surfaces</u>.

    A. caused by running on hard surfaces.
    B. caused with running on hard surfaces.
    C. caused by his having run on hard surfaces.
    D. which he caused by running on hard surfaces.
    E. due to the fact of his running on hard surfaces.

2. In the "Help Wanted" section of the local newspaper, <u>they post ads listing after-school jobs for high school seniors who need to earn extra money.</u>

   A. they post ads listing after-school jobs for high school seniors who need to earn extra money.

   B. they post the ads that list after-school jobs for high school seniors who need to earn extra money.

   C. ads listing after-school jobs for high school seniors who need to earn extra money.

   D. ads list after-school jobs for high school seniors who need to earn extra money.

   E. the ads that list after-school jobs for high school seniors who need to earn extra money.

3. Dr. Jonathan Stein soon revealed that he <u>was not only a skilled eye surgeon but also had a compassionate bedside manner.</u>

   A. was not only a skilled eye surgeon but also had a compassionate bedside manner.

   B. not only was a skilled eye surgeon but also had a compassionate bedside manner.

   C. was more than a skilled eye surgeon but also had a compassionate bedside manner.

   D. was not only a skilled eye surgeon but also was compassionate in his bedside manner.

   E. was both a skilled eye surgeon who also had a compassionate bedside manner.

4. The American novelist Herman Wouk, <u>who is the author of *The Caine Mutiny* and *The Winds of War*, and who will receive</u> the lifetime fiction award from the Library of Congress.

   A. who is the author of *The Caine Mutiny* and *The Winds of War*, and who will receive

   B. who is the author of *The Caine Mutiny* and *The Winds of War*, and has received

   C. is the author of *The Caine Mutiny* and *The Winds of War*, and who will receive

   D. being the author of *The Caine Mutiny* and *The Winds of War*, and who will receive

   E. the author of *The Caine Mutiny* and *The Winds of War*, will receive

5. Surfing the net and watching <u>television has created</u> a nation of overweight teens and adults.

   A. television has created
   B. television have created
   C. television, creating
   D. television creates
   E. television is creating

6. <u>Having spent the last of her allowance,</u> Nancy was forced to break into her piggy bank to pay for her mother's birthday gift.

   A. Having spent the last of her allowance,
   B. She spent the last of her allowance, therefore,
   C. By spending the last of her allowance,
   D. Because of spending the last of her allowance,
   E. Because she spent the last of her allowance,

7. The president proposed an economic bail-out plan for the auto industry <u>for the reason of its being healthy is essential</u> to the economic welfare of this country.

   A. for the reason of its being healthy is essential
   B. because its health is essential
   C. because being healthy is essential
   D. on account of its health is essential
   E. in which its health is essential

8. Many American crocodiles, members of a species recently removed from the endangered species list, <u>lives in a heavy guarded nuclear power facility</u> owned by Florida Power and Light.

   A. lives in a heavy guarded nuclear power facility
   B. live in a heavy guarded nuclear power facility
   C. have lived in a heavy guarded nuclear power facility
   D. lives heavily guarded in a nuclear power facility
   E. live in a heavily guarded nuclear power facility

9. <u>Encouraged by the government to develop alternative energy vehicles, an energy-efficient electric car will be available to consumers by 2011 by many of the major automobile companies who are committed to creating it.</u>

   A. Encouraged by the government to develop alternative energy vehicles, an energy-efficient electric car will be available to consumers by 2011 by many of the major automobile companies who are committed to creating it.
   B. Encouraged by the government to develop alternative energy vehicles, many of the major automobile companies who are committed to creating it, an energy-efficient electric car will be available to consumers by 2011.
   C. Encouraged by the government to develop alternative energy vehicles, many of the major automobile companies are committed to creating an energy-efficient electric car that will be available to consumers by 2011.
   D. Many of the major automobile companies are encouraged by the government to develop alternative energy vehicles and as a result they are committed to creating an energy-efficient electric car that will be available to consumers by 2011.
   E. Being encouraged by the government to develop alternative energy vehicles, many of the major automobile companies are committed to creating it, an energy-efficient electric car available to consumers by 2011.

10. Those Missourians who live in St. Louis are proud of their city's history: both the 1904 Olympic Games, the first ever held in the United States, and the 1904 World's Fair were held in their city.

    A. Those Missourians who live in St. Louis are proud of their city's history: both the 1904 Olympic Games,

    B. Those Missourians who live in St. Louis are proud of their city's history: because both the 1904 Olympic Games,

    C. Living in Missouri, those Missourians are proud of their city's history; both the 1904 Olympic Games,

    D. Those Missourians who live in St. Louis are proud of their city's history, the 1904 Olympic Games,

    E. Those Missourians who live in St. Louis, proud of their city's history, both the 1904 Olympic Games,

11. Although her mother is Russian, Cristen does not speak the language and has never visited there.

    A. Cristen does not speak the language and has never visited there.

    B. Cristen does not speak the Russian and has never visited there.

    C. Cristen is not speaking the language and has never been visiting Russia.

    D. Cristen does not speak the language and has never visited Russia.

    E. Cristen has not spoken the language and has never visited there.

12. Studies of attendance patterns of elementary school students have shown that absenteeism at charter schools in this country are less than in other public schools.

    A. absenteeism at charter schools in this country are less than in public schools.

    B. absenteeism at charter schools in this country is less than in public schools.

    C. absenteeism at charter schools in this country are less than those in public schools.

    D. absenteeism at charter schools in this country are lesser than in public schools.

    E. absenteeism at charter schools in this country is less than that in public schools.

13. William Faulkner, relatively unknown during his lifetime, winning the Nobel Prize for Literature in 1949 for writing stories set in mythical Yoknapatawpha County, Mississippi.

    A. winning the Nobel Prize for Literature in 1949, for writing stories set in mythical Yoknapatawpha County, Mississippi.

    B. won the Nobel Prize for Literature in 1949 for writing stories set in mythical Yoknapatawpha County, Mississippi.

    C. winning the Nobel Prize for Literature in 1949, writing stories set in mythical Yoknapatawpha County, Mississippi.

    D. winning the Nobel Prize for Literature in 1949, as he wrote stories set in mythical Yoknapatawpha County, Mississippi.

    E. has won the Nobel Prize for Literature in 1949 for writing stories set in mythical Yoknapatawpha County, Mississippi.

14. To portray an accurate portrait of deceased rapper Notorious B.I.G. for a documentary film, <u>fellow rapper Jamal Woolard learned everything he could about the murdered singer, memorizing the words to all his songs, studying videotapes of his mannerisms, and he worked closely with acting coaches to capture the subtleties of character</u>.

   A. fellow rapper Jamal Woolard learned everything he could about the murdered singer, memorizing the words to all his songs, studying videotapes of his mannerisms, and he worked closely with acting coaches to capture the subtleties of character.

   B. fellow rapper Jamal Woolard learned everything he could about the murdered singer, memorizing the words to all his songs, studying videotapes of his mannerisms, and he was working closely with acting coaches to capture the subtleties of character.

   C. fellow rapper Jamal Woolard is learning everything he could about the murdered singer, memorizing the words to all his songs, studying videotapes of his mannerisms, and he worked closely with acting coaches to capture the subtleties of character.

   D. and to learn everything he could about the murdered singer, fellow rapper Jamal Woolard is memorizing the words to all his songs, studying videotapes of his mannerisms, and he worked closely with acting coaches to capture the subtleties of character.

   E. fellow rapper Jamal Woolard learned everything he could about the murdered singer, memorizing the words to all his songs, studying videotapes of his mannerisms, and working closely with acting coaches to capture the subtleties of character.

IF YOU FINISH BEFORE TIME IS CALLED, CHECK YOUR WORK ON THIS SECTION ONLY. DO NOT WORK ON ANY OTHER SECTION IN THE TEST.

Answer Key

Section 2: Critical Reading

1. B	7. B	13. C	19. E
2. C	8. A	14. B	20. E
3. C	9. B	15. E	21. B
4. B	10. D	16. B	22. B
5. A	11. C	17. A	23. C
6. E	12. A	18. D	24. C

Section 3: Mathematics

1. C	6. D	11. C	16. B
2. D	7. D	12. C	17. A
3. A	8. C	13. C	18. C
4. D	9. A	14. C	19. C
5. E	10. B	15. C	20. C

Section 4: Writing

1. D	6. E	11. C	16. B	21. E	26. E	31. C
2. B	7. B	12. D	17. D	22. C	27. A	32. B
3. C	8. D	13. B	18. D	23. E	28. D	33. C
4. A	9. C	14. C	19. B	24. D	29. C	34. D
5. D	10. E	15. E	20. D	25. B	30. D	35. A

Section 5: Critical Reading

1. E	7. E	13. A	19. D
2. E	8. D	14. D	20. C
3. B	9. C	15. C	21. B
4. A	10. C	16. A	22. A
5. E	11. D	17. D	23. C
6. B	12. A	18. E	24. D

Section 6: Mathematics

1. B	6. E	11. 12	16. ½
2. B	7. B	12. 48	17. 21 or 23
3. C	8. E	13. 69	18. 32
4. B	9. 12	14. 6	
5. B	10. 2	15. 3	

Section 7: Critical Reading

1. E	6. A	11. C	16. A
2. D	7. A	12. B	17. E
3. B	8. B	13. C	18. A
4. A	9. B	14. D	19. D
5. B	10. C	15. E	

Section 8: Mathematics

1. E	5. E	9. B	13. B
2. C	6. C	10. B	14. B
3. B	7. B	11. C	15. A
4. A	8. E	12. B	16. C

Section 9: Writing

1. A	5. B	9. C	13. B
2. D	6. A	10. A	14. E
3. B	7. B	11. D	
4. E	8. E	12. E	

Answer Explanations

Section 1: Essay

To determine your essay score, look at the rubric (following the Diagnostic Test) and compare your essay to the scored essays on the Diagnostic Essay. Try to be objective when you evaluate your writing and give yourself an honest score between 1 and 6. If possible, have your English teacher evaluate your essay.

Section 2: Critical Reading

1. **B** The clue that "scientists remain skeptical" indicates that they don't believe in the existence of the Yeti. The signal word *consequently* sets up the second clause of the sentence as a result of the first clause. Because they don't believe, scientists have *relegated* (moved to a position of less importance) the Yeti to legend.

2. **C** The signal word *because* sets up the relationship in the sentence. Since "the microbes may help fight infection," it would be *detrimental* (harmful) to destroy them.

3. **C** The explanation after the colon indicates that many students engaged in plagiarism; thus, it is the *pervasiveness* (state of being widespread) of cheating that has surprised school officials.

4. **B** The clue word is *pejorative* (negative). The answer must be a negative word that would go along with the idea of being *insipid* (bland; uninteresting). *Trite* (dull; uninteresting) is the only negative word in the choices.

5. **A** The clue "proof of political trickery" defines the missing word, *chicanery* (trickery).

6. **E** If the nature of the evidence is such that it would lead the jury to acquit, it cannot be solid evidence. This suggests that the prosecuting attorney does not have solid or *factual* evidence. Evidence that is *circumstantial* (based on inference rather than conclusive proof) would "lead the jury to acquit the defendant."

7. **B** Characterizing the executives as "ruthless" and indicating that they "embezzled" suggests they were motivated by *avarice* (greed).

8. **A** The structure of the sentence sets up a relationship of opposites. If the committee fears a quality in the mayor, it would want to replace her with a person who had opposite qualities. Choice A has the only set of opposites, *abrasiveness* (a rough, irritating quality) and *conciliatory* (bringing together in agreement).

9. **B** According to the passage, the statement "there is nothing temporary in his dramas" refers specifically to Shakespeare, not to other poets or to the time period. The end of the sentence, "truly did he dwell amidst the elements constituting man in every age and clime," explains that his works are universal and people of every age can relate to them.

10. **D** The author uses these men to contrast with Shakespeare. Because the author has made the point that Shakespeare transcends his time period, these men, in contrast, are closely linked to the time periods in which they lived.

11. **C** The author offers more than one possible explanation for the origin of the moon.

12. **A** The author uses the green cheese to provide a transition from the composition of the moon to the theories of its origin.

13. **C** The author clearly states (lines 1–2), "That government is best which governs not at all." He reiterates this point throughout the passage.

14. **B** The phrase *many and weighty* refers to the beginning of the sentence, "The objections which have been brought against a standing army" (lines 11–12).

15. **E** The word *expedient* suggests something convenient and practical. Throughout the passage, however, the author emphasizes his point that government interference is undesirable. Thus, while he reluctantly admits that government is a necessary tradition (line 26), he would rather see men rule their own lives.

16. **B** The context of the line suggests the *mode* is the "method which the people have chosen to execute their will."

17. **A** The author repeats *it* in order to show what the government does not do in contrast to what the character of the American people can do. The clue is in the next sentence: "The character inherent in the American people has done all that has been accomplished."

18. **D** The author points out that legislators have put obstacles in the way of trade and commerce (lines 49–57). The reference to India rubber is used to show that trade and commerce are flexible and capable on "bouncing" over the obstacles.

19. **E** The context suggests that unity would make the Militia stronger; thus, *strength* is the best choice.

20. **E** The author mentions all four as goals for the Congressional deliberations. He states that Congress should try to make the "smallest expense possible of time, of life, and of treasure and to infuse" power into the militia.

21. **B** The author states, "The organization and discipline of the Army are effective and satisfactory." All the others he mentions as problems.

22. **B** The author of the first passage states, "The objections which have been brought against a standing army, and they are many and weighty, and deserve to prevail," while the second author states, "The organization of the militia is yet more indispensable to the liberties of the country."

23. **C** The author of passage 2 strongly believes "the militia is yet more indispensable to the liberties of the country" and would completely disagree with the assertion of the author of passage 1.

24. **C** The author of passage 1 repeatedly states his objection to a standing army and would find any argument supporting the establishment of one as having questionable validity.

Section 3: Mathematics

1. **C** Note that 75% is $\frac{75}{100}$ or $\frac{3}{4}$. Thus, $\frac{3}{4}n = \frac{3}{4}$. Multiply both sides of the equation by $\frac{4}{3}$ and you get $n = 1$. *(See Chapter X, Section B.)*

2. **D** This is a Pythagorean triplet 3, 4, and 5. Substitute numbers in the five choices and see which one will give you positive integers for x and y. *(See Chapter XI, Section B.)*

3. A Multiply both sides of the equation by 2, and you get $\frac{x}{y} = 8$. But $\frac{y}{x}$ is the reciprocal of $\frac{x}{y}$. Thus, $\frac{y}{x} = \frac{1}{8}$. *(See Chapter XI, Section A.)*

4. D If $2x + y > 18$, then $y > 18 - 2x$. Since $x < 5$, we have $2x < 10$ and $(18 - 2x) > 8$. Thus, $y > 8$. *(See Chapter XI, Section C.)*

5. E Note that the sum $(x + y)$ can be either even or odd. However, $2(x + y)$ must be even. Thus, $2(x + y) + 1$ is odd. *(See Chapter X, Section C.)*

6. D Substitute 3 for k in the expression $(4k + 5)$ and you get 17. Divide 17 by 7 and you have a remainder of 3. *(See Chapter X, Section D.)*

7. D Since $AB = AC$, $m\angle B = m\angle ACB$. The sum of the measures of three angles of $\triangle ABC$ is 180°. Thus, $m\angle C + m\angle ACB + 80° = 180°$, and $\angle ACB = 50°$. Also, note that $\angle ACD$ and $\angle ACB$ are supplementary. Therefore, $m\angle ACD = 130°$. *(See Chapter XII, Section A.)*

8. C Because there are four points, and each point can be connected to three other points, there are $4(3) = 12$ line segments. However, the line segment from A to B is the same as the line segment from B to A. Thus, there are $\frac{12}{2} = 6$ line segments. *(See Chapter XIII, Section A.)*

9. A If $a > 90$ and $a = c$, then $c > 90$. Thus statement II is false. We know that $a + d = 180$ because the angles are supplementary, so statement III is false. Also, $a + b = 180$ and since $a > 90$, $b < 90$. So, statement I is true. *(See Chapter XII, Section A.)*

10. B Begin with 4 # 0 and we have $(4)(0) - 2(0) = 0$. Then 0 # 3 = $(0)(3) - 2(3) = -6$. *(See Chapter XIV, Section A.)*

11. C Note that $(x^2 + y^2)^2 = x^4 + 2x^2y^2 + y^4$. Therefore, you have $(5)^2 = 10 + 2x^2y^2$ and $2x^2y^2 = 15$. *(See Chapter XI, Section E.)*

12. C The average of the members of Set A is $(-4 - 2 + 0 + 2 + 4 + 6 + 8) \div 7 = 2$. Because the members of Set B are 7 times the members of Set A, the average of Set B is $7(2) = 14$. *(See Chapter XIII, Section C.)*

13. C Evaluate $g(3)$ and obtain $3(3) - 3 = 6$. Thus, $3g(3) = 3(6) = 18$, and $3g(3) + 3 = 18 + 3 = 21$. *(See Chapter XI, Section H.)*

14. C Rewrite 4^3 as $(2^2)^3 = 2^6$ and 8^2 as $(2^3)^2 = 2^6$. Thus, $4^3 + 8^2 = 2^6 + 2^6 = 2(2^6)$. Because $2(2^6) = 2(2^n)$, $n = 6$. *(See Chapter XI, Section F.)*

15. C Note that B is approximately -1.5 and $2D$ is approximately 1. Thus, $B + 2D$ is closest to -0.5 or point C. *(See Chapter X, Section A.)*

16. B Because $\triangle ABC$ is equilateral, $\triangle ADB$ is a 30-60 right triangle. Leg $\overline{AD}$ is opposite $\angle ABC$, whose measure is 60°. Thus, leg $\overline{BD}$ is opposite $\angle BAD$, whose measure is 30°. Using the 30-60 right triangle relationship, $BD = 6$ and $B = (-6,0)$ and $h = -6$. *(See Chapter XII, Section G.)*

17. A

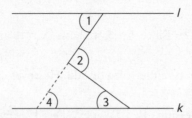

By extending a line segment as shown in the accompanying diagram, we have two alternate interior angles, $\angle 1$ and $\angle 4$, and $m\angle 1 = m\angle 4 = 2x + 4$. Also, $\angle 2$ is an exterior angle to the triangle. Thus $m\angle 2 = m\angle 3 + m\angle 4$, which means $4x = m\angle 3 + (2x + 4)$, and $m\angle 3 = 2x - 4$. *(See Chapter XII, Section A.)*

18. C From Smithtown to Glen Cove, there are $(2)(3) = 6$ ways. However, returning from Glen Cove to Smithtown, there are $(1)(2) = 2$ ways, because we don't want to be on the same road again. Thus, the total number of ways to travel from Smithtown to Glen Cove and back is $(6)(2) = 12$ ways. *(See Chapter XIII, Section A.)*

19. C Renting 10 videos costs $\$4 + 10(\$2) = \$24$. The average cost per video is $\$24 \div 10 = \$2.40$. *(See Chapter XIII, Section C.)*

20. C Since $\overline{EOF}$ is a diameter, $\angle D$ is inscribed in a semicircle, and thus $\angle D$ is a right angle. Thus, $\triangle EDF$ is a right triangle. Also, $m\angle DFE = 2m\angle DEF$, and the sum of their measures is $90°$. Therefore $m\angle DFE = 60°$, $m\angle DEF = 30°$, and $\triangle EDF$ is a 30-60 right triangle. Note that leg $\overline{DF}$ is opposite the $30°$ angle, $DF = \frac{1}{2}(12) = 6$. *(See Chapter XII, Section B.)*

Section 4: Writing

1. **D** The sentence lacks parallelism. Changing the underlined portion to *as . . . as* will provide parallel structure.

2. **B** The sentence contains a shift of pronoun from *one* to *you*. Since the *you* is not underlined, you must change the *one* to *you*.

3. **C** The sentence contains a modification error. It begins with a modifying phrase, *Usually busy transporting needed supplies,* which should be followed by what the phrase modifies: *huge, supertankers.* Only choices C and D begin correctly. Choice D is awkward and contains the vague phrase, *filled with oil.* Only Choice C is correct.

4. **A** The sentence is correct as written.

5. **D** The sentence contains the awkward verb phrasing *are to help.* Choice D uses the correct verb phrase *have been formed.*

6. **E** The sentence contains a comma splice error. Choices B and D incorrectly use the semicolon, because they do not have two main clauses. Choice C has an incorrect tense shift.

7. **B** The sentence is wordy and awkwardly phrased. Conciseness is a goal, so using appositive phrases rather than clauses will tighten up the sentence. Choice C is wordy, Choice D is a run-on, and Choice E contains a misplaced modifier.

8. **D** The sentence correctly uses the colon but contains an error in parallel structure. Choice D corrects the parallelism error.

9. **C** The sentence contains a pronoun-antecedent error. *Each* is a singular indefinite pronoun and must use the singular form *it*. In addition, since *deer* is used in its plural form (identical to the singular form), the verb *were* is necessary.

10. **E** The sentence has a subject-verb agreement error (*depth . . . exceed*) and is wordy, repetitious, and awkwardly phrased. Choices B and D both contain subject-verb errors. Choice C is repetitious (*studying . . . studied*).

11. **C** Choice A and B are incorrect because the conjunction *neither* must be followed by the conjunction *nor*. Choice D contains a redundancy (*sufficient enough*) and Choice E has a subject-verb agreement error (*are*).

12. **D** Pronoun-antecedent error: the pronoun *it* has no clear antecedent.

13. **B** Error in adjective-adverb confusion: the adverb *smoothly*, not the adjective *smooth,* is needed to modify the verb *had gone.*

14. **C** Idiom error: the correct idiom is *comment on,* not *comment about.*

15. **E** The sentence is correct.

16. **B** Pronoun case error: the pronoun *I* is a nominative pronoun, used when the pronoun is the subject of a sentence or a predicate nominative. In this sentence the correct pronoun to use is *me* (object of the preposition *except*).

17. **D** Comparison error: the *plays* of Christopher Marlowe must be compared to the *plays* of Shakespeare, not just *Shakespeare.*

18. **D** Comparison error: when comparing two things, the correct form is *more,* not *most.* Use *most* to compare three or more things.

19. **B** Subject-verb agreement error: the subject of *grows* is *trees* (plural). The plural form of the verb is *grow.*

20. **D** Idiom error: the correct idiom is *prefer . . . to,* not *prefer . . . more than.*

21. **E** The sentence is correct.

22. **C** Subject-verb agreement error: since *neither* is a singular indefinite pronoun, the correct form of the verb is *was.*

23. **E** The sentence is correct.

24. **D** Tense error: The sentence states that Ricardo *was studying* (past tense). To show action that occurs before past tense, the correct tense to use is the past perfect, *had been studying.*

25. **B** Diction error: the correct word is *allusions,* not *illusions.* An *allusion* is a reference; an *illusion* is a false perception of reality.

26. **E** The sentence is correct.

27. **A** Diction error: the correct idiom is *contrary to* rather than *opposite to.*

28. **D** Tense error: when an action takes place over a period of time, and it began in the past and continues into the present, the correct tense to use is the present perfect, *have staggered.*

29. **C** Pronoun-antecedent error: the antecedent *avalanches* is plural and needs the plural pronoun *they*.

30. **D** The first paragraph provides an introduction into the rest of the essay. It does not contain any personal anecdote (Choice A) nor does it explain a misconception (Choice B), set up a contrast (Choice C), or argue a position (Choice E).

31. **C** Choice A uses *which* instead of *who* to refer to the men. Choice B is not a complete sentence. Choice D uses the incorrect form of the verb *unearthing*. Choice E is in the wrong tense.

32. **B** Choices A and D are run-on sentences. Choice C does not identify *they*. Choice E does not subordinate the last clause as it should.

33. **C** Choices A, B, D, and E all use illogical transitional words.

34. **D** The point has been previously made in sentence 6, which states that the figures were made of baked clay.

35. **A** This sentence is the best choice to conclude the essay. Choice B begins with a vague modifying phrase. Choice C has an agreement error (*are*). Choice D switches from *you* to *a tourist*. Choice E begins unnecessarily with *In conclusion* and contains an agreement error (*have*).

Section 5: Critical Reading

1. **E** It is clear from the logic of the sentence that since Bart is going to behave properly, he wants to remove or *expunge* (to erase or remove from a record) the black mark.

2. **E** The clue *diverse styles of art* should lead you to *eclectic* (varied).

3. **B** The clue *Aromas of the holiday season* should lead you to *redolent* (smelling of).

4. **A** The clue *Unable to determine the authenticity* defines the missing word; *apocryphal* means untrue or of doubtful authenticity.

5. **E** The sculptures are *whimsical* (playful, fanciful) and contrast with the seriousness of the palace. They are placed in the palace with the serious art, so they are *juxtaposed,* or put next to each other for the purpose of comparison.

6. **B** Both passages emphasize that beauty lies in simplicity.

7. **E** The words *no sham, nor ostentation* correspond with the idea in passage 1 that more ornate objects do not require better workmanship. In fact, the opposite is true.

8. **D** Passage 2 uses anecdote (personal narration) which is absent from passage 1.

9. **C** Both passages indicate a preference for simple furnishings.

10. **C** The passage is a character study of Dorothea.

11. **D** The author suggests that Dorothea's "plain garments" gave her "the impressiveness of a fine quotation from the Bible . . . in a paragraph of today's newspaper." The comparison suggests her clothing is like the words of the Bible, simple and enduring.

12. **A** The author remarks that Dorothea is very clever, but then qualifies (limits or restricts) this statement by pointing out that Celia had more commonsense.

13. **A** It would take a close observer to notice the *shade of coquetry* (flirtatiousness) in Celia's dress.

14. **D** The context suggests that *shade* means hint.

15. **C** The author compares Dorothea's eyes to her "religion, too unusual and striking."

16. **A** The author implies that Dorothea was embarrassed by her enjoyment of riding (she had "conscientious qualms") and "looked forward to renouncing it." Thus, Choice A would weaken the author's argument.

17. **D** If a man did not come to see Mr. Brooke, Dorothea concluded "that he must be in love with Celia."

18. **E** Dorothea gave her sister credit for "having attractions altogether superior to her own." Therefore, in context, *adorned* means credited.

19. **D** The author emphasizes Dorothea's passion and naïve, childlike quality (ingenuousness).

20. **C** The author refers to 1988 and 1968 to show the radical changes in the realm of environmentalism and to predict that more changes are to come. To be successful in business, one must be alert to trends; the author believes an understanding of environmental markets will be critical to the business landscape.

21. **B** The author explains the system which places "a cap on the total amount of air or water pollution that may be emitted." The only choice that does not emit air or water pollution is an electric car.

22. **A** According to the passage, an allowance is equivalent to "the total amount of air or water pollution which may be emitted."

23. **C** The author mentions "public relations" (I) and "corporate responsibility" (II) as reasons for a company to become carbon neutral in the absence of government regulations.

24. **D** The author would clearly agree that "increasing rates of per capita consumption will result in increased value placed on any activities which lessen the impact of development on natural systems."

Section 6: Mathematics

1. **B** Solve the equation $2x + 1 = 3$ and obtain $x = 1$. Substitute $x = 1$ into the expression $-2x + 1$ and get -1. *(See Chapter XI, Section B.)*

2. **B** If 25% of the students are boys, then 75% are girls. Set up a proportion with s being the number of students in the class. We have $\frac{12}{75\%} = \frac{s}{100\%}$ or $\frac{12}{0.75} = \frac{s}{1}$ or $s = 16$. *(See Chapter X, Section B.)*

3. **C** This is a geometric sequence with the common ratio $r = 2$. The formula for finding the nth term is $(a_0)(r^{n-1})$, where a_0 is the first term. Thus, the 5th term is $(1)(2)^4 = 16$, and the 10th term is $(1)(2)^9 = 512$. Thus, the 10th term divided by the 5th term is $\frac{512}{16} = 32$. *(See Chapter X, Section E.)*

4. **B** Since l is perpendicular to line m, the triangle shown is a right triangle. The measures of the 2 acute angles are x and y due to vertical angles. Thus, $x + y = 90$ or $y = 90 - x$. *(See Chapter XII, Section B.)*

5. **B** Ten years from now, Janet will be m years old and her father will be $2m$ years old. Today, Janet's and her father's ages are $(m - 10)$ and $(2m - 10)$, respectively. The difference is $(2m - 10) - (m - 10) = 2m - 10 - m + 10$ or m. Another approach to the problem is as follows: The problem stated that ten years from now, Janet will be m old and she will be exactly half her father's age. This implies that ten years from now, Janet's father will be $2m$ years older. Therefore, he'll be $(2m - m)$ or m years older than Janet. Thus, he is also m years older than Janet today. *(See Chapter XI, Section A.)*

6. **E** Between '06 and '07, the increase is 2 million, the greatest increase. *(See Chapter XIII, Section D.)*

7. **B** Factors of 8 are 1, 2, 4, and 8. Thus, $8^2 = (1)(2)(4)(8)$, and 8 is a member of Set S. *(See Chapter X, Section F.)*

8. **E** The area of rectangle $DCGH = (2)(6) = 12$, rectangle $CBFG = 2(4) = 8$, and rectangle $EFGH = (4)(6) = 24$. The 3 rectangles have an area of $12 + 8 + 24 = 44$. However, for each of these rectangles, there is another rectangle parallel to it (front and back, left and right, and top and bottom). The total area is $2(44) = 88$. *(See Chapter XII, Section E.)*

9. **12** We use a proportion, $\frac{18}{9} = \frac{24}{x}$. Thus, $18x = 9(24)$ or $x = 12$. *(See Chapter XI, Section G.)*

10. **2** Since $g(x) = h(x - 2)$, $g(3) = g(3 - 2)$ or $g(3) = h(1)$. Looking at the graph, we have $h(1) = 2$. *(See Chapter XI, Section H.)*

11. **12** The distance from A to B is 4 and from B to C is 3. Also, $\triangle ABC$ is a right triangle. Thus, using the Pythagorean theorem, $AC = 5$. Therefore, the perimeter is $3 + 4 + 5 = 12$. *(See Chapter XII, Section G.)*

12. **48** A three-digit number greater than 200 must have the digits 2, 3, or 4 in its hundreds place. The tens and the units places could be any one of the four digits. Thus, the total number of three-digit numbers greater than 200 is $(3)(4)(4) = 48$. *(See Chapter XIII, Section A.)*

13. **69** Since the average is 90, the sum of the four tests is 360. The highest score is 98; therefore, two of the other scores could be 97 and 96. The fourth score is $360 - (98 + 97 + 96) = 69$. *(See Chapter XIII, Section C.)*

14. **6** Since $h(x) = x - 1$, you have $h(n^2) = n^2 - 1$. Thus, $2h(n^2) = 70$ becomes $2(n^2 - 1) = 70$ or $n^2 - 1 = 35$. Then $n^2 = 36$ and $n = 6$ or -6. Since n is positive, $n = 6$. *(See Chapter XI, Section H.)*

15. **3** In general, given a single equation with two variables, the solution set to the equation contains infinitely many ordered pairs. For example, the equation $y = x + 2$ has an infinite number of solutions. For the equation $\frac{2k}{k^{\frac{2}{3}} - 1} = \frac{16}{m}$, k and m are given as positive integers, which might limit the number of solutions. One approach to find positive integer values of m and k is to solve for m in terms of k and then use guess and check. In this case, $m = \frac{16\left(k^{\frac{2}{3}} - 1\right)}{2k} = 8k^{-\frac{1}{3}} - \frac{8}{k}$. Because the equation contains a cube root, we try perfect cubes for k, such as 1, 8, 27, and so on. When $k = 8$, you have $m = 3$.

An easier approach is to enter the equation into a graphing calculator by letting $y_1 = m$ and $x = k$, and $y_1 = \frac{16\left(x^{\frac{2}{3}} - 1\right)}{2x}$, then look at the table of values for positive integer values for m and k.

A third approach that often works for these equations on the SAT (but not necessarily for all proportions) is to set the two numerators equal. Then you have $2k = 16$ or $k = 8$. Substitute $k = 8$ into the expression $\left(k^{\frac{2}{3}} - 1\right)$ and you have $(8^{\frac{2}{3}} - 1)$ or $(4 - 1) = 3$. Thus, $m = 3$. This is a unique approach to solve a single proportion with two variables. It can lead to a quick solution so it is worth trying first, but it doesn't always work. *(See Chapter XI, Section B.)*

16. **k = $\frac{1}{2}$** Begin with the equation $k^2 = \frac{k}{2}$. Rewrite and you have $k^2 - \frac{k}{2} = 0$. Multiply both sides by 2. You get $2k^2 - k = 0$ or $k(2k - 1) = 0$. Thus, $k = 0$ or $k = \frac{1}{2}$. Since k is positive, $k = \frac{1}{2}$. *(See Chapter XIV, Section B.)*

17. **21 or 23** Note that 100% of *h* is simply *h* itself. Thus, we have $40 < (h + h) < 50$ or $40 < 2h < 50$ or $20 < h < 25$. Since *h* is odd, *h* is either 21 or 23. *(See Chapter XI, Section C.)*

18. **32** The area of the circle is 16π. Since $16\pi = \pi r^2$, the radius of the circle is 4 and the diameter is 8. The diameter is also a diagonal of the square. The area of the square can be obtained by (side)^2 or (diagonal)$^2 \div 2$. Thus, the area of the square is $(8)^2 \div 2 = 32$. *(See Chapter XII, Section F.)*

Section 7: Critical Reading

1. **E** The logic of the sentence indicates the missing word is the opposite of *starkly modern geometrical form*. The closest opposite in the choices is *traditional*.

2. **D** The clue *shifted the focus of her experiments* leads you to look for a word that contrasts with *theoretical*. *Practical* is the closest opposite in the choices.

3. **B** A "swelling water table" would prevent *subterranean* (underground) burial and create a need for above ground tombs.

4. **A** In this definitional sentence, clue words are *magic* and *emotionally painful*. Choice A is correct because *mystical* means magical and *poignant* means emotionally painful.

5. **B** The clue is in the first half of the sentence: Dr. Noah David wants to avoid "conclusions based on unwarranted assumptions." This fits with *fallacious* (false) data leading to "unjustified conclusions."

6. **A** Since something *soporific* leads to sleep, the professor's style must be dry and dull, which a pedantic lecture would be. This is far from *scintillating* (sparkling).

7. **A** The author offers physiological (legs, feet, brain) evidence and based on this evidence, speculates about the predatory propensities of early man.

8. **B** The author speculates that prehistoric men lived and competed with large beasts: "the protohuman was out there competing in the open among big and dangerous beasts, and winning its share of the contests."

9. **B** The author describes the experiment in which the two unarmed researchers went into the "predator-rich plains" of Africa in "search of carrion and game."

10. **C** According to the passage, the hunting and scavenging lifestyle gave rise to "human hallmarks such as family groups and divisions of labor."

11. **C** In context, the best meaning of *cache* is to store the meat.

12. **B** The author credits the hunting lifestyle with creating the need "for the rudiments of speech and the process of planning."

13. **C** The author uses the term revolution to describe the gradual changes that occurred in the physiology of early man.

14. **D** The phrase *relative heartbeat* refers to the million years between the *australopithecines* and *Homo sapiens*. In evolutionary time, this is a very short period, hence, the heartbeat.

15. **E** According to the passage, "the most important vehicles blazing the hunter's path may have been his own legs."

16. **A** The author describes various physiological changes in prehistoric man that make his body more suited for running upright to support his assertion that *Homo sapiens* has a history as a runner.

17. E All of the choices support the assertion that *Homo sapiens* was born to run except Choice E. The author states that the running man was the "antithesis of the pig-necked, bowlegged, knuckle-shuffling chimpanzee life-form."

18. A An important point in this passage is that prehistoric man was a predator who scavenged and hunted for meat. The discovery that "they did not have the capacity to chew and digest meat" would weaken his argument.

19. D The best choice to describe the tone of the passage is *amusingly informative*. The author has a clear position to present about man as a predator, but he enlivens his prose with humorous examples (bipedaling across the plain, a hopeless slowpoke plodding about the plains, "Meet me on the far side of the water hole. Limping zebra there.")

Section 8: Math

1. E The numbers on a die are 1, 2, 3, 4, 5, and 6. Three of the numbers are even. Thus, the probability is $\frac{3}{6} = \frac{1}{2}$. *(See Chapter XIII, Section B.)*

2. C If $2|x| < 2$, then $|x| < 1$. The only integer that satisfies the inequality is $x = 0$. *(See Chapter XI, Section D.)*

3. B Rewrite $2^3 + 2^3$ as $2(2^3)$ or $(2^1)(2^3)$. Adding their exponents, you have $2^{(1+3)}$ or 2^4. Thus, $2^4 = 2^n$ or $n = 4$. *(See Chapter XI, Section F.)*

4. A If the average of x and y is 10, then $\frac{x+y}{2} = 10$ or $x + y = 20$. Similarly, $\frac{x+y+z}{3} = 8$ implies $x + y + z = 24$. Substituting $(x + y)$ with 20, you have $20 + z = 24$ or $z = 4$. *(See Chapter XIII, Section C.)*

5. E "Directly proportional" implies $\frac{a_1}{b_1} = \frac{a_2}{b_2}$. Only the table from Choice E satisfies this proportion: $\frac{-3}{-12} = \frac{1}{4} = \frac{3}{12}$. *(See Chapter XI, Section G.)*

6. C If $m = -n$, then $m^2 - n^2 = (-n)^2 - n^2 = n^2 - n^2 = 0$. *(See Chapter XI, Section F.)*

7. B Parallel lines $\overline{HK}$ and $\overline{NP}$ give you two similar triangles: $\triangle HMK$ and $\triangle MNP$. Thus, you can use a proportion, $\frac{x}{4} = \frac{x+2}{8}$, where $x = HM$. You have $8x = 4(x + 2)$ or $8x = 4x + 8$ or $x = 2$. *(See Chapter XII, Section C.)*

8. E Slope is $\frac{y_2 - y_1}{x_2 - x_1}$. Thus, $\frac{k-0}{2-(-4)} = 2$ or $\frac{k}{6} = 2$ or $k = 12$. *(See Chapter XII, Section H.)*

9. B The area of the circle is πr^2 or 36π. Since $\triangle AOB$ is equilateral, $m\angle AOB = 60°$, and the area of sector $AOB = \frac{1}{6}(36\pi)$ or 6π. The area of an equilateral triangle can be found by $\frac{s^2\sqrt{3}}{4}$. Thus, the area of $\triangle AOB$ is $\frac{(6)^2\sqrt{3}}{4}$ or $9\sqrt{3}$. The shaded area is $6\pi - 9\sqrt{3}$. *(See Chapter XII, Section F.)*

10. B If a two-digit number is divisible by 5, it must have either a 5 or a 0 as its units digit. In this case, there are five choices for the tens digit and only one choice for the units digit: 95, 75, 55, 35, and 15. Thus, there are five two-digit numbers that are divisible by 5. *(See Chapter XIII, Section A.)*

11. C Since the area of the larger circle is 36π, then $\pi r^2 = 36\pi$ or $OA = 6$. The length of $\overline{OB} = 6 - 2 = 4$. Thus, the area of the smaller circle is $\pi(4)^2$ or 16π. *(See Chapter XII, Section F.)*

12. **B** If $a + b = 1$, then $b = 1 - a$. Substitute $b = 1 - a$ in the equation $ab = -6$. You have $a(1 - a) = -6$, or $a - a^2 = -6$, or $0 = a^2 - a - 6$. Factor and you have $(a - 3)(a + 2) = 0$, and $a = 3$ or $a = -2$. Since b is positive and $ab = -6$ and $a = -2$. *(See Chapter XI, Section E.)*

13. **B** The graph in the diagram is a translation of four units to the left of $x = y^2$. Thus, the equation is $y^2 - 4$. Another way to identify the equation is to check the three given points $(-4,0)$, $(0,2)$, and $(0,-2)$ with each of the equations in choices A through E. *(See Chapter XII, Section I.)*

14. **B** Since the area of the sector is 4π, the area of the circle (which is four times the area of the sector) is 16π. The area of a circle is πr^2. Thus, $\pi r^2 = 16\pi$ or $r = 4$. Since $ABCD$ is a square, $AB = BC = 4$. Arc AC is $\frac{1}{4}$ the circumference of the circle. The measure of arc $AC = \frac{1}{4}(2\pi 4) = 2\pi$. Thus, the perimeter of the shaded region is $4 + 4 + 2\pi$ or $8 + 2\pi$. *(See Chapter XII, Section F.)*

15. **A** Since $h(2) = -4$, you have $n(2)^2 + (2) - 2 = -4$ or $4n = -4$ or $n = -1$. Thus, the function is $h(t) = -t^2 + t - 2$, and $h(-2) = -(-2)^2 + (-2) - 2 = -4 - 2 - 2 = -8$. *(See Chapter XI, Section H.)*

16. **C** Factor $4x^2 - 4x + 1$ and you have $(2x - 1)(2x - 1)$ or $(2x - 1)^2$. Thus, $m = 2$ and $\frac{h}{2} = -1$ or $h = -2$. Therefore, $m + h = 2 + (-2) = 0$. *(See Chapter XI, Section A.)*

Section 9: Writing

1. **A** The sentence is correct.

2. **D** The sentence contains a vague pronoun reference (*they*) as does Choice B. Choices C and E are sentence fragments.

3. **B** The sentence contains a parallelism error. Correlative pronouns (*not only . . . but also*) must be followed by parallel elements. Choices A, C, D, and E all have errors in parallelism.

4. **E** The sentence has incorrect structure: as written, it is a sentence fragment. Choices B and D are also sentence fragments. Choice C is too wordy.

5. **B** The sentence has a subject-verb agreement error (*surfing and watching has created*). Choices D and E both have subject-verb agreement errors, and Choice C is a sentence fragment.

6. **A** The sentence is correct.

7. **B** The sentence is too wordy (*for the reason of its being*). Choice C has a vague modification problem. Choice D is wordy, and Choice E is illogical.

8. **E** The sentence has a subject-verb agreement error (*crocodiles lives*) and an error in adjective-adverb confusion (*heavy guarded*). Choices B and C have the same error in adjective-adverb confusion (*heavy guarded*). Choice D has the subject-verb agreement error.

9. **C** The sentence has a misplaced modifier error. Choice B has a vague pronoun reference (*it*), Choice D is too wordy, and Choice E is a run-on sentence.

10. **A** The sentence is correct.

11. **D** The sentence does not have a noun as a reference for the word *there*. Choices B and E have the same problem. Choice C has awkward verb phrasing.

12. **E** The sentence has a subject-verb agreement error (*absenteeism are*) and an unparallel comparison error (comparing *absenteeism* to *public schools*). Choices C and D have the agreement error, and Choice B has the comparison error.

13. **B** The sentence is a fragment as are choices C and D. Choice E has a tense error (*has won*).

14. **E** All the choices except Choice E are unparallel.

Scoring Worksheets

Critical Reading

	Number Right	Number Wrong
Section 2		
Section 5		
Section 7		
Total		

Raw score = Number right – (Number wrong ÷ 4) = _____ – _____ = _____

Round the raw score to the nearest integer: _____.

Scaled score range: _____

Note: To find your scaled score range, use the following chart.

Critical Reading Raw Score Conversions							
Raw Score	**Scaled Score Range**	**Raw Score**	**Scaled Score Range**	**Raw Score**	**Scaled Score Range**	**Raw Score**	**Scaled Score Range**
67	800	48	580–640	29	470–520	10	340–400
66	760–800	47	580–640	28	460–520	9	330–390
65	740–800	46	570–630	27	450–510	8	320–380
64	720–800	45	570–620	26	450–510	7	300–380
63	700–790	44	560–620	25	440–500	6	290–370
62	680–780	43	550–610	24	430–500	5	280–370
61	670–770	42	540–610	23	430–490	4	260–360
60	660–760	41	540–600	22	420–480	3	250–340
59	660–740	40	530–590	21	410–480	2	230–330
58	650–720	39	530–580	20	410–470	1	220–320
55	630–700	36	510–570	17	390–450	–2	200–270
54	620–700	35	500–560	16	380–440	–3	200–240

Raw Score	Scaled Score Range	Raw Score	Scaled Score Range	Raw Score	Scaled Score Range	Raw Score	Scaled Score Range
53	610–680	34	500–560	15	380–440	–4	200–230
52	600–680	33	490–550	14	370–430	–5	200–210
51	610–670	32	480–540	13	360–420	–6 and below	200
50	600–660	31	480–540	12	350–410		
49	600–650	30	470–530	11	340–410		

Mathematics

	Number Right	Number Wrong
Section 3		
Section 6		
Section 8		
Total		

Raw score = Number right – (Number wrong ÷ 4) = _____ – _____ = _____

Round the raw score to the nearest integer: _____.

Scaled score range: _____

Note: To find your scaled score range, use the following chart.

Mathematics Raw Score Conversions					
Raw Score	**Scaled Score Range**	**Raw Score**	**Scaled Score Range**	**Raw Score**	**Scaled Score Range**
54	800	34	530–610	14	390–450
53	760–800	33	520–600	13	380–440
52	720–780	32	520–580	12	360–430
51	700–780	31	520–580	11	350–430
50	680–770	30	510–570	10	320–420
49	680–750	29	500–560	9	300–420
48	670–730	28	490–550	8	300-410
47	660–720	27	480–540	7	300–400
46	650–700	26	480–530	6	290–380
45	630–700	25	470–530	5	280–380
44	610–680	24	460–520	4	270–370

continued

Mathematics Raw Score Conversions *(continued)*

Raw Score	Scaled Score Range	Raw Score	Scaled Score Range	Raw Score	Scaled Score Range
43	620–670	23	460–520	3	260–340
42	610–670	22	440–510	2	240–340
41	600–650	21	440–490	1	230–320
40	580–650	20	430–490	0	210–310
39	570–650	19	430–480	−1	200–290
38	550–640	18	420–480	−2	200–280
37	550–630	17	410–460	−3	200–250
36	540–630	16	400–460	−4	200–220
35	540–610	15	400–450	−5 and below	200

Writing

	Number Right	Number Wrong
Section 4		
Section 9		
Total		

Multiple choice raw score = Number right – (Number wrong ÷ 4) = _____ – _____ = _____

Round the multiple choice raw score to the nearest integer: _____.

Look on the Multiple Choice Raw Score Conversion Chart to determine your score range.

Writing Multiple Choice Raw Score Conversions

Raw Score	Scaled Score Range	Raw Score	Scaled Score Range	Raw Score	Scaled Score Range
49	800	30	540–640	11	360–450
48	770–800	29	530–630	10	350–440
47	740–800	28	520–620	9	340–430
46	720–800	27	510–610	8	330–420
45	700–790	26	500–600	7	310–400
44	680–780	25	490–590	6	300–390
43	670–770	24	480–580	5	300–380
42	660–760	23	470–570	4	290–340
41	660–740	22	460–560	3	280–330
40	650–720	21	450–550	2	270–320

Raw Score	Scaled Score Range	Raw Score	Scaled Score Range	Raw Score	Scaled Score Range
39	640–720	20	450–540	1	250–300
38	630–710	19	440–540	0	200–290
37	630–700	18	430–530	–1	200–270
36	620–700	17	420–520	–2	200–240
35	590–680	16	410–510	–3	200–280
34	580–680	15	400–500	–4	200–260
33	570–670	14	390–490	–5	200–230
32	560–660	13	380–480	–6 and below	200–220
31	550–650	12	370–470		

To find your total writing score, estimate your essay score using the rubric (attached to the diagnostic test explanation of answers.)

Essay score (1–6): _____

Use the following chart to find your scaled score ranges. Find your multiple choice raw score in the first column. Then look across the top for your essay score. The intersection of these two scores is your writing score range.

Writing Conversions							
Multiple Choice Raw Score	0	1	2	3	4	5	6
49	650–700	670–720	690–740	710–770	750–800	770–800	800
48	630–690	640–720	660–740	690–770	720–800	740–800	770–800
47	600–690	620–720	640–740	660–770	700–800	730–800	750–800
46	580–690	600–710	620–730	650–750	680–770	700–790	720–800
45	570–690	580–720	600–740	630–750	660–760	680–770	690–790
44	560–680	570–710	590–730	620–740	660–750	670–760	680–780
43	540–660	560–690	580–710	610–730	640–740	650–750	660–770
42	530–660	550–680	570–700	600–720	630–730	640–740	650–760
41	530–650	540–670	560–690	590–700	620–720	640–730	640– 750
40	520–640	530–670	550–690	580–710	620–710	630–730	640–740
39	510–630	520–660	540–680	570–700	610–700	620–720	630–730
38	500–620	510–650	530–670	560–700	600–690	610–710	620–720
37	490–610	500–640	520–660	550–690	590–680	600–700	610–710
36	480–600	490–630	510–650	540–680	580–670	590–690	600–700
35	480–590	490–620	500–640	520–650	550–660	570–670	580–680

continued

Writing Conversions *continued*							
Multiple Choice Raw Score	0	1	2	3	4	5	6
34	470–590	480–600	500–620	510–630	530–640	560–660	570–670
33	450–570	470–600	490–610	500–620	540–630	550–650	560–660
32	440–570	460–590	470–600	490–610	520–620	540–640	550–650
31	440–560	460–570	470–590	480–600	510–610	530–630	540–640
30	430–550	450–560	460–580	470–590	500–600	520–620	530–630
29	430–540	440–550	450–570	460–580	490–600	510–610	520–620
28	420–530	430–540	440–560	450–570	470–590	500–600	510–610
27	410–520	420–540	430–550	440–560	460–580	480–590	500–600
26	400–510	410–530	420–540	430–550	450–570	470–580	490–590
25	390–500	400–520	410–530	420–540	440–560	460–570	480–580
24	380–490	390–510	400–520	410–530	430–550	450–560	470–570
23	370–480	380–510	400–510	400–520	420–540	440–550	460–560
22	370–470	380–500	390–510	390–520	410–510	430–540	450–550
21	370–470	380–500	390–500	390–510	410–510	430–530	450–550
20	360–460	370–490	380–500	390–500	400–510	420–520	440–540
19	350–460	360–490	380–500	390–500	400–510	420–520	430–530
18	340–450	350–480	370–490	380–490	390–500	410–510	420–520
17	330–440	340–470	360–480	370–480	380–500	400–510	410–510
16	320–440	340–460	350–480	360–480	370–490	400–500	410–510
15	310–430	330–450	340–480	350–470	360–490	390–490	400–500
14	300–420	320–440	330–460	340–470	350–480	390–490	400–500
13	300–410	310–430	320–450	330–460	340–470	380–480	390–490
12	290–400	300–420	310–440	320–450	330–460	370–470	380–480
11	280–390	290–410	300–430	310–440	320–450	360–460	370–470
10	270–390	280–400	290–420	300–430	310–440	350–450	360–460
9	260–380	270–380	280–410	290–420	300–430	340–440	350–450
8	260–370	270–370	280–400	280–410	290–420	330–430	340–440
7	250–370	270–360	280–390	280–410	290–410	320–420	340–430
6	240–360	250–350	270–380	270–400	280–400	310–410	330–420
5	220–350	240–340	260–370	260–390	270–390	300–400	320–410
4	210–340	230–330	250–360	250–380	260–380	290–390	310–400
3	210–310	220–320	240–330	240–370	250–370	280–380	290–390
2	210–300	220–310	220–320	230–350	240–360	270–370	280–380
1	200–290	210–300	220–310	230–340	240–350	250–350	260–370
0	200–270	210–280	210–300	210–320	220–320	230–330	240–350

Appendix: Using the TI-89 Graphing Calculator

The TI-89 Graphing Calculator is a versatile tool. Many of the features are useful in solving SAT math questions. For example, the TI-89 graphing calculator can be used for:

- Solving an equation
- Solving an equation involving an unusual symbol
- Solving a system of equations
- Solving an equation involving absolute values
- Solving an equation involving functional notations
- Evaluating or factoring an algebraic expression
- Comparing the numerical values of two expressions

In this appendix, we offer ten examples of how to use the TI-89 graphing calculator to solve SAT math questions.

Solving an Equation

From Chapter XI, Section B, Practice Problem 2

If x is a real number, how many values of x satisfy the equation $(x + 10)^2 = 25$?

A. 0
B. 1
C. 2
D. 3
E. 4

C TI-89 solution:

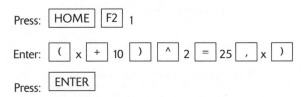

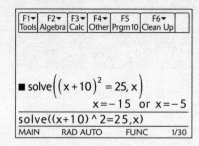

Solving Equations Involving Absolute Values

From Chapter XI, Section D, Practice Problem 5

If n satisfies both of the equations below, what is the value of n?

$$|2n - 4| = 10$$
$$|3 - 2n| = 11$$

7 TI-89 solution:

Press: HOME F2 1

Enter: CATALOG A ENTER 2 x − 4) = 10 CATALOG

Select: ▷ *and* ENTER

Enter: CATALOG A ENTER 3 − 2 x) = 11 ,

x)

Press: ENTER

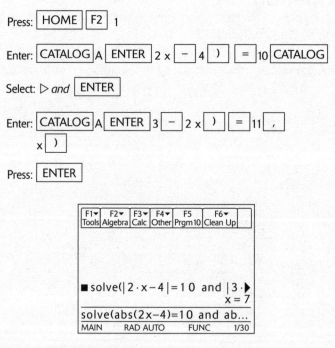

Note: It is more convenient to use the letter x instead of n, because the letter x has its own designated key while, for n, you have to first press the ALPHA key and then press n.

Solving a System of Equations

From Chapter XI, Section E, Practice Problem 1

If $2a - 2b = 5$ and $a^2 - b^2 = 10$, what is the value of $a + b$?

A.   4
B.   5
C.   10
D.   20
E.   100

A TI-89 solution:

Press: [HOME] [F2] 1

Enter: 2 x [−] 2 y [=] 5 [CATALOG]

Select: ▷ *and* [ENTER]

Enter: x [^] 2 [−] y [^] 2 [=] 10 [,] x [)]

Press: [ENTER]

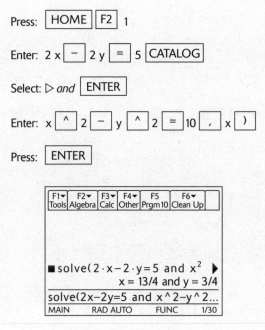

Note: It is more convenient to use the letters x and y instead of a and b, because the letters x and y have their own designated keys. In contrast, for a, you have to first press the ALPHA key and then press a, and then repeat the same procedure for b.

Solving an Equation with a Variable in the Exponent

From Chapter XI, Section F, Practice Problem 1

If $3^n + 3^n + 3^n = 9^6$, what is the value of n?

A. 2
B. 3
C. 4
D. 11
E. 12

D TI-89 solution:

Press: HOME F2 1

Enter: 3 ^ x + 3 ^ x + 3 ^ x = 9 ^
        6 , x)

Press: ENTER

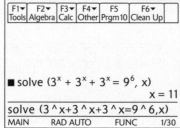

■ solve $(3^x + 3^x + 3^x = 9^6, x)$

$x = 11$

solve $(3 \wedge x + 3 \wedge x + 3 \wedge x = 9 \wedge 6, x)$

MAIN   RAD AUTO   FUNC   1/30

Note: It is more convenient to use the letter x instead of n, because the letter x has its own designated key while, for n, you have to first press the ALPHA key and then press n.

Solving an Equation Involving a Function

From Diagnostic Test, Problem 23

If $p(x) = x^2 + 2x$, and $p(2h) = 8h$, and $h > 0$, what is the value of h?

A. -4
B. -1
C. 0
D. 1
E. 4

D TI-89 solution:

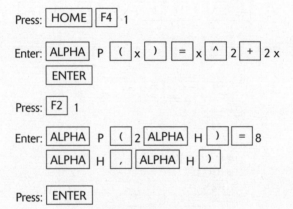

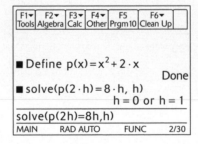

Solving a Problem Involving an Unusual Symbol

From Chapter XIV, Section A, Practice Problem 5

Let @p be defined as $2^p - 1$ for all integers p. What is the value of @ ((@3)?

127 TI-89 solution:

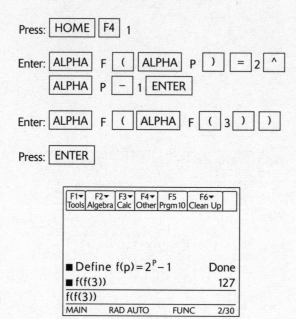

Solving Problems Involving Functions

From Chapter XI, Section H, Practice Problem 1

If the function f is defined by f(x) = 2x − 6, which of the following is equivalent to 5f(x) + 10?

A.   10x − 40
B.   10x − 20
C.   10x + 4
D.   10x + 20
E.   7x + 4

B TI-89 solution:

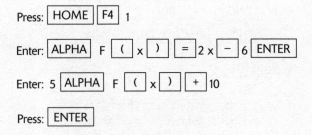

Press: | HOME | | F4 | 1

Enter: | ALPHA | F | (| x |) | | = | 2 x | − | 6 | ENTER |

Enter: 5 | ALPHA | F | (| x |) | | + | 10

Press: | ENTER |

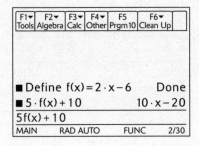

| F1▾ | F2▾ | F3▾ | F4▾ | F5 | F6▾ |
| Tools | Algebra | Calc | Other | Prgm10 | Clean Up |

■ Define f(x)=2·x−6   Done
■ 5·f(x)+10   10·x−20
─────────────────────────────
5f(x)+10
MAIN   RAD AUTO   FUNC   2/30

Working with the Distance Formula

From Chapter XII, Section G, Practice Problem 5

In a coordinate plane, the distance between point A(10,5) and point B(–2,b) is 13. If b > 0, what is the value of b?

10 TI-89 solution:

Note: It is more convenient to use the letter y instead of b, because the letter y has its own designated key while, for b, you have to first press the ALPHA key and then press b.

Press: | HOME | F2 | 1

Enter: | 2ND | √ | (| 10 | − | (−) | 2 |) | ^ | 2 | +
| (| 5 | − | y |) | ^ | 2 |) | = | 13 | , | y |)

Press: | ENTER

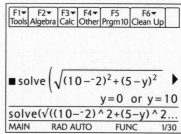

Working with Inequalities

From Chapter X, Section A, Practice Problem 1

In the accompanying diagram, five points, A, B, C, D, and E, are on a number line in the positions indicated. Which point has m as its coordinate if $m < m^3 < m^2$?

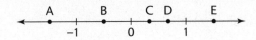

A. A
B. B
C. C
D. D
E. E

B TI-89 solution:

Press: │ HOME │

Enter: x │ 2ND │ ∠ x │ ^ │ 3 │CATALOG│

Select: ▷ *and* │ ENTER │

Enter: x │ ^ │ 3 │ 2ND │ ∠ x │ ^ │ 2 │ │ │ x │ = │

Now you enter each of the given 5 choices, one at a time, and see which one produces a true statement.

Let A = −1.12, B = −0.5, C = 0.3, D = 0.6, and E = 1.3.

Enter: │ (−) │ 0.5

Press: │ ENTER │

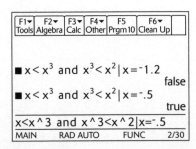

Note: It is more convenient to use the letter x instead of m, because the letter x has its own designated key while, for m, you have to first press the ALPHA key and then press m.

Simplifying a Numerical Expression

From Chapter X, Section A, Practice Problem 6

What is the numerical value of $\dfrac{\frac{1}{2}+\frac{1}{3}}{\frac{1}{6}}$?

5 TI-89 solution:

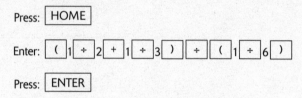

Press: HOME

Enter: (1 ÷ 2 + 1 ÷ 3) ÷ (1 ÷ 6)

Press: ENTER

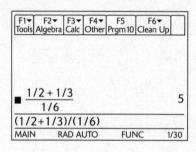

CliffsNotes® To Go!

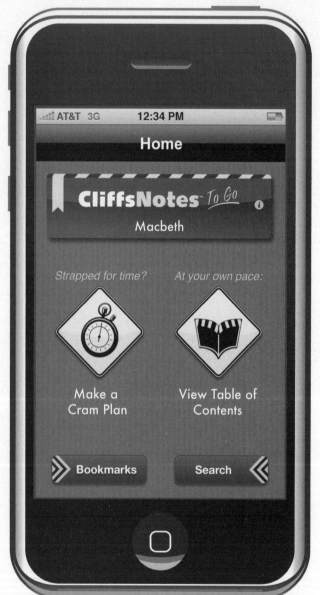

From *Romeo and Juliet* to the *Adventures of Huckleberry Finn*, **CliffsNotes® To Go** has the classics covered—wherever you go.

- **Audio overviews of the work**
- **Study plan that fits your timeline**
- **Detailed chapter summaries**
- **Interactive character maps**
- **Quizzes and questions**
- **And more!**

Cliffs Notes® To Go literature study guides are available for $1.99 per application from Apple's App Store. For more information visit **www.cliffsnotes.com/literature /cliffsnotes-mobile**

CliffsNotes®